LEAVES FROM AN INDIAN JUNGLE

LEAVES FROM AN INDIAN JUNGLE:

GATHERED DURING THIRTEEN YEARS OF A JUNGLE LIFE IN THE CENTRAL PROVINCES, THE DECCAN, AND BERAR

A. I. R. GLASFURD

GYAN

Published by

GYAN

Gyan Publishing House
5, Ansari Road
Daryaganj, New Delhi-110002
Phone: 011-47034999, 9811692060
E-mail: books@gyanbooks.com

Distribution Network
gyanbooks.com
India, USA, Canada, UK, Australia

ISBN: 978-93-7169-242-7 (PB)

First Published, 1903

2nd Impression 2025

Printed at: Gyan Press, Delhi.

LEAVES FROM AN INDIAN JUNGLE
Author: A. I. R. GLASFURD

LEAVES FROM AN INDIAN JUNGLE

Hot weather—the mid-day halt.

LEAVES FROM AN INDIAN JUNGLE

GATHERED DURING THIRTEEN YEARS OF
A JUNGLE LIFE IN THE CENTRAL
PROVINCES, THE DECCAN,
AND BERAR.

BY

A. I. R. G

WITH TWENTY ORIGINAL ILLUSTRATIONS BY THE AUTHOR.

1903.

CONTENTS.

LIST OF ILLUSTRATIONS.

ACKNOWLEDGMENTS.

The acknowledgments of the writer are due to the Editors of the *Indian Sporting Times*, the *Indian Field*, and the *Asian*, whom he has to thank for their courtesy in permitting him to make use of such of these articles as have previously appeared in their columns.

To the management of the *Times of India*, Bombay, he is especially indebted. It is largely due to their help, particularly with regard to the reproducing of the illustrations by their photozincographic department, that he has been enabled to carry out his ideas.

INTRODUCTION.

Prefatory remarks to these Jungle Sketches would be out of place were it not for the fact that some sort of apology, some foreword, seems necessary in bringing forward yet another publication on Indian sport.

The subject is a well-worn one, and must be so tired of by most readers, that to meet the weary sigh of—"What? *More* nullahs—*more* beaters—*more* shots clean through the heart?"—that may greet his essay, the writer feels that he must advance a detaining hand, and hasten to plead as follows:—

Teak, bamboo, *jámún*, *sál* and others—these leaves have been gathered by a wandering *shikári* on the banks of forest streams, in the moonlit *machán*, under the banyan's grateful shade, for those who love the jungle; and in their quiet colouring there is no place for a record of expensive 'bags' or tall yarns.

All they aim at is to present, in a style true to Nature, the silent charm of their native hills and plains, and the comings and goings of the *fauna* that inhabit them.

They are scattered here in the hope that to some they may prove reminiscent of the attractions of *shikár* in a manner devoid of the objectionable diary style and those wearisome stereotyped accompaniments that have only an irritant effect—especially on seasoned *shikáris* of wide experience, who shoot much, but are silent as to their performances.

To this end the recital of a somewhat limited experience has been kept, as far as possible, in the background, an effort being made to bring out rather those apparently unimportant details, the light and shade, so to speak, that, apart from the mere gratification of a hunting instinct, go so far to form the pleasurable whole of a hunter's wanderings. It is also hoped that, aided by the illustrations, these 'leaves' may give a nearer and more detailed view of some of India's jungles and sport to those who have not visited the country. If, however, it is a guide-book, a compendium of knowledge, that the latter require, they should turn to the well-known works of famous authors on Indian *shikár*.

The writer is aware that the illustrations—especially some of the animal figures—fall below artistic standards; but the animals, feebly depicted though they be, will not be found posing in those conventional 'Indian' surroundings which exist solely in the fertile imagination of the untravelled artist, or may have been elaborated by him on the rough suggestions of those who possess the necessary local knowledge without the power of expressing it in a useful way. No care has been spared to make the sketches true to Nature, and to present wild beasts as they are actually found at home; and, for this purpose, scenes have been revisited for the express purpose of securing truth in the smallest details. All the landscapes are *fac-similes* of actual localities as they exist at the present moment.

Photographs have been avoided, as only high-class work on a large scale would serve the purpose of the writer.

From those who, like the exasperated Frenchman, "abhor the beauties of Nature," some indulgence is craved. There is a place for everything; and what would be but sickly sentiment in the more strenuous walks of life comes naturally enough when we enter the silent vistas of untrodden forest and become susceptible to those elemental influences, old as humanity itself, that still exercise some sway over the most civilized mind.

The critical reader should therefore allow the rustlings of these leaves to draw him within their quiet shade, forgetful of the fact that his guide is neither 'mighty hunter' nor boasts much wider experience than is sometimes afforded by the earlier years of 'a soldier, therefore seldom rich.'

ERRATA.

A few obvious errata have crept in while this publication was in the press—some minor errors in punctuation here and there.

p. 26, for '*spurf-owl*' read *spur-fowl.*

p. 39, line 21, should read—

. . . . .

. . . . *After that, the tree !*
Interposed by, etc. . . . .

p. 54, line 24, for *lines* read *Lines.*

p. 101, line 31, after *Pipalda* insert *are.*

p. 107, line 30, for *herd* read *head.*

pp. 117 *et sequitur*, for *Cantonments* read *Cantonment.*

AT HOME.

AN INDIAN SUMMER'S DAY.

Morning.

"Koël! Ko-yel!" from the feathery tamarinds. The faint breeze accompanying an Indian dawn has died away, and a burning March sun is climbing into a hard blue sky, casting hard blue shadows across the smooth, white, tree-bordered road of the little Cantonment.

"Tok—tok—tok—tok!" from the glossy new *pipal* leaves hammers the little barbet, all head and beak—if you can see him—punctuating each monotonous note with a sidelong nod, now right, now left.

Soon Nature will lie wrapped in the noontide silence. The hot weather has come once more, and the exile girds up his loins for resistance, passive though it may be, till relieved at the bursting of the next monsoon rains. The *punkah* has recommenced its weary flap; and many an unhappy individual, uncheered even by that priceless thirst which is now his right, is settling into a quiet hypochondria.

But to the *shikári* come no discomforting thoughts. Let the sun do his fiercest, and the "brain-fever-bird" his worst, while parched leaves eddy in the scorching blast; they only remind him that his time of promise is nigh. Unfold the map; visit each old haunt afresh; mark as likely those yet unvisited; welcome the men returned with hopeful news; settle the route, and overhaul rifle and gun. Hurrah! for April jungles and all they hold in anticipation; there are compensations for an Indian summer after all.

Noon.

Hot dry jungle crackles under a vertical sun, and the dust of the forest road lies away in a long grey riband behind the rythmic hoof-beats of our third change of horse-flesh as a long ride draws to its destination.

Ahead, quivering in the heat-haze, a dip in the low woody hill country, indicative of a line of river, with those glimpses of dark green groves along its banks. Mother Tapti at last!

The track curves down to cross a tributary stream, and we walk the good mare across its shingly bed, under the low branches of gnarled and hoary mango trees, up which spring and whoop the grey apes that we have disturbed at their midday drink. Far up-stream the fresh green of *jámún* covert; down-stream great rocks, with some peafowl scuttling away from a little water-hole. A likely place indeed!

We ascend the far bank slowly in deep shade; then off on a final canter. Jungle thins, and gives place to a narrow clearing, its diminutive fields lying reaped and bare; the barking of village curs is heard, and a humble Korku hamlet stands on its knoll, overlooking a fringe of dark trees that border the river below. Our hoof-beats bring out one or two of the jungle men, who, grinning in a friendly way, point to a bend up-stream. There, romantically situated in the deep shade of a spreading many-trunked banyan, is the little 80-lb. tent. A *mandwa*, or thatched, open-sided shelter, has been erected adjoining it, 'neath which on snowy napery tiffin is ready laid!

We sink into the inviting arms of a long cane-chair.

"Yes, my excellent Abdul, you may remove my boots; but, before all, bear swiftly hither a chalice brimming over with nectar such as the *sahibs* do love!

"*Al-hamdu-l-illah!* but that's well worth a thirty-mile ride!

"Two tigers located here, did you say? and the men away preparing for my honour's hunting? and the luke-warm tub is ready? The gods be propitious indeed!"

NIGHT.

The glare of a long hot weather day is past, and the misty river breathes cool airs that stir the lighter foliage. An excellent dinner, prepared by the faithful "Bulbul Amir," is just over, and a long cheroot glows peacefully as the grateful smoke curls slowly aloft. *Cicadæ* and crickets maintain their ceaseless songs, and from the margin of the pool beyond that dark bank rises the occasional croak of a wakeful frog.

We are set out in the open, away from the now heat-retaining trees, and may gaze straight up into the serene, star-pricked arch of the sky. The moon is up, turning the jungle into fairy-land, and its inhabitants, that have hidden in silence during the heat of day, are now abroad, wandering in search of food and water throughout this wonderful tropical night. The nightjars that sail mysteriously about during the crepuscular hour, uttering a strange cry of "Chyeece—chyeece!" have taken up their nocturnal call, and "Chuckoo—chuckoo—chuckoo!" continuously to each other across the broad shingly river-bed. Very faintly, so far down-stream is he, may be heard the distant braying of a *chital* stag.

Even the presence of aboriginal man seems but to add to the sense of contented peacefulness, a soft "rub-a-dub, rub-a-dub," proclaiming the Korkus awake in their rude hamlet, beyond which the sleeping hills slope down to the narrow valley.

Over there a glow of little fires shows our men occupied with their evening meal, and a murmur of voices behind the camp others, who are engaged in rubbing wood-ashes into a certain broad peg-stretched skin.

Yes! It has been a lucky day, and the first tiger is already bagged. Happy thought that prompted the placing of an extra "stop" at the very spot which he should choose to break out of the beat, and a fatal pause that which he made, right under our tree.

A shy, game-killing, jungle beast, what long weary ways his tracks had led us that hot day, until we "ringed" him, at home, so far from his "kill" of the previous night!

And so he is slain over again. Anticipation, realization, fond recollection, threefold charm of these forest scenes—pleasures that will be ours long after the jungle knows us no more!

The white sheets look invitingly cool in the moonlight; and the cheroot can be finished there.

"Call me at five o'clock, Abdul!"

How delicious to stretch one's pleasantly fatigued limbs on the smooth linen, and gaze up at the thought-bringing stars, while dreams of the morrow's sport trail gentle sleep in their train.

So the East doth call to us who are her foster children.

That fatal pause.

TOLD BY THE DOCTOR.

It was a wet night in the rains, and late. Most of our fellows had left the mess, and the Doctor and we two, after several games of "Snookers," had passed into the ante-room and flung ourselves into deep chairs.

The conversation turned to *shikár*. Ours was a little station where much of the after-dinner talk did hinge on shooting topics, for many of us were keen sportsmen, and there was more game to be had in the neighbourhood than is to be found round and about most military stations now-a-days.

We were recalling reminiscences of by-gone days, and each had some little anecdote to relate of past shooting seasons, which led us away into a series of discussions and controversies that lasted well into the already far-spent night, when the Doctor, calling for a fresh cigar, said: "Well, boys, I'll spin you a yarn that I seldom care to relate, for the truth is that, looking back now, I myself can scarcely believe that it ever occurred. I don't ask you to believe a word of it, mind you—let it pass as a yarn. But wait—"

"*Qui hi?*"

"*Hazur!*"

"Three big whiskies and sodas!"

Our dear old Doctor was one of the real old school, and although, in deference to the latest innovation, we called him "Colonel" in public, it was with relief that we reverted, when we could, to the name by which we had known him for many a year—and the relief was mutual.

"*Colonel!*" he would say. "D—— your Colonels! Have I been your "sawbones" all these years to have *that* flung at my head in my old age?"

This to such of us as were the more intimate of his friends.

After a pull at the long glasses we leant back, and the worthy old medico began :—

"It was in the 'seventies,' I must tell you, that the experience I am about to relate befell; and it was not very far from here. (The old boy named a district that had borne a great name for tigers.)

"I was out on my usual hot-weather shoot, and arrived one day at a village near which I had been informed there was a solitary tiger of great age and enormous size that had frequented those jungles for a great many years. He had been fired at and hit by both *sahibs* and Kolis—the *shikáris* of those parts—and bore a reputation for unfailing cunning. He was also a 'very bad tiger,' and had killed his three or four men. His latest performance in this line had taken place not long before my advent, when he had strolled out of the jungle in full daylight, and removed the top of the skull of an old woman who was picking up *mhowa* flowers under a tree. Not that he was in any way a man-eater. His performances in the man-killing line were evidently merely in revenge for the harm done him by mankind : he was lame of one leg, and carried a matchlock ball in his back.

"The jungle he frequented was quite impossible to beat, if indeed one could ever have persuaded beaters to enter it. The very sight of a buffalo tied up as a bait drove him away for days, and he never approached a natural kill or any water-hole without making a complete circle round it and carefully examining all the adjacent trees. He would stop all traffic along the jungle tracks in the neighbourhood for days at a time,—in fact, he was a perfect *shaitán!*

"Now there are lots of tigers with more or less similar habits ; but I had bagged several of the kind, and felt that, given patience, time and luck, I should assuredly remove this one's skin to the security and comfort of my bungalow or to that of my aunt Priscilla's drawing-room at home. You see I have no other relatives, and my aunt is a lady to keep in with. I may have my moor and salmon river yet!"—and, gently closing his eyes, the doctor reflectively blew an enormous cloud from his Mayo cheroot.

"Well, I started trying for that tiger.

"His special bit of jungle was a little level valley encircled by an amphitheatre of low rocky hills and drained by a winding *nála*—a beautiful *nála*; its bed of smooth, clean, golden sand, overhung by charming trees and green bushes, broken here and there by outcrops of sandstone boulders, and holding, at the mouth of the little vale, marked by the big tamarinds as the deserted village site of Páldi, one solitary pool of crystal clear water. This snug retreat the brute had entirely to himself, for he would permit no other felines to share it, and the wood-cutters of the villages in the vicinity, the only people who ever went that way, never dared so much as to pass the little gorge by the water-hole that led to his sylvan fastness.

"I saw at once that ordinary methods would not prevail, so after a day or two spent in cautious reconnaissance of the scene of future operations, I at length prevailed on some of the inhabitants of the villages round about to lend me the services of their cattle, and so possessed myself of a 'scratch herd' of bovines of decidedly mixed appearance, mostly very scraggy. This motley assemblage I had driven, one evening about five o'clock, through the dreaded pass and into the little strath I have already described.

"A forest fire had swept over a portion of the glade, and the half-starved kine, their senses ravished by a sight of the fresh green grass that sprouted from the blackened ground, lost no time in scattering themselves all over the place, the cowbells tinkling merrily in a way that was doubtless peculiarly fascinating to a tiger. I immediately ascended to my *machán*, which had been erected with great care in the branches of a big *mhowa* tree that flung its boughs over the pool, and all the men at once returned to camp ; the cowherds intensely relieved, as they had done their work in fear and trembling even under the protection of myself and my orderly with rifles.

"I may remind you of my invariable custom of sitting up at night *alone*.

"As the sun sank in a bank of murky clouds and a fitful wind began sighing through the forest, I began to make up my mind that I was in for an all-night vigil of the fruitless kind we know so well, for I could hear the cowbells tinkling nearer and nearer as the instinct of their wearers led them to make tracks for home, and they approached the narrow outlet to the valley on their way ; shortly a bony old cow, the most knowing of the lot, hove in sight, then another, and another, each pacing slowly forward with rythmically nodding head and swinging tail. The cunning plan had evidently failed, and the striped autocrat was presumably 'not taking any.'

"Just, I say, as I was reconciling myself to the idea of sitting the night out, on the chance of the tiger coming to drink, there was a sudden mighty commotion in the rear of the herd ; and a moment later a sea of tossing horns, stampeding hoofs, and upraised tails passed under my tree, as a crowd of wild, mad, panic-stricken cattle scurried through the pass and out beyond, where the frenzied clacking of their bells died away in the direction of the nearest village. I felt that they *must* have left one of their number behind, and there came over me that self-same thrill that charms the heart when a big salmon takes one's 'Jock Scott' with a rush, and one enters on the nervous work of playing him on light grilse tackle.

"'Hooked' the tiger was; but whether I should ever bring him to the 'gaff' was quite another question.

"After the exciting flurry that had just taken place, the jungle recovered its wonted calm with extraordinary rapidity; and as the pool at my feet was the only water for some two miles around, I had no lack of company to interest me so long as light lasted. Birds of all descriptions, jackals, flights on flights of the painted sandgrouse dropping swiftly over the trees on to the moist cool sand, and, after drinking, rising again as suddenly with their clucking call; and then a large company of that marvellously wary bird, the pea-fowl, followed by a timid, hesitating herd of spotted deer. As night fell all these gradually departed, and, after the loud cries exchanged across the valley by the roosting peacocks, a silence descended that could be felt.

"Later on a breeze sprang up, and, while carrying the human taint well away in the right direction, served to drown any suspicious sounds which might scare away a shy animal. You know the extraordinary way *machâns will* creak in a dead calm!

"The waning moon was not due till about 11 p.m., so I produced my spoon, and untied my frugal meal of potato-pie which my servant had provided, after which a draught from the water *chágal* prepared me for a long vigil.

"It was an extremely dark night, for heavy lowering clouds in dense masses blotted out the stars, and gave me many a foreboding as regards having a clear moon later on. I settled my back against a branch, and gave myself up to reflection. I wondered how the tiger was getting along, and if he'd drink soon or late; or perhaps he might pay more than one visit to the pool during the enjoyment of his meal. What a funny old fellow was that Koli *shikári* with whom I had had a talk that day; and how solemnly he had given me a quite unnecessary warning 'not to sleep on any account!'

"A thousand memories and fancies chased each other through my mind, as they will do on such occasions, and meanwhile a languor stole over the corporeal portion of me while my brain continued alert and unceasingly active. The end of it was that after starting violently once or twice from this borderland of dreams, I found myself admitting that after all a nap till moonrise would do no harm, and—I fell asleep.

* * * * *

"You know that way one has, when the mind is prepared and expectant, of passing from sound sleep to absolute wakefulness—clear, sharp, wide-awakefulness? Well, in response to the light but firm pressure *of a hand on my arm* I was instantly awake!

In a flash, with dismay, I noted that the moon was not only up but floated in a serene and cloudless sky, flooding the pool below me in pale clear light, while at my side *a figure sat* and pointed with a strangely bloated and swollen, bandaged arm at a dark mass that broke the silvered surface of the water below! They say the 'ruling passion is strong in death.' At any rate, acting on my first impulse (the whole scene, though lasting but a second, is indelibly imprinted on my memory), I raised the rifle that lay in my lap, and, getting the white card night-sight on the tiger's shoulder, fired.

"The brute rolled over on the sand, plunging, grunting, and struggling; and as it did so there came two light pats of an approving hand on my back, a deep drawn sigh, and the still air was filled with the most appalling odour, which

A dark mass broke the silvered water.

I at once recognised as the peculiar smell emanating from a body in the last and hopeless stage of pyæmia or blood-poisoning!

"I whipped round! The *machán* was empty! I was absolutely alone; not a sound disturbed the pale silence but a choking gasp from the expiring tiger. An owl hōoted far up the glen. But that dreadful unhallowed reek of rotting, festering humanity hung still, thick, choking, almost palpable, over, under, and around me!

"Why I spoke in English then I know not, but I leant over, and said in a low voice, 'Who's there?' then, recollecting myself, '*Kaon hai?*' Again I repeated, in a voice that I scarcely recognised, 'Ho! *Kaon hai?*'

"The silence was paralysing and unbearable.

"I will ask you to imagine the horror of the situation. I am, as you know, not imaginative. I have seen strange things in my time; but the awful, petrifying effect of that moonlit dread, with its disgusting physical accompaniment, upset all the man in me, and I felt as a child feels when it starts quaking and whimpering from the terrors of nightmare to the black throbbing blackness of night.

"I bore up awhile in a rapidly increasing fear that quite mastered me; and then I could stand it no longer, and, untying the cord I kept wound about my *chágal*, I let my rifle down to the ground, and followed myself, regardless, thoughtless of barked shins and palms, fell the last few feet on my face, picked up my rifle, and, with a glance at the dead tiger, made my way to camp, vainly trying to reconcile the scene I had just passed through with the fancies of a brain suddenly dragged from slumber.

"Reaching the sleep-steeped camp at 3 a.m., I helped myself to a stiff peg and a cheroot, and lay smoking till dawn. I had a cup of coffee then, and accompanied my men back to the dead tiger. Half ashamed, I found myself looking about the base of the tree in which I had spent the night; not a mark in the soft soil but those of my men and myself, and in that clear sweet morning light, remembering that the odour of a well-fed and lately-fed tiger would be sufficient to account for what had persuaded my nocturnal fears, I caught myself smiling at the strange fancies that will come to a man in the hours of darkness. Leaving the men to skin the tiger, which was one of the largest I have ever seen, I strolled back towards camp, shooting a couple of peafowl *en route.* The old Koli came with me. I could see he wanted badly to say something, and shortly out it came—

" 'The *sahib* returned very early,' he said. I assented. A silence.

" 'Did the *sahib* keep awake all night?'

" The pertinacity of the old man annoyed me unaccountably, and I answered shortly and evasively.

" 'Without doubt,' he replied, 'the *sahib* is a rajah and I a poor man!'

"Nearer camp he spoke again. 'I will show the *sahib* something if he will follow me; and he led the way into a tangle of low thorn and scrub; chopping a prickly tendril with his *kulhári*, he dragged aside a mass of creepers, and there lay at our feet a weather-beaten rectangular laterite slab.

" In its upper surface was cut an oblong depression, in which lay traces of mortar.

" 'Marble slabs make nice curry-stones,' thought I.

" 'What was the *sahib's* name?' I said, seating myself on a boulder.

" 'How should I know?' was the reply. 'When I was so big'—and the old Koli lowered his skinny hand— '*he* came here and wounded a tiger—*that* tiger they say; but it jumped on him, and in two days he was dead. And the servants put him in the earth here. Next year another *sahib* came, and he brought a smooth white stone, and had this big one cut, and put it on the top, and departed. There are *badmash* people who might steal such stones, *Sahib*; who knows!'

"'Paldi was a *basti* then. It has now long been deserted, many days—many days!'

"Moved by a sudden shamefaced curiosity I put him a question—

"'You are a Koli?'

"'*Sahib!*'

"'A *shikári?*

"'*Sahib!*'—with another inclination of the head in assent.

"'Do you ever sit up at night here for game?'

"He lifted his head, as he squatted at my side, and looked me keenly in the eye; then—

"'It is my bread, *Sahib*, and I have many children. There is much game in this jungle—sámbar; *rohis*; *chital*; much game!' And he sighed. 'But I do not often sit now, *Sahib*, not *here!* but when I *have* to sit, *Sahib*, when times are hard, *I never sleep!*' and he gave me another queer look.

"'But what do I know, *Sahib*; your honour is a rajah and I a poor man, but it may be that now I may sit—and sleep too—in peace!'

"This was all I could get out of the old man, so I returned to my breakfast; but as I went I murmured to myself—'There are more things in heaven and earth than are dreamt of in *your* philosophy!'"

TEAK AND BAMBOO.—(THE SAMBAR.)

"Dhánk!"

Which is my name, in the language of the Korkus, and the most appropriate of all my names, expressing my voice as nearly as can any human word—that abrupt, sonorous, trumpet-like note, which, once heard, ringing through the gorges of my native hills, can never be forgotten.

"Dhánk!" What memories it conjures up! The shimmering surface of the moonlit jungle pool, where the ripples widen about our feet: the bell of alarm from some watchful hind, warning, perchance, of the forest king's midnight approach: the first rosy shafts of the rising sun, touching the solemn peaks that rise in solid grandeur far across the tumultuous sea of forest-clad hills, in whose dark deep valleys long *rausa* grass drips chill dews: the little open glade on the *salai*-studded slope of some precipitous spur, where the saplings show frayed and red from the rubbing of our stags' antlers.

It was amid these Central Indian hills that I first saw the light—at the head of a deep glen, where the arching trees, roped together by the long, thick tendrils of the *mahúl* creeper (*Bauhinia scandeus*) met their green canopy far above our heads, and the sunlight, filtering through a well-nigh impenetrable mass of verdure, fell here and there in broken patches on the tangled mass of undergrowth—for I was born during the rainy season.

I remember the first time my dam led me out on the little game-path winding along the steep mountain sides that hemmed in our retreat: above us the hill-tops were lost in

At the head of a deep glen.

driving mist, while from below rose the deep booming of a torrent in angry spate, as it leapt, turbid and yellow, over a short basalt cliff, and roared down the valley to join the swollen Tapti.

Elsewhere it was still and oppressive, and the remains of the last downpour dripped heavily off the sodden teak leaves. Far down the valley a thin curl of blue smoke behind the trees marked the huts of some hill-folk, while away out beyond the low foot-hills lay the distant clear-cut line of the plains, meeting the sky like the horizon of a vast sea.

Our life is seldom a stirring one: we live in quiet retirement in our lonely forests, not often seeing more of the outer world than the little Korku hamlet at the mouth of our valley affords when it lies wrapped in sleep, and we wander nightly to visit the few *bêr* bushes in its vicinity, or when we hear the distant chopping of some solitary woodcutter's axe.

To live thus is to be sombre, deliberate, almost melancholy; and any one who has studied our habits must know this to be our nature, although he will also have had experience of our keen perceptions and extreme natural watchfulness.

During my earlier days my dam and I seldom wandered beyond the limits of the glen where I was born, and which was inhabited by only a few more of our species, including one stag. I saw him now and again only, for he wandered little, and showed a great reluctance to pass through the forest while his horns were in the sensitive velvet stage. Among the more interesting neighbours were a couple of our little cousins, the *khákar*, or barking deer, whose ruddy little coats were to be seen in the grass bordering the thicker copses, their white, rabbit-like tails raised in ridiculous fashion as they darted in play behind the tree stems;

while the valley resounded at dawn and eve with the shrill "Kuckkaa—kiya—kuck'm!" of our cheery friends the grey jungle-cocks.

As time passed the rain ceased, and the sun began his work on the jungles: the leaves fell, the *salai* trees stood out gaunter and barer each day, and the fast-yellowing grass seeded its vicious crop of tiny spears, which, strange to say, are looked on as a titbit by the stags, who, about this time, are beginning to roar and collect in view of the approaching rutting season.

Early one morning, as we stood by the yet running waters of our glen, we were startled by the sharp bark of our neighbours, the *khákar*. "Aaow—aaow!" sounded their little voices, as they rapidly threaded the well-known thickets, and shortly there rang out the deep bell of a sámbar hind, as the whole ravine waked to sudden panic, and the jungle crashed before the irresistible rush of the large deer. Darting to my dam's side, with cocked tail, I found her trembling, facing down the bed of the stream, her large ears spread to catch the slightest sound, and then, as some little reddish forms appeared slinking round a far rock, we turned, and swiftly passed through a bamboo coppice, up over a steep knoll, and suddenly stopped short again. A pattering sound swept up the banks, and a glimpse of our ruthless foes, the wild dogs, vanishing up-stream, where the rest of the herd had pursued their mad flight. Again we swiftly climbed, and at last stood, with heaving flanks, to hear a faint, far off yelp, before we crossed the ridge and plunged into the jungle slopes of another great *khora*; nor did we stay our way till yet another ridge and glen divided us from our erstwhile home.

Descending more leisurely at length, there suddenly appeared before us the great head and neck of a large stag,

Stood, with heaving flanks.

who regarded our advent with lordly surprise, his sweeping antlers springing from a head poised grandly on a massive, shaggy-maned neck. The bristles on his broad back were raised, and his tail stuck stiffly out as he faced us, and then, curling his lip and drawing his breath with a slight hissing noise through his teeth, he slowly bent his neck, and with a powerful stroke of his horns, to which there still adhered some strips of rough skin, scored a deep gash on the stem of a *salai* sapling.

"The Red ones!" he growled. "Ah! they were here yesterday: how these ill weeds increase; it is not like old times when they were scarce!" And in spite of bravado his tone betrayed a tinge of suppressed fear. Passing down-hill, I stopped a moment to gape at him, as he bent his great strength against the frayed sapling that groaned under his antlers, and rained red strings of peeled bark on the grass below; when he paused, and again lifting the corner of his mouth, and distending his eye-pits, from which there exuded a strange sickly-sweet odour, edged majestically towards me and slowly lowered his sharp tines. His temper was evidently uncertain; so, with a skip, I rejoined my mother, and we wound down a slippery grass slope to take up our new quarters.

We found ourselves in a much finer glen than that we had left; it ran up right under the precipices buttressing the mighty Bairat, which raises its flat-topped bulk 4,000 feet above the sea. A stone detached from the cliffs fell crashing into the dry leaves at our feet, and the faint whoops of the great grey apes sounded far above our heads as they sprang in play among the bare white branches of a torchwood tree which jutted from a ledge in the sheer face of black basalt. In the cool depths of bamboo thicket high up the ravine side was our day retreat, where the wild plantain grew in the rocks overhanging us, and the sun scarcely ever penetrated; while at the *dêwar*, where one ravine met another, the valley expanded into a charming little glade, dotted with the *aola* trees that bear our favourite berries. A little farther down were the pools of "twelve-month" water, and the *lotán* where the stags rolled nightly in mire; while in many spots the numerous peeled trees and trampled dusty earth betokened the *akhára*, or arenas, where they met on moonlight nights; when their challenging roar echoed through the silent forest, and the hinds, their feet crackling the great dry teak leaves, trooped out like spectres to watch.

Such was the Jámgarh *khora* in the old time, and there I passed my uneventful youth; which period I will pass over without comment, save that I twice experienced a "beat," when the line of yelling Korkus passed up the *khora*, and I received my first sharp lessons in the art of breaking back—a highly simple and successful operation when properly carried out.

It takes us many long years to arrive at maturity and our full strength of limb and antlers; and six years passed before I began to hold up my head with reason.

My horns fell regularly, every spring, until they approached their present proportions; since then I have noticed that I retained them unshed for longer periods.

My present pair, of which, I may remark, there is reason to be proud, have not fallen since they grew the summer before last; nor will they be shed this year if I am any judge; however, all of us may not fare similarly.

Our great size and the difficulty of concealing ourselves when once we are noticed, added to the heat of the day, have necessitated very nocturnal habits; and, wandering all night in search of food as we do, it is needful for us to hide and sleep when the sun is up.

Our eyesight is very keen, even on dark nights, and, combined with a highly developed sense of smell, serves to protect us from such noxious animals as wander by night.

By sundown we are on the move; it may be towards some patch of *kútki*, tilled on the level uplands by the Korkus, who vainly rattle empty kerosine tins, or pull an ingenious arrangement of wooden clappers all night, or through the forest in search of fallen fruits. And so, feeding all night, we drink at some pool before daybreak, and at sunrise are well on our way to our *baitak* or "form." Personally I like a good mud-bath, after which I scrape the caked mire off my sides against some handy tree, or shake myself like a dog; then, culling a toothsome morsel here and there as I slowly wander up the damp bed of the stream, the first rays of the sun tempt me to loiter in their gentle warmth, till awakened Nature reminds me that the night is past, and I mount the familiar hillside, to settle down in my favourite couch overlooking the valley by the pollard teak tree or, if it be summer, under the bamboos higher up.

If it is seldom that you see me, you must blame your eyesight ; and remember that on our hills to move is to be seen, to stand motionless is to hide, and that of this our race is well aware. "To see without being seen" is the motto for our jungles, and I have often stared right in your face, your eyes all but meeting mine, as you passed on, noting in wonder the numerous traces of my horns and hoofs.

The memory of my first big fight? Ah, it seems as yesterday!

I had been away from my *khora* the previous day, having wandered some distance during the preceding night. I remember when night fell, and the evening glow gave place to a moonlight almost as bright, I descended the sheering mountain side, and, winding down a tremendous open grassy spur that sunk swiftly to the hazy depths of Jámgarh below, paused ere entering the path of teak scrub, half way down, with its heavy heads of green and thick leaves—for the season was early November.

Hark! a faint roar rose from the glen. I stood listening with tense nerves, and then recognised a rival's voice: indignant, I hastened my descent.

Reaching and passing up the bottom of the ravine, I again clearly heard the hoarse challenge, and halted. "Dhánk!" my lusty young voice burst forth in fierce acceptance, and with hastening steps I clattered over the boulders and sprang up the bank. A fringe of thick coppice surrounded the large *akhára* of our glen, and through this I forced my head and shoulders and glared forth into the arena.

There, facing the moon, whose cold rays fell on his wild eyeballs and bristling mane, stood a hoary old stag. Throwing up his muzzle he gave vent to a hoarse, whistling, broken-voiced bellow, displaying in that motion a throat and chest livid with deep scars. The tips of his thin, sharp-pointed horns—for he was past his prime—gleamed dully against the dark background, where the indistinct forms of some hinds mingled with the shadows cast by the trees.

The scene roused me to an unutterable fury, and I slowly emerged from the copse and faced him. He turned his bloodshot eyes on me; and thus we glared at each other, every hair erect, tails stiffly raised, and wide-opened eyepits glistening with the sickly-smelling secretion of the rutting season. A sudden silence fell—the jungle seemed to wake and hold its breath—a nightjar "Chuck, chuck, chuckoo'd" in the distance—we each paced forward slowly—and then, with one swift rush, our antlers crashed together! Round and round, now back, now forwards, as one or the other gained some momentary advantage, raged the furious battle: the earth was torn up under the spurning of our widespread feet; saplings snapped under our mad, blind rushes; sticks and leaves flew as though a whirlwind caught them up. At length we paused for breath, horn to horn, leaning against each other, open-mouthed, eyes showing white, and blood clotting our manes or dripping on the dried leaves below. Then at it again, forced to our knees, heaving up again, resisting and boring, horn grating on horn, scoring the ground deep with the mighty thrusts of our hind feet, till, almost despairing myself, I felt my antagonist weaken. But with indomitable fury the veteran resumed the onslaught.

At length, his gasping breath whistling in his parched old throat, and contesting every foot with untameable purpose, I gathered up all the reserve of my vigour, and with a huge effort bore him backwards; on the edge of the steep fall came the last blow, his footing slipped, and, driving a sharp tine deep into his labouring chest, he rolled down into the river-bed, accompanied by a shower of earth and loose stones.

Staggering to the edge I looked down. There stood the old warrior, muzzle to the ground, and ears drooped in the humiliation of defeat; and, as I gazed, he slowly turned, and with a bubbling groan tottered away into the black shadow of a great mango tree that arched the *nála* lower down.

Then, flinging back my bloodstained antlers, one deep, exultant bell, in which were concentrated all my pent up feelings, rang through the forest and died away on the silent night—"Dhánk!"

The next morning, as I took my accustomed way up the *khora*, and paused ere facing the steep slope to my favourite form, accompanied by a few hinds, my eye caught a swift movement in the now dry *nála*-bed; we had sighted each other simultaneously, and it was in vain that the tiger flattened his belly against the yellow sand, for my deep voice gave forth a sharp warning, and, with answering barks of alarm, the hinds crashed through the crackling carpet of leaves, and stood stamping their fore feet, while nothing escaped their large ears, which were spread to catch any suspicious sound, as they moved them first in this direction, then in that. With a baffled look on his cunning face the tiger rose, and disappeared round a bend in the ravine.

Some days after this I saw a *sahib*, accompanied by two Korkus, coming up the glen. They were walking up the bed of the stream and pointing to the pugs of the tiger: something made me move my head as I gazed down on them from among some dry bamboos on the top of an overhanging bank, and in an instant a Korku clutched the *sahib's* sleeve and, directing his attention to me, whispered, "*Burra dhánk!*" but I, ever wary, had risen and withdrawn from view. Suddenly a sámbar's bark rang out from the *nála*—at the time I noticed nothing peculiar in it except that it sounded weak—and then another. In a moment of curiosity I stepped forward to investigate this strange occurrence. One of the Korkus had his hands up to his mouth, and the *sahib* had disappeared. Again came the bark, apparently from the Korkus, and I turned to plunge into the jungle; as I did so, a rifle exploded among the trees to my right, and I was felled to the ground.

Being on the edge of a steep fall, I rolled some distance ere I could regain my feet and stand up, paralysed with a numbing pain. Steps rushed towards me through the loud leaves, and, with an effort, I tottered down-hill and gained the thicket bordering the stream, as the Korkus rushed up to turn me, waving their arms and shouting. With a frantic plunge I passed them, and, crossing the bed of the *nála* with a clatter, disappeared among the trees, just as a second bullet buried itself with a thud beyond me in the bank. A few steps more and I came to a standstill, feeling faint and sick; then, seeing a small side *nála*, I crept a short distance up it, and had barely squatted in its sheltering grasses, and pressed my head to the ground, when my enemies came in sight, and, passing close by my hiding-place, their eyes fixed intently ahead, rapidly receded up-stream.

There were now two *sahibs*, one of whom was gasping out as he ran—"A perfect monster!—a forty-five incher!" Their footfalls grew faint in the distance, and at length I was able to creep from my nook, and, with horns laid back, stealthily retrace my way, and take a jungle-path that led me finally, limping, halting, out of that glen and into the next.

Proceeding thus, my fears and the smart of my wound ever pressing me on, I drank at a pool, and, going stronger, had put some miles between me and the scene of the disaster before I crept under the thick tangle of a woody hillside and laid me down. My hurt was painful, but had long since ceased bleeding, being caked with leaves. Lying thus, the rapid twilight closed in, the pink glow died from the opposite hillside, and a single star trembled in the deepening sky. A big owl sent its weird quavering cry floating over the hushed forest, and was silent.

The sleepy croak of a frog rose on the still air; and the jungle sank to rest.

When the waning moon rose, about midnight, I staggered to my feet, and crept stiffly down-hill to the cold raw valley, where the surface of a pool lay silver between black rocks. Wading in, I stood deep in its cooling waters, licking my wound clean.

After a deep draught and a roll in the damp sand I felt better, and stood listening. It was indeed good to live again—to feel once more the grand unbroken solitude of my native wilds—to smell the resinous perfume of the *salai* trees standing in their ghostly array up the hillside—to see the hills slumbering under the moon, and hear the jungle stir in its sleep—the distant call of some wakeful night-bird, or the rustle of a dried teak leaf, as it floated, twirling, lightly to the ground.

I did not fully recover from this day's trouble for many long weeks and lost condition. It was difficult to get at the wound and keep it clean of flies and maggots.

I thought deeply also on the hind's bark that had worked so nearly fatally on my curiosity, and have since learned that the cry of our species can be fairly well imitated by the Korkus, who hold a leaf of the *palás* to their mouths and blow on it: this I have from my old pal Bhálu, the black one, whom I found the other morning digging out an ants' nest. We are good friends, and it is only during the *mhowa* season that our interests clash. Bhalu is quick-tempered, and when we see his shaggy coat moving at midnight under the *mhowa* trees and hear him sucking and slobbering over the luscious flowers, we know better than to poach on his preserves, although, after all, his angry demonstrations are little better than a pretence, and laughable at that.

He keeps us merry too on moonlit nights, when he and Mrs. Bhalu fall out and wrangle, and the *gúbars,* the tiny owls, wake to chortle and hideously chuckle as they sit demurely side by side in the branches overhead.

One more adventure, *Sahib*, and I have done. It concerns those vile little foes of ours from whom there is seldom escape—the wild dogs. When I tell you that forest reservation has so increased their numbers that for every one during the old days there are now ten, and remind you that each pack, numbering about a dozen individuals, often more, must be fed and fed well, you will begin to understand the enormous losses inflicted on the herds of deer during a single season.

Increasing numbers have even altered the wild dog's retiring nature, and he now boldly appears where he would not have dared show himself a few years ago.

Sahib, you are steadily driving us from our home in these hills. Why is the grass never fired now, and why left to die down season after season till it cumbers the earth with such a mildewed and powdery carpeting as none but the rankest herbage may penetrate when the rain comes down? The bison are going, and we follow; and at no very distant time these hills will stand yet more desolate, deprived of all that once gladdened their solitude.

I could tell you many another tale—of Dádu and Khátu, the Korkus, *shikáris* in the old days, but now—well, flesh is scarce in these regions, and in response may be to a knowing look from the "Jamadar *sahib*" they take their long *bandúks* from the thatch and enter the *bandi*. Sámbar, whether stag, hind or fawn, is good; but a fat young bison-cow—*Wah!*

But the wild dogs!

It was at the end of the fierce summer drought, when the first premonitory storms had grumbled for some time over the hills, and great violet-black masses of heavy rain-clouds came trailing up from the south-west. A fitful wind, moisture-laden, blew up the *khora*, and the cool grey morning tempted me to loiter under the trees, which, in anticipation of their approaching function, had put forth a fresh head of green young leaves.

A light pattering sounded behind me. I turned in surprise to see the lean head of an old wild bitch quickly withdrawn in the grass! Then came a yap, and a scampering in the jungle; then another yap; and, paralysed with fear for a moment, I laid my antlers craftily back, and crept away at right angles. In vain! A long line of my fierce little hunters were extended in a fan, and, overlapping me, were swiftly closing in!

Turning, I lumbered up the *khora*, and, breaking into a panic-stricken gallop, glanced behind to see the horrid, mute line of leaping, skulking red forms pouring from the woods in grim earnest.

What a chase! Climbing over spurs—dashing down the far side—scattering the clucking spurf-owl—bursting through the brittle jungle!

Once I sought to turn aside, but their flank was thrown swiftly forward, and headed me back. Realising that the easily loping brutes behind were driving me as they listed, I grew desperate and made a sudden dash for a side glen: the scraggy old bitch I had first seen came up with a rush, and her jaws closed like a vice on my belly; then, as I frantically plunged through some bamboos, was torn away, the blood pouring from the red gash.

On I clattered over the boulders, among which there now began to trickle a thin muddy stream, and, turning a bend, the fresh smell of rain-soaked earth struck my nostrils, as, carrying on its breath a distant peal of thunder, the first wild rush of the monsoon struck the groaning forest!

Large drops of rain met me as I laboured at a wearying gallop up the deep-cut ravine, and at length sighted the refuge I had sought—a deep pool under a little ledge of basalt, over which now poured an ever-thickening stream of red, earth-stained water.

Into this I plunged and turned in time to meet the leader of the pack, whom I struck under the water, my sharp fore foot cutting deep into his entrails: the rest surrounded me in an instant, finding their tongues for the first time, and bursting into a chorus of savage, whining yelps. Twice was I borne down, madly striking right and left with antlers and feet, and rose again, my cruel tormentors literally covering my bleeding form. The deepening, swirling pool was churned into yellow foam, the sharp snouts of the dogs sowing here and there as they swam ashore, and whined from the rocks, leaping out again to seize or be struck under.

At last down came the spate with a booming roar; and we were all caught up and hurried headlong downstream: my foes were swept away like corks, and I, with difficulty feeling ground, breasted the raging torrent an instant, and then dragged my harried body up the bank.

Yes, they were all gone, save a few that had followed down the opposite bank. Yet, what was this? The drowned and battered carcase of one of them yet hung from my chest, his bared fangs closed in the grip of death! Shaking myself free, blind with a furious fear, I impaled the dead body, and pinned it to the bank again and again—then I crawled under the lashing trees, and disappeared in driving sheets of rain.

* * * * *

Seat yourself on that rock, *Sahib*, and let your gaze wander over my forests spread out below. That distant mist rising beyond those low grey-blue hills marks the deep-sunk valley of the Tapti; before you the rolling sea of jungle stretches unbroken to the horizon, and beyond it to the sources of the Narbada; while at your feet the bamboo-tangled mountain-side descends well-nigh sheer to that broad shingly river-bed two thousand feet below, rising again to those lofty flat-topped sentinels beyond. The untiring voice of the green barbet floats up from the valley—"Kotúru—kotúru!" A jungle-cock sends his five clear notes into the calm evening air. The warm sky is full of the sunset gold.

And here I leave you. Farewell! and———"Dhánk!"

MELURSUS "DIABOLICUS."

Ursus labiatus, alias *Melursus ursinus* as he is now called, the common "Sloth" bear of India, appears to be an animal of varied accomplishments and strange contradictory character.

Scarcely any two of the sportsmen to whom we are indebted for information regarding the habits of Indian game appear to be of one mind with respect to the temper and general bearing of this interesting quadruped in such dealings as he may have with man. A quiet, inoffensive vegetarian, say some,—although this would hardly agree with the experiences of the forty and two children torn by the bears introduced to them by one Elisha,—a poor old blundering buffoon of the woods, fleeing from a shadow, receiving his death wound with quiet resignation, and remonstrating with plaintive ululations alone: a nasty-tempered quarrelsome brute, say others: a persevering enemy that will not leave his victim the semblance of humanity, says the native.

It appears however that the character of this bear, with respect to man, depends largely on locality. On the Central India plateau he is an object of great dread to the native, more to be feared than any tiger or panther. Instances of his totally unprovoked attacks on human beings are here frequent. A belated villager, some poor creature squatting in the woods to gather the fallen flowers of the *mhowa* tree, the traveller pausing by some jungle pool —any of these will do. The face and head of the victim are almost invariably chosen as his objective by this infernal brute, and he will not usually leave the poor flesh until it is difficult to tell to whom it once belonged. That this picture is not too highly coloured may be proved by anyone travelling in those parts. Gruesome objects, jawless, scalped horrors, are at the present moment to be seen in the hamlets of the forest region referred to. These are instances of the somewhat incomplete handiwork of *Melursus.*

Fewer accidents occur to the sportsman through the agency of bears than by that of felines. This is to be attributed to various reasons. *Melursus* is not so quick, and his armament is inferior to that of tiger or panther : the ground he chooses as his resort often abounds in points of vantage for the hunter on foot : his black coat will not permit him to hide in a handful of twigs—all this, added to the fact that some of our books on Indian sport make light of and poke fun at him, induces the ordinary sportsman to undertake operations against the sloth bear without, perhaps, that seriousness which would accompany his actions when tackling more dangerous game.

However, it is a dangerous thing to underrate one's adversary ; and nasty, sometimes fatal, accidents have before now occurred to sportsmen, who have discovered too late that the so-called sloth or "Honey" bear can on occasion wake up, and attack with remarkable vigour, inflicting wounds as severe, though not so dangerous, as those dealt by the *felidæ.*

She-bears of this variety, with cubs, are apparently the offenders in most cases of unprovoked assault, although it is the writer's experience that, when wounded, bears have been more aggressive as a rule than similarly wounded felines.

Bear stories are so common, and have figured so largely in tales of Indian sport, that in sympathy with the reader one must at the outset cry—"Halt !" But the narrative of an extraordinary escape the writer had when once fairly in the clutches of one of these black, hairy, yelling brutes is too tempting to pass by.

As has been hinted at, there was a time when he held but scant respect for *Melursus;* but up to that date it had not been his privilege to make acquaintance with the sub-family "*diabolicus.*"

It was during a singularly ill-chosen expedition to a certain district of the Central Provinces, that once bore a great name as a hunting-ground, that camp was pitched not far from a rocky range of sandstone hills named "Chitra-Kátra." Thither the writer found himself riding out at dawn one morning in the merrie month of May. The men had gone on overnight, and were to watch the hillsides from before daylight for the bears which I was assured I should find.

I should hasten to make it plain that, being a "family man," my methods of *shikár* have to be tempered with a due regard to the avoidance of a too intimate or personal acquaintance with wild beasts in their live and kicking state. A "foot" *shikári*, of the tree-and-rock-roosting species, I had hitherto gone scatheless through episodes—some tame, others exciting, all happily without harm to any of the people accompanying me—which had imbued me with a cock-sureness that ordinary prudence was all that was required to justify me in assuring those anxious for my welfare that no risks could or would be run.

On reaching the foot of Chitra-Kátra hill not long after sunrise, a distant whistle and vigorous beckoning brought me scrambling happily to the top, where I was informed that a large she-bear with a cub had been seen loafing about, and had, just before my arrival, disappeared behind some rocks half-way down the hillside. Creeping along, I met the other *shikári*, and was joined by two of my men with rifle and gun.

It appeared that there were some caves below those rocks. I then went cautiously forward, and found myself on top of a long terrace of perpendicular sandstone, about twenty feet high, running along the face of the hill. At the foot of this cliff came a narrow ledge, and below this again a sloping face of smooth rock that, becoming ever steeper, at length dropped over the edge of a cliff. At the bottom of this lower cliff was a mass of big boulders, and thorny jungle crept up thus far from the surrounding woods.

I had previous experience of she-bears, which I had known to come viciously charging up fifty yards of rocky hillside for nothing at all but the sound of a human voice; so I stood quietly there to elaborate some scheme by which the old lady might be "drawn" without compromising anybody's safety. As I did so, I heard a bear snuffling and grunting, about a hundred yards off, nearer the foot of the hill; so I ran on tiptoe along the rocks to find that the beast, which had evidently become suspicious, was making off into the jungled plain below. I followed the noises for about half an hour without coming up with the bear, then lost them, and returned to the hill, rating the *shikáris* for not having marked the game down with greater accuracy.

Since only one bear had been seen, and the hill and caves had been watched from before dawn, it was natural to conclude that that bear was the one I had heard going away, and that the caves were vacant; so I came climbing up in a slanting direction and joined the men; after which we all clambered on to the narrow ledge before described, and began looking for marks along it, out of curiosity to see the place.

I had quite given up all hope of any sport that morning, and was ruminating on the shockingly gameless condition of the country in which I had already wasted a useless fortnight. I went slowly along the ledge, followed by the *shikáris* and men, looking into little recesses below the perpendicular face of sandstone, and under the impression that there was no hiding-place sufficient for a bear. The *shikáris*, local men, were now of opinion that there *was* no cave here.

After a time there came a corner, round which curved the ledge we were following, and passing this I suddenly found myself in front of a large low-roofed cave.

At the far end of this antechamber, into which the morning sun shone brightly, were two dark apertures leading into the bowels of the hill. On the sandy floor of the entrance to the cave were the fresh ingoing marks of a bear, and none leading out!

We had halted, I suppose, for a few seconds, and I had let fall a word or two, in a low tone, to the effect that a bear was there all right and it was no place for us.

Next to me was the local Gónd *shikári*, and behind him a young Ját non-commissioned officer of my regiment; while another of my men had been posted on the terrace above us to act as a look-out.

Our position was a sufficiently hazardous one from the nature of the surroundings, as will be noted by a glance at the sketch of the episode—itself copied from a photograph secured during a subsequent visit to the scene of disaster. It did not take long for a mental appreciation of that situation to form itself, and the next moment we were quietly retracing our way.

Round the corner whence we had come was a little room for expansion, so to speak, where the precarious ledge widened slightly, and formed a kind of niche or platform overhung by rock. For this vantage ground we were now making; and, had we reached it, I think that bear might, with a fair amount of certainty, have been defeated and precipitated into the depths below. But unfortunately there was a "but" in the case: scarcely had we taken one step in retrogression when a horrible subterranean disturbance occurred in the depths of the cavern we had just left.

This accelerated our movements somewhat; but they were as nothing compared to the rapidity of the eruption that was going on behind us, and in less than no time a disgusting outcry belched forth from the dark opening in the face of sheer rock, and a furious bellowing announced that the brute was on us! So close were we to our little haven round the corner that my own man had already arrived; but for those in rear of him—time was up! The Gónd leapt like any ape up some narrow cleft just ahead of me; while for me there was nothing but a swift whip round to face this horrid trouble, my rifle not even permitted to reach my shoulder. To right—a blank wall of smooth cliffside; to left—a swift descent to the unknown over the edge of a slope scarcely less sudden than that of an ordinary church steeple; and in front—a raging, roaring, mass of black hair shooting towards me with the speed of a runaway motor-car!

Bang! goes my rifle right into and touching the brute's back—and next moment I am in some strangely slow-moving nightmare, one of the most vivid of its kaleidoscopic memories being the peculiarly smooth-brushed appearance of *Melursus*' forehead as her jaws close on my right thigh, and seem to remain there for ages!

Then, curiously enough, I am upside down; and everything whirls round and round in a freak-like dance! Through clenched teeth I remember breathing some desperate remark such as "Done for *this* journey!"

There came a sudden shock.

With fingers gripped tight in some harsh long hair, or clutching at elusive rock-slopes, we bump and whirl swiftly downwards—instinctive ideas of the cliff awaiting us darting through my whirring brain!

To a certain extent a species of unconsciousness then seems to have supervened; for it appeared to be long after this that there came a sudden shock, and a numb sensation seized my back and side. In a kind of mist I saw the shaggy body of the bear hurled far from me into space; and then there came a distant deep thud and, after it, a faint rattling crash—ah! my poor dear rifle, that was you; was it not?

Slowly I became conscious that I was clutching something: things seemed all anyhow. Yes; it was a little tree that was gripped in the strength of despair, and I was hanging on to it, head downwards, on the face of the cliff itself!

My Ját orderly's voice soon sounded in my ear. "Oh, *Bhagwán! Bhagwán!*" I heard him pant, "he is saved!" The plucky fellow had crawled down that awful slope, having in the first place, ere ascending the fatal hill, luckily enough removed his shoes. And now he managed to seize one of my hands, I was somehow drawn upwards, and, getting on to the curve of the slope, was assisted up to the ledge, where I sat down.

My first thought, I must confess, was "Bear!" and a weight seemed suddenly lifted off my chest as I realized that the brute would find it impossible to reach me again. After that a feeling of resentment supervened, bitter and cruel in its intensity, and, as my eyes fell angrily on the jungle below, I eagerly stretched out a hand for my weapon. But alas! had I not heard its splintering crash in that terrible fall!

Then it was that my gaze fell on one tiny, solitary tree—less than a sapling—that clung to the cliffside. And I thought of bears no more, seized with a silent amazement at that miraculous escape!

That little branch, no thicker than a man's ankle, but of wondrous toughness, rooted in some mere chink in the rock, was the only break in all the smooth face of sandstone around. There was no other tree within many yards! Ever since its chance seed germinated in that minute niche had it grown towards the fulfilment of a noble mission; and behold to-day the realization thereof!

Flourish there, little lonely tree! Swing in naught but caressing breezes from thy sun-kissed root-hold; and would that they might all be moisture-laden! Increase and multiply thy grateful spreading boughs! But this is not thy destiny—for 'tis only an obscure little jungle plant called "*Bhiria*,' whose name I would set big on a scroll of honour.

Remembering now that the bear had seized me, and that I seemed to have no right leg at all when I crawled back to safety, I glanced down.

* * * * *

It should be noted that absolutely no sense of pain had accompanied my late adventure. It was therefore with a kind of humourous incredulity that I stared at what met my astonished gaze—the thin shooting breeches hanging in gory tatters round a limb that was soaked in blood from groin to ankle!

Off came the breeches, and the marvel only grew. One, two, three, four great holes in my leg—my own good right leg! It seemed incredible. I wiped away what obscured the wounds, and felt their gaping edges with at first gentle then bolder fingers. I gauged their depth with probing fingers, lifting up in my curiosity a flap of tunnelled muscles ; and still no pain of any kind ! I uncorked my water-bottle of clean boiled water, and directed its stream from some height into the ragged apertures ; examined them again, cleaned them out, and bound the leg round with a pocket handkerchief and strips of *pagri* cloth—and I never felt fitter in all my life !

The Ját, Mulloo, was meanwhile regaling the party with a vivid description of the catastrophe, and his solemn round eyes and broad-mouthing speech so tickled me, as he explained, with very illustrative gestures, how I had fallen forwards and, fixing my hands in its shaggy coat, mounted that howling, horrified bear, before, accompanied by our satellites the hat, rifle, and little bear, we had gone revolving down, that I leant back and roared with a laughter that went a long way in allaying the fears of the faithful fellows attending me.

The only now practicable way off the hill was *past the cave again*, and down a rough mass of boulders, and sufficiently arduous it was indeed. Meanwhile the *shikári*, who had gone down to pick up the pieces of my rifle, brought up the carcase of the bear cub, with my bullet hole in its forehead. The little brute, clinging to its mother's shaggy shoulders, had intercepted or at least set up the bullet considerably. Whether the she-bear got any of it is not known. She went slowly off round a spur of the hill, halting twice *en route*, say the men.

Camp, six miles off, was reached at last on a stretcher made of two poles and a *pagri*. Here to my concern it was found that most of the perchloride of mercury mixture I had brought with me had leaked from the glass-stoppered bottle ; but a little was left, and, making up the solution, I washed and syringed out the wounds, now feeling faint from pain.

A day of "Loo," or roaring hot winds, was succeeded by a calm cool night, and I was carried ten miles farther. By this time my back had stiffened from my fall of the morning, and it was impossible to obtain rest for a moment, nor could I, though incessantly sitting up and lying down again, draw breath without pain. To ease the back I tried to turn on my side; but at that such a cramp seized the lacerated muscles of the thigh that the horrified bearers of my bed almost dropped me at the sharp expletive which rose involuntarily to the sky.

All next day was spent at a roadside bungalow: the wounds had glazed over, and it was necessary to open them up and dress them again, which at last I forced myself to do with my penknife. At night came torture at the hands of the little native assistant surgeon summoned to treat me. A night of morphia-induced slumber, and twenty-five miles more on the bed, brought me to a small civil station, a friend in need and comparative rest—comparative, for here came chloroform and an operation. Though a mauling from a bear is not so dangerous as one from a carnivorous animal, there was considerable apprehension of pyæmia setting in: but the fact of being in hard condition averted that from the outset.

In one single bite the bear, seizing the leg sidewise, had made all her four canine teeth almost meet. In that wound practically all the muscles of the lower part of the thigh were involved; and a considerable portion of them, forming a dangerous flap, had to be subsequently removed by the surgeon's knife. One fang penetrated to and almost severed the very tubing in which runs the femoral artery.

Two months on one's back, surrounded by hospital smells, afforded scope for thought; and in reviewing the affair the following points suggested themselves.

In the first place, the unlucky position that placed me at that bear's disposal was one of sheer deception.

Secondly, as the bear had some yards in which to get up a rattling pace, and a sharp curve round which to approach me, completely under cover until within a few feet, it was impossible to stop her in time. Indeed, had I brained her, she must have got me once somewhere, being straight head on to me and coming so fast. The only thing that could have averted a catastrophe would have been a projectile of sufficent energy to at once overcome and arrest *her* energy of, say, 250lbs. travelling at 25 miles per hour, and it is not possible to carry a one-pounder Vickers-Maxim everywhere!

So far, we see, all the luck was on the side of the wild beast; but when she seized me it was my lucky star that rose. The bear caught me where I could best afford it—the big muscles in front of the thigh.

Again, the precarious foothold saved me. Our impact and my fall on her back upset the brute, and our rapid descent of the slope prevented her from losing her grip and seizing me again; it would doubtless have been my face and head then!

After that, the tree interposed, by a truly extraordinary piece of luck, in the small of my back—the only place to stop my whirling descent; it saved me doubly, for had I possibly escaped death by falling, the bear, finding me still with her, would undoubtedly have polished me off in her own hideous way.

The melancholy forebodings of a "dot-and-carry-one" action, and those horrid-looking boots with the ultra-Parisian heels, were fortunately not realized; and the leg is almost as good as new. But the lesson has been worth the learning. Bhalu may be a vegetarian: but to presuppose a general mildness of temperament thereby seems misguided, and hardly good enough.

PAKHAL NADDI OF THE PALM TREES.

The literature of hog-hunting is already so complete, and has been dealt with by such past masters in the sport itself as well as in its portrayal, that the subject is to be approached with the greatest diffidence. All that can be said on this grand, engrossing, hunting topic must needs savour too much of what has gone before ; and yet reminiscences of bygone days at "Junglypur" would be incomplete without some reference to what the old place afforded us of this very quintessence of the hunter's sport.

Hog-hunting played a great part in the woodland sports of Ancient England, if we are to judge by the preponderance of the "boare," the "wylde swyne," in the hunting pictures and poetry of a certain period of those olden days. The lines of Chaucer and of other contemporary poets testify to the hunter's joy in partaking of what was evidently considered the "blue riband" of that old time *shikár*—his pride and boast of conquest over the "fearsome tuskyd beaste."

In the lay of "Syr Eglamoure of Artoys" (dated 1570) we have a wonderfully spirited account of hog-hunting three hundred and thirty years ago, which will show pigstickers of to-day that there is little "new under the sun :—"

Syr Eglamoure wened well to do,
With a speare he rode him to,
As fast as he myghte ryde.
Or yf he rode never so fast,
The good speare asonder brast,
It wolde not in the hyde.

(from which we fear that Syr Eglamoure had failed to keep his hogspear keen, as all good pigstickers should.)

> That boare dyd him wo ynoughe,
> His good horse under him he sloughe,
> On foot than must he bide!

However, Syr Eglamoure had a second weapon on which to fall back—hys good swerde—and so probably fared better than would the hog-hunter of the present day, when—

> "On foot than must he bide."

Shakspere's Venus foretells the death of her Adonis should he encounter with the "boare"—

> —with javeling's point a churlish swine to goare,
> Whose tushes, never sheathed, he whetteth still,
> Like to a mortall butcher bent to kill.
> His brawnie sides with hairie bristles armed
> Are better proof than thy spear's point can enter
> *   *   *
> Being irefull on the lyon he will venter.

So when we are told that pigsticking in India was evolved from bear-spearing, that that its superiority was not discovered till the supply of bears had run out, we cannot restrain an exclamation of doubt. It does not seem likely that the earliest Indian pigstickers would have required such guiding towards a sport of their ancestors; besides which, hog-hunting was already recognised and indulged in by the chiefs of Hindostán.

Long years though they be since the "wylde swyne" dwelt in English copses, those fortunate enough may still enjoy his pursuit in this land of their adoption. We whose lines were cast awhile at "Junglypur" were lucky enough to get the sport first hand from Nature—so to speak—at our very doors; and, above all, without that much-to-be-deplored expenditure which has gone far to bring pigsticking towards the level of Indian racing.

Our hog-hunting cost us nothing—no two thousand rupee racehorses—no heavy tent club mess bills. But we got our pig!

As the rider canters over the level cultivated plains four miles due west of Junglypur, there rises to meet him, over long stretches of cotton and millet, a line of nodding, slender-necked date-palms, their drooping plumes hanging above the tangled coverts of a little stream known as "the Pakhal Naddi."

The name of this beautiful piece of pig covert is perhaps derived from the word *pakhál*, meaning a *bhisti's* water-bag; and a happy simile it is, for the stream watering it may aptly be likened to a never-failing *massak*. Throughout the driest hot-weather season its springs well forth in the midst of a parched and dusty plain, and break away in a deep cool stream, meandering over a muddy bed from pool to pool, the still dark depth of which reflect the graceful overhanging forms of shady boughs.

This covert is extremely thick, and of the kind known so well to Deccan hog-hunters as a *sindhibund*, where the undergrowth is largely composed of dwarf date bushes, intermingled with *lantána* and *karúnda*, and where impenetrable masses of dense green creepers, encouraged by the moisture-soaked soil, swarm tumultuously up the highest palms, flinging thick canopies of verdure over their drooping plumes, and smothering the underwood in an all-pervading embrace. Hard by, irrigated by little channels led off the main stream, are several betelnut, sugarcane, and other gardens, affording a cover scarcely less secure than the palm *nála* itself; the whole, in sooth, forming a retreat calculated to lull the most suspiciously inclined porker with soft dreams of high feeding and undisturbed peace.

We first essayed our luck with the denizens of the Pakhal Naddi not long after our first arrival at Junglypur—now many years ago—and since few of us had ever before been able to indulge in the glorious sport, our methods would have horrified anyone accustomed to an orderly tent-club way of conducting affairs! Most of us had yet to blood our virgin spears, and it was on this our first day "every man for himself and the devil for the hindmost." We were accompanied by a motley rabble of dogs, both small and great—hounds and mongrels, terriers and long-legged lurcher-like brutes, which one of our number termed his "greyhounds." All the same we had no sooner entered a scrubby fallow patch *en route* to the Pakhal Naddi, one early morning, than the fun began.

Aroused by the annoying yap-yapping of a diminutive fox-terrier at his ear, a good boar rose from a grass patch, and made for an adjoining bit of garden cultivation; whereat a hubbub arose that baffles description. Strong men yelled, spears flashed in dangerous proximity to neighbours' ribs, bushes crashed, hedges burst asunder, greyhounds were trodden on, ridden over, and wailed vociferously, and the main body of the pursuers, gathering strength as it went, hustled off after the pig; while, in quite another direction, a somewhat timorous individual, who had been persuaded to accompany us on the ground that it was the right thing to pig-stick, was to be seen, pale as death, balancing precariously on the neck of his country-bred mare, as he was swept away over the yet misty fields into, apparently, the "ewigkeit."

What an uproar there was in that garden patch where the perplexed pig took refuge as the storm of hoofs swept o'er him! Full of little irrigation drains, tall castor-oil plants, and various other garden products, it was not long ere stirrup-leathers were torn from saddles, and excited sportsmen deposited in more or less damp spots with a celerity that spoke volumes for the efficacy of the entanglements. "Where is he? where is he?" gasped a hunter who was pale with hurry, and at whose belt hung various knives and other lethal weapons. "Where is he?" we bellowed, in English and the vernacular, to the scandalised and horror-stricken tender of the garden land, who stood on one leg, with his hands joined despairingly, as we swept through the lush vegetation.

A howl, and a small white terrier flung from out a bush, put us on the track once more, and this first of "first spears" was scored by a lucky jab downwards, as the boar rushed with a vicious lunge right and left between our horses' legs. "'Ware blind wells!" we yell, and the chase is resumed, to finally merge into a furiously struggling mass of stamping hoofs, angry grunts, and upraised spear-shafts, where the harried pig, gnawing a fetlock or two and desperately fighting to rise, gives up the ghost with evident relief and, in the spirit, is fled from the horrible inferno which, in the body, he could not escape.

Our local "cowboy" now dismounted, and, despite remonstrances, "killed" the already dead boar several times over, by shoving a large species of knife into the limp carcase.

Being the first time we had worked the Pakhal Naddi the ground was more or less unknown to us, and a good pig got away, unseen, in the direction of the Chandrabhaga—a river that comes down from the hills about a couple of miles to the west, and which was the nearest haven of security for pigs driven from the Pakhal.

There now ensued a long period of inaction and patient waiting. In time, however, the faint popping of *kawit* bombs and the crack of blank cartridge sounded nearer, mingled with the music of the kerosine tins; and after a while the bushes parted, close to where I had been posted with another spear—H.—and an enormous grey pig emerged, halted, eyed us an instant, and with a "humph!" of churlish disgust turned, and trotted coolly along the covert side, to disappear again into its shelter as he made off up-stream. He was shortly followed by a fine black boar, a shade bigger if anything, who pursued the same casual tactics with even less hurry. However, they must have put on the pace after this, for a few seconds later, two natives, who had been cutting brushwood quite two hundred yards away, rushed from the *nála* in suppliant attitudes; and we understood thereby that the pigs were taking a line straight away through the *nála* for the now familiar Chandrabhaga. Crossing the stream at a little clearing therefore, H. went up the far side, while I trotted up mine: the others had taken up unlucky positions and could not be seen.

Near the head of the *sindhibund*, where it ceased and the ordinary dry *samalu*-bushed watercourse began, I halted and awaited events; but my luck was out, for the boars did not come out so far up, and I shortly spied two rapidly moving objects half a mile away, and made out H. riding a big pig single-handed.

To gallop across the shingle, and set the mare going in this direction, was the work of a moment; and, my mount being fresh, I rapidly approached the scene of action, just too late however, for, as we forged alongside, H. scored first spear—a bit "abaft o' the mizzen" though, and the boar, the heaviest I had yet seen, and evidently our black acquaintance of a few minutes before, jinked across my front. Gallantly the little mare responded, and, with a bound forward, the spear point entered behind the small ribs, high up, and stood out from his brawny chest. None of us were rich in spears in those early days, so, fearing a smash, I let go ; and the pig, with the magic wand swaying from his flank, charged H., missed his horse, stumbled, recovered desperately, stumbled again, and fell on his knees, to sink slowly with a sigh on his side, and roll up the whites of his game little eyes—dead.

Meanwhile a more animated scene was being enacted nearer covert.

A big boar, so fat that he had only cantered a short distance into the open before lying up in wrath under a bush, had been attacked ; but, in spite of several severe wounds, had cut one horse, and regained the shelter of the thick *nála*. As we arrived on the scene, he had just made good his retreat down-stream, leaving a beater nursing his thigh, down which there trickled a thin red stain ; while, further on, a rider, more rash than the rest, had fallen, horse and all, over a steep bank, and had just been propped up, gazing vacantly into space. However, a bottle of soda soon pulled him round.

An uproar arising still further down-stream we hurried thither, and found the old pig, weak from loss of blood, standing behind some thick bushes. Edging round, I found him facing me down a tiny path in the jungle, his small eyes blazing with fury, and drew up the mare and lowered the spear point none too soon, for instantly making up his mind, and acting on his resolution like the good pig he was, out he came. Had he been fresher I fear there would have been good reason to bewail the folly of trying to take a charge at the halt, as it was only by thrusting downwards, with all the strength at my command, that I kept him down as he passed under the mare's belly, and *crack!* went the stout bamboo shaft, snapping in two just above the blade, as a rustle behind told us he had regained his sanctuary.

This boar was never found, although we had the covert hunted through for him next day, and so must be added to the list of 'wounded and got away.'

The beat, being resumed, was carried out to the end of the palm grove. Partridges whirred by in numbers; a jackal came slinking out and loped away across the open; and, at the last moment, a big sounder of sows and squeakers broke, and sped off in a long line northwards.

This brought our morning's sport to a close, and, cantering down past the *pân* gardens, there —a welcome sight— stood the tent, with the white figures of servants flitting about, preparing the breakfast to which we were soon doing ample justice amid the popping of soda-water and the gurgling of well-earned "pegs." Cheroots and a chat, and the opening meet of the Junglypur Tent Club broke up, as we drove off home the four miles to Cantonments.

Many a capital morning or afternoon did we enjoy here— and many a blank day, too—the proceedings often graced by the presence of the ladies of the station. The sport that we had been led to believe was to be had with the pig in other parts of the surrounding country never came up to our expectations however. In spite of capital bits of cover here and there, a very mistaken policy had filled every hamlet with licensed guns, and it was only regular strongholds like the Pakhal Naddi that could defy the systematic poaching of village *shikáris* and professional netters.

As I have already hinted, one day's hog-hunting *reads* very like another; so, in perplexity, one turns from the difficulties of prose to the snare of blank verse. It is by no means the first time that the metre of Longfellow's 'Hiawatha' has been murdered in adaptation, so apologies are perhaps superfluous.

The last time I saw the old 'Pakhal' four good pigs were laid out in a row by the Mess tent. Under the soft drooping foliage of the big tamarind trees by the ruined *fakir's* tomb, the good horses were being rubbed down, preparatory to being led home. The declining sun touched the surrounding fields with gold.

As we finished our 'pegs,' lit up cheroots, and got into the dogcart, I took a last look at the long line of gracefully-posed palms, now standing out black and sharp against the flaming western sky, in the quiet evening air. A moment later we swung round a bend in the road; and, with a sigh, realised that the Pakhal was a memory of the past!

PAKHAL NADDI OF THE PALM TREES.

In the Plain beneath the Mountains,
Mountains seven, wild Satpuras,
wells a rivulet—the Pakhal—
Pakhal Naddi of the palm trees.
Palm trees nodding o'er the copses;
copses full of creeper tangle;
tangle drooping ever downwards,
drooping, green, to kiss the surface,
surface of dark, placid Pakhal!

Darksome are those slimy thickets,
thickets of the Pakhal Naddi.

Waning moon not long since risen,
yellow o'er the eastern levels,
shimmers faint on winding covert,
covert sleeping soft, where crickets,
crickets, cicadæ, are trilling.

O'er the fields a solemn silence,
silence of the coming gilding,
green and golden, of the morning,
to eye-rubbing, yawning, waking,
stirring, waking Mother Nature.

Trembles higher star of morning;
grows soft light ere first false dawning;
stir the birds, cry "Chee!" in brambles;
dim lie fields beyond the brambles—
bare reaped fields beyond the brambles—
Where the grey and fleeting shadows,
prowling jackal, foul hyæna,
slink before compelling fingers,
first pale fingers of the morning.

From the trees beyond the river
flutes the koël—koël fluty;
scream they, early flying parrots;
stream they, arrow-like, o'erhead to
join their fellows mid the *bér* trees.
Partridge wakes—"Ka-teetur; tee-
tur!"
Antelopes, capricious moving,
yellow flanks turn towards the morning.

Far o'er furrow, through *paláti*—
dry-stalked, cotton-picked *paláti*—
comes a slowly moving darkness;

darkness growing ever nearer,
twining, halting, crackling, snuffing;
darkness of suspicious bodies,
bodies of suspicious darkness,
looming ever bigger, nearer,
till the snouts of snuffling '*dookers*,'
'*dookers!*'—pigs they, wild, of jungle—
snuff and gruntle slowly onwards.
Piggies full of sweet potatoes,
stolen sweetstuffs, luscious juices!
luscious they—the cane-stored juices,
slobbered canes of luscious sugar,
crunched up by the teeth of piggies
in that field beyond the river!
Lean sows grunting to their hoglets,
small brown hoglets squealing answer;
youthful boars assuming graces,
graceless pranks they ne'er had tried on
were he present—Grey-Boar, master!
Sterns retreating, tails a' twitching,
passes on the champing sounder,
sounder of the jungle '*dookers*,'
seeking shelter mid the Pakhal.

Entering the prickly covert,
covert closing tight behind them,
covert smiling in the sunshine,
level rays of dawning sunshine,
showing ne'er a sign of piggies,
innocent it smiles. Of '*dookers*'
what does it know? Peaceful Pakhal!

In the distance sounds a thudding,
cantering of useful 'tattoos';
ponies carry *sahibs* to hunting,
canter on till, dust subsiding,
sees them drawing rein o'er yonder,
under tamarinds so shady,
where the hunters—Arab—Waler—
switch their tails, by syces tended.

Thither, too, the scouts repairing.
Shortly see hog-hunters issue—
(champing curb-chain, glancing spear-tip),
cross the fields o'er, pass the ford by,
some to right and some to left hand
(and a couple with the beaters).

Roosting like some mangy vulture
in the branches of a *bábul*—
thorny tree that wild acacia —
sits a figure—stands a figure—
ape-like gibbers mid the branches,
branches of the thorny *bábul*;
pointing, beckoning—beckoning, pointing,
joins dusk hands before the *sahib*,
points into the Pakhal's shelter.
"There he lies, the horrid *sooar*!
"Oh! the rascal—Ah! the villain—
"may his destiny be blasted,
"and his female relatives all,
"nose-clipped hussies, may they shamed be!

"See! The swine came from the sugar,
"sugarcane of my own planting,
"trampling—crushing—masticating,
"night-long ravages in champing!
"When the *sahibs* were changing horses,
"burst he all my fence asunder,
"passed he thence into that thicket—
"thicket of the Pakhal Naddi.
"Where yon mango tree's dark shadow
"falls aslant the prickly palm-brake
"lies he daily—cursed '*dooker!*'

"See! I call my fellow-toilers
"(hasten Bápoo! hurry Ráma!)

" and, to aid your honour's hunting,
" join with them your beaters yonder."
In the thickest of the covert,
e'en at midday, fall but rarely,
chequered patterns of a sunlight
filtering through the verdure arching,
glancing rare on placid pool-face.
There the branches—very scratchy—
of the prickliest sort of *sendhi*,
trailing downwards, form a bower,
sweep the earth with lowered lance-points;
'neath this haven, ploughed and furrowed,
soft-tossed earth—the moistest, coolest
resting-place for grey-boar's tummy!
Grey-boar stretched out on his tummy,
hind legs trailing, snout soft 'nuzzling,'
snuff on sniff and sidewise 'nuzzling,'
turning up damp soil luxurious—
comfort for a hairy tummy!
Not too near that nagging party—
lean sow nagging, hoglet squeaking—
peaceful dreams of nightly visits,
long night visits to the sugar,
sugarcane or sweet-potato,
carrot yellow, onion juicy.
Not one earthly care he careth;
not one enemy he feareth
finger's snap for. Panther, Tiger,
when they mark him, cat-like, make as
though they failed at all to see him;
feign some previous engagement!
Grey-boar, therefore, scarcely stirreth
sleepy eyelid, ear slow twitching,
when a distance-mellowed clamour—
throb of tom-tom, howl of beater—
wafts so faintly on the breezes,
breezes balmy of the morning;
but, in somnolence, contemptful,
grunts he, on his side reclining—
" Nasty little shrill mosquitos!
how you bother with your pinging!"
'Length the beat, a corner turning,
coming near the likeliest covert,
swells out to a diapason,
swells the dusky throats of beaters.
Pops the squib! *bang—bangs!* blank cartridge,
rattle empty tins from Baku!
thwack with bamboo, poke with bamboo,
Hoo the '*dooker*'—Ha! the '*dooker*'—
rout him out, the tusky '*dooker!*'
See! On down-curved wing comes whizzing
driven partridge, bush-quail screeching;
wheels scared nightjar; shrieks the lapwing;
halts the lobbing hare, upsitting,
hearkens to the din behind him.
Then the bushes, gently shaking,
part, and void the motley sounder:
lean sows grunting to their hoglets,
hoglets hurrying swiftly after,
hurry past the prickly arbour—
Grey-boar's green and shady harbour.
Grey-boar, on his side extended,
hind legs draws up, eyebrow raises,
raises up his mighty headpiece,
meditates in formidable
bristly-whiskered indignation—
" What a most unseemly hooting!
" tins a' rattling, horns a' tooting!

Bursting from the prickly covert.

" (Hoo ? the '*dooker*'—Ha ? the
'*dooker*')—
" why the devil such a hurry ? "
Gone ! my swift stampeding sounder,
fled the hare and flown the partridge !
(Sudden sounds a shriller screaming—
" Oh ! I see him—Ah ! I see him.")
" Really this is too outrageous !
" What about a dart among the
" dusky shins of yelling beaters ? "
Bangs a sudden bomb behind him—
stinging, reeking, vile saltpetre—
helps to make for him his mind up.
Grey-boar surly walks from covert,
leaves his enemies a bouquet—
scarcely that of rose or lily—
odour of the bristly '*dooker !*' ;
passes down those aisles o'er arching
Pakhal Naddi of the palm trees.
Where a little knoll uprising,
bush-encumbered, palm-frond studded,
gives a view towards the westward—
westward to the Chandrabhaga—
shingly-bedded Chandrabhaga—
lurk the hunters, hidden almost,
flashing spear-tip, hidden almost ;
hidden quite the Arab, Waler,
ears a' twitch and bits a' champing,
waiting grace of Pakhal Naddi.
Hark ! The distant throb of drumming !
(tighten chin-strap, grasp the spear-haft)
anxious watch yon covert, prickly
covert-side of prickly Pakhal.
See him there ! our brother-hunter—
Rufus of the scanty top-knot,
cunning rider, rider leary—
keeping fairly near the exit,
easing gee-gee, lest it weary,
slipped off earthward from the saddle,
stands dismounted by his gee-gee.
See him ! watch him ! wily Rufus
gathers up his reins so artless ;
artless Rufus, so nonchalant,
places casual foot in stirrup !
Where's he broken ? Rufus leary,
foxy brother—awfully wily—
we know what your little game is—
going to tell us when you're mounted
Grins he, unabashed, the culprit,
grins a grin, and points a lance-tip.
There they go ! the motley sounder,
lean sow lobbing, young boar trotting,
snouts set straight for Chandrabhaga—
shingly, bushy Chandrabhaga !
And behind them, breaking covert,
bursting from the prickly covert,
looms a shape ! Ribs sudden thumping,
thumps the heart, and throbs the temple—
Shades of *Sooars—what a whopper !*
Black as night that brow umbrageous !
grizzly-grey those 'chaps' outrageous !—
and that mighty head, dividing
ploughshare-like the thorns deriding.
Steals he strangely, smoothly, forward,
(twinkling legs screened all by grasses)—
halts ! And never sidewise turning,
roves his little keen set optic,
right and left his twinkling optic.
Softly ! softly ! brother hunters
(reins so ready, spurred heels twitching).
Prithee ! note that plain so stretching,

full two miles before us stretching:
grace awhile! The grey-boar trotteth
to his doom on plain far stretching.
Grace awhile! Till grey-boar trotteth
just too far to regain Pakhal,
not too far to gain the Chandra—
two miles hence the Chandrabhaga—
ere we catch him. Wait! Now *RIDE!*

'Neath strong hoofbeats furrow flying—
rushing wind in ears roar-roaring—
dart we from that knoll uprising,
bush-encumbered, palm frond-studded,
dart out on that plain far stretching.
Now the hunter, Arab, Waler,
neck and neck shall prove their mettle.
In a moment fly to meet us
prickly bush and hedgerow thorny;
just a pull to steady Arab,
bounds into the air our Waler,
hedgerow thorny's far behind us!

When the blood so madly courses,
to the lips a yell it forces;
yell of rushing, tearing gallop—
howl of glorious exultation
in this tearing, fighting gallop.
Grey-boar, lobbing there before us,
looming ever nearer, nearer,
hears that yell of exultation!
hears that rushing, tearing gallop!
slackens in his lazy lobbing—
halts! And never sidewise turning,
roves a sudden glittering optic.

Just too far the kindly Pakhal!
rather far, dear Chandrabhaga!
Grey-boar, swiftly meditating,
scarcely he an instant waiting,
springs out stoutly once more westward—
westward for dear Chandrabhaga!
But that deadly instant's pausing
brought swift hunters straining nearer,
till that grisly back, see-sawing,
scarce a spear's length vantage drawing,
seems to threaten with its bristling
fierce, and truculent see-sawing:
so, awhile, the hunted, hunters,
straining—racing—fly on forwards.
But the pace too good to last is—

See! His bounds seem getting shorter;
every leap his loins stretch longer;
angry boar, like lightning turning,
propping hoofs the light dust spurning,
crosses, like some swift torpedo,
foaming bows of rushing cruiser—
Then it was that spear-point harmless
sped into the furrow—bloodless—
and the Arab's knees, thud-thudding,
'gainst old Grey-boar's side struck thudding.
On his side comes Grey-boar angry—
down goes Arab—soars the rider!
turning turtle, mighty toss takes!

Lucky he! That Grey-boar rising,
stubborn, fierce, on plain arising,
marks a second foe—or truly
shared he fate of poor Adonis!
Flying, spurring, closely after,
comes the swiftly pounding Waler—
much too solid to knock over!—
rushes neck-stretched, thudding Waler,
rush to meet her, Grey-boar foaming—
red his furious glinting optic—
bristles upright, grey 'chaps' foaming,
onwards—upwards—bounds at Waler.

"*Hough—hough—hough!*" the Grey-boar foaming!
True bites spear-point, point of shoulder
passing—like a stroke of lightning—
such the force of that mad impact—
glances far and deeply through him;
but the speed of such an impact,
Grey-boar up the haft it hurls him;
cleanly keen, tush slices stifle—
stifle of the sturdy Waler;
cracks stout bamboo, splinters spear-haft,
foaming Grey-boar's left behind us—
standing sternly ominous, and grimly,
like some tide-set rock the surges
rushing over leave behind them.

So it comes—last fierce finale,
reins all tugging—wrenching—wheeling;
dry lips panting—wide eyes staring—
spurring back on Grey-boar reeling—
"*Hough—hough—hough!*" brave boar! still fighting—
grunting—charging—tushes tossing
fiercely upward! Let 'em *all* come!
Till at last—foes ever facing—
comes some strangely weary faintness,
dies the light from eyes courageous,
sinks to earth boar—grey and glorious!

• • •

Home o'er brown fields quietly jogging—
passed hot gallop—passed fierce killing—
let us ponder on this killing.
" How he must have felt that killing,
" grim old Grey-boar! brave old Grey-boar!
" rather I the kindly bullet—
" sudden, thudding, numbing bullet—
" than that chill blue lance's probing.
" Ugh! the gory lance so probing.
" Cruel fate thine! poor old Grey-boar
" (falls o'er eyes a misty feeling.)

" *Not a bit, dear boys!*—believe me,
" in a tearing, fighting gallop,
" when the end comes—comes it glorious!
" for in such a fight uproarious,
" where is dread anticipation?
" dead to pain is all sensation!
" Just one rushing—slashing—roaring—
" howling—maddening exultation—
" then Oblivion. Drops some Curtain.
" At its brightest, life's lamp broken.
" But the flame that's so extinguished,
" naught *it* knows when—how—extinguished!"

Therefore, give us, good old Pakhal!—
dear old palm-fringed Pakhal Naddi!—
Boars in plenty—gallops glorious,
many such a fight uproarious—
Pakhal Naddi of the Palm Trees!

THE MAN-EATER OF BELKHERA.

Hidden away in a corner of the little-known province of B——, and about one hundred miles due west of the capital of the Central Provinces, lies the little station of—let me call it—"Junglypur." Lying in the *terai* of the Satpúra mountains, Junglypur faces the steep wall-like ramparts of this range of hills at a distance of some five miles. Behind, to the southward, lie extensive, level, and fertile plains of cotton-producing fame.

In the old days the jungle almost surrounded the little Cantonment, flowing down from the hills over the *terai* country, unbroken save for a few patches of rough cultivation. In those times game of all kinds was very plentiful, and within easy reach of the station. It is on record that an officer of one of the native infantry regiments at Junglypur bagged a tiger in a field of *túr* on the spot now occupied by the rifle range; while a party of sportsmen shot three tigers before breakfast in the then dense coverts of the Chandrabhaga river, which issues from the hills six miles to the west. In the jungles along the lofty Bairát ranges bison used to be plentiful, and sámbar and bears were everywhere abundant. Panthers of course were common, and in those good old times they were even known to enter the native bazaars, and sometimes the Lines, in search of dogs, goats, or other prey.

Time has of course altered all this, its effects being felt even in an out-of-the-way place like Junglypur, and much of the charm of its situation has in consequence departed. The ploughshare has bitten deeply into the once jungle-smothered lands ; roads have opened up the erstwhile impenetrable depths of the "Mélghát," as the hilly forest region lying within the Satpúra range is called; improvements in firearms have thrown a large quantity of muzzle-loading muskets in the way of the natives of those tracts ; and game has greatly diminished in numbers.

However, when I was quartered at this queer, little, old-fashioned station, some years ago, there was still a fair amount of *shikár* to be had—if one cared to work pretty hard for it, and had sufficient patience to put up with a somewhat disheartening proportion of blank days. In this connection I refer to "big game:" antelope, *chinkára*, and such smaller game were really plentiful, and not difficult to get at.

I will however pass over a description of the sport obtainable in the vicinity of little Junglypur, confining myself to the story of the Belkhera man-eater, a recital of whose misdeeds and bold ferocity may prove more interesting.

It is an accepted fact that a large number of man-eaters in Central India and the Deccan are panthers. No man who has even a short experience of panthers and tigers will deny that the former animal is the more dangerous of the two. The tiger is, as a rule, a gentleman. The panther, on the other hand, is a bounder. The tiger is not infrequently a blunderer ; but *Felis pardus* knows exactly how to combine the two attributes of dashing pluck and almost unerring discretion, which are his by inheritance.

The panther moreover—his habits leading him to the vicinity of villages—is much more familiar with man, and in consequence holds him in greater contempt than does the tiger, whose acquaintance with the biped is generally confined to a yelling band of demons and a terrifying explosion from some tree-top. It is therefore not surprising to find that, where their numbers are nearly equal, the spotted cat is a greater *connoisseur* of human flesh than is his striped congener.

During the time that I was a resident of Junglypur there was usually one man-eater at least at his fell work in the Mélghát and surrounding hilly districts, and he was pretty certain to be a panther. A favourite ground for these operations was the low hilly country bordering the Tapti river, whence the attack would be conducted, and toll taken in the small Korku villages situated on the rich and cultivated strips of alluvial land on its banks. One such man-killer was credited with a bag of twenty-seven victims, including a misguided native *shikári*, who sat up for him in a tree, but was, in his turn, cleverly stalked. All that his friends found of this unfortunate were the soles of his feet and a coil of blood-stained hair. At last this dreaded marauder was shot by a plucky little Korkúni as it was dragging her husband out of his hut in a field at night.

In the neighbourhood of a hill village named "Asalwara," not far from the old fort of Narnála, another man-eating panther made his appearance; and after eight grass-cutters—members of a gang who had come up from the plains to ply their trade—had been mysteriously made away with, he was wounded by a brother-officer of mine and disappeared. From this it was concluded that he had died of his wound. However, man-killing began not long afterwards on the banks of the Tapti once more.

From my own observations I have formed a theory that, unlike the tiger, who once a man-eater is often always a man-eater, the panther, with his superior cunning, is not so incautious as to enter on such a career in too exclusive a manner. He probably exercises the greatest circumspection in choosing his human victims, only taking advantage of them when satisfied by patient observation that he can do so with comparative impunity, and spreading his depredations in the human line over wide areas. Between times he must, therefore, fall back on his normal habits—feeding on jungle-pigs, village goats, cattle, &c. These habits it is, probably, which make it so difficult to tell whether the real offender has been brought to book.

One evening in the cold weather a Korku appeared at my bungalow, and informed me that a man from his village, Belkhéra, had been caught—by tiger or *shér*, of course—while cutting bamboos up the precipitous sides of the Mahadeo *khora*. He was quite sure that it was a tiger: had seen it looking at him from some rocks, and its "pugs" were *so* big—spreading out his hands as he spoke: so I was equally certain that it was a panther.

Belkhéra is a small Korku village four miles from Junglypur, and at the foot of the hills. It is situated on the banks of a large *nála* that runs up for nearly four miles into the heart of the mountains. At the far end of this long deep glen is the aforesaid Mahadeo *khora*, or ravine. Nothing therefore could be attempted that night, especially as there was no moon.

Next morning, however, I rode out to Belkhéra, before it was light, and the first streaks of dawn found us half-way up its long glen. It was bitterly cold, and the deep-sunk valley was drenched in heavy dew. The little jungle track lay alternately over the trap boulders of the shrunken stream and through long patches of red *rausa* grass. To the right and left the hillsides soared almost sheerly up, clothed with bamboo thickets, and thickly dotted with innumerable *salai* trees, which at this season were shedding their autumnal-tinted leaves. High over the surrounding spurs the curious pyramid-shaped peak of the Chór Pahár (Robbers' Hill) jutted into the sky. Further on, rising to a height of about 3,500 feet, were the twin hill-tops of Jhákra, and under them lay the precipice-girdled Mahadeo *khora*. It was here that the panther had seized the woodcutter on the previous day.

At last we arrived at this ravine. The scene of the tragedy was pointed out, and I crept quietly forward to reconnoitre the spot. It was possible that the panther might still be near his victim's body.

The unfortunate man had been seized and strangled, without so much as a cry escaping him, while engaged in chopping male bamboos out of a small thicket of these plants; and his body appeared, by the tracks, to have been dragged along the hillside into the bed of the steeply-falling ravine, and then carried further up it. We now arrived at a place over which pours a small cascade during the rainy season; and here the tracks ceased. I had ascended this ravine once before, and was therefore able to make a guess at the most likely place for the panther to lie up in. This was a deep pocket in the smooth-worn rocks, over which hung the roots of an old banyan tree that clung to the cliffside higher up, sheltering a small pool of stagnant rain-water. Wearing cotton-soled stalking boots as I was, there was little difficulty in climbing up to this spot without a sound, and slipping back the cartridges into the breech of my rifle, I crawled forward and peered round the corner.

The place was deserted; and not a sound disturbed the silence, except the rustle of some dried leaves as a small brown squirrel ran up the rocks. The green scum on the surface of the water had been disturbed, however, and the rock at its edge had been freshly wetted.

I was proceeding to examine this, when a stone fell from the cliffs up-stream, and an exclamation from one of the Korkus caused me to glance up. A large panther was in the

He clung to the rock,

act of clambering up another dry waterfall. He clung to the rock just at the top, and was glancing back before springing out of sight beyond it. At this moment I fired.

The brute slipped, recovered, clung again, and, an instant later, disappeared before a second shot could be put in.

We had a difficult climb out of the ravine; but I felt sure I had hit the panther, and that I should find him not far away; and at last we stood looking down on the spot where he had clung and disappeared. With due precautions this place was examined, and, further on, a few drops of blood were found. They led us up and on to a little game-path, continued here and there for about a hundred yards, and then failed.

Two hours afterwards we gave up the search in despair, and returned to the pool. There, neatly tucked away in the knotted roots of the banyan tree, were the remains of the miserable woodcutter. All his clothes had been stripped off him, and the legs, backs of the thighs, and all soft parts having been eaten and torn away, the corpse presented the most ghastly appearance. The head was stiffly bent backwards; the teeth projected in a frightful grin. Even in life the poor Korku is no beauty.

The throat of this poor creature bore marks of extra ferocious treatment, and was simply covered with deep, gaping wounds. A peculiar feature of his injuries was that he had been partially scalped!

As may be imagined, I lost little time in getting away from this dreadful spectacle.

That afternoon I returned, with a number of men, and very thoroughly beat the surrounding ravines and jungle; but with no greater success. It could only be hoped, therefore, that the man-eater had taken himself off to die in some distant spot.

* * * * *

Almost exactly one year subsequent to the above events, I was again informed of a human " kill " near the ill-fated Belkhéra.

This time the victim was an old woman. She had been seized half-way up the main glen, near a place named " Béra Páni." Béra Páni was a kind of rendezous for grass-cutters, where they collected their grass bundles to be carted down to the village.

This poor old lady had come up the valley with a party of Korkus, who had scattered in search of grass. Her son, a child of ten or so, was with her. Son and mother separated during their work. At mid-day the boy heard the sound of a fall, and a kind of gurgle, but thought it was his mother throwing down a heavy bundle of grass and then clearing her throat. There were grasscutters all over the hillsides, who called out to each other occasionally, and from the ravine hard by, down at Béra Páni, came the cheerful tinkling of bells as the bullocks stood grazing near the carts.

In the late afternoon the boy carried his load of grass to the carts, but his mother did not appear. Becoming anxious after a while, he went up-hill again in search of her, and came on her grass bundles, then on her sickle. Further on he saw blood-smears on the grass stems, which so terrified him that he bolted like a deer back to the Béra Páni, screaming, " Tiger ! tiger ! ! "

In a moment the cry had spread to the grasscutters yet on the hill, who rushed huddling together, and were shortly afterwards chattering and gesticulating round the motherless boy. After a while half-a-dozen men banded together, and, armed with sticks and hatchets, followed the tracks of the kill and drag, shouting and beating trees up a side *nála.* First they came on the woman's *sári*, then on the body itself—one leg eaten. The panther was slinking off up-hill, having been actually seated tearing at his prey when disturbed. One of the Korkus, having been employed by me previously on my excursions in these hills, had the presence of mind to persuade his companions to leave the body as it lay and send for me. A bungle however was made, and I did not get the news until next day at 2 o'clock.

Shortly after 4 o'clock I was walking up the Belkhéra glen. As I turned a corner I came on a number of the villagers, among whom sat two native policemen, solemnly taking down the evidence of the *pancháyat* which had just been held on the corpse of the ill-fated woman. Here I learnt that during the night the panther had returned, and dragged the body of his victim far up the hillside. Of course, as usual, it was a *bágh*—an enormous tiger with paws *so* big, &c.—but I had discovered the pugs of a large panther close to the stream by this time. After a talk, in order to discover how the land lay, my Pathan orderly and I, led by a guide, proceeded to climb the hill, followed by men with *kulharis* (small hatchets) and rope.

The man-eater had removed the corpse about five hundred feet up the hillside; and being guided to the spot and ascertaining, by creeping quietly in, that he was not in the immediate vicinity, I found it poked away under a small bamboo clump. Its appearance was still more horrible than that of the Korku killed the previous year, but somehow not so revolting, the remains bearing small resemblance to humanity. The entire lower half of the body had been devoured, with the exception of the shins and feet; the knee-joints had been crunched apart like the knuckle-bones of a chicken, and lay twisted out of all semblance to human shape; one arm had been chewed; and the other lay extended, with the pewter bracelets still encircling the withered old wrists.

The nape of the neck, the shoulders, and throat were fearfully mauled, and bore witness to a ferocity of "savaging" that must have been quite unnecessary, considering the helpless weakness of the poor old victim.

As I looked down at these poor relics I suddenly noted, for the first time, that this victim, too, had been *partially scalped!*

Was it then that my poor shot last year was indirectly responsible for at least another human life? Had that panther escaped to claim at least this other victim?

The sun had sunk over the opposite hillsides, so I turned with relief from such discomforting thoughts to superintend the building of the *machán* in which I was to spend the night.

Not a single good tree was to be found: all were either stunted *salai* or other small wood. However, the difficulty was surmounted by cutting three long poles in the neighbouring ravine; and, lashing them upright to supplement the flabby boughs of the nearest *salai* tree, a rough platform was erected at a height of some fifteen feet from the ground. Some bran was scattered round the remains of the old woman, which had been dragged away from the shadow of the bamboos and tied firmly by the arm to a sapling.

It was rapidly getting dark when the men moved off; and my orderly and myself were left sitting, listening to their footsteps dying away in the fallen leaves.

As a rule I sit alone for panthers; but on this occasion I preferred the company of my orderly, which, as events proved, was a fortunate decision on my part.

It was a dark night: that is to say, we should have no moon until about four in the morning; and then only a thin and waning sickle. I had fitted my night-sight to my gun, in which I had placed a couple of cartridges loaded with slugs. This night-sight consisted of an ordinary visiting card, into the end of which a V-shaped cut had been made. When this card has been fastened to the top rib of one's gun by a couple of rubber rings, the bottom of the V fitted against the barleycorn, or foresight, and the ear-like flaps raised, I know of few better aids to accurate shooting by night, provided there is some glimmer of light. Aim is taken by getting the object between the flaps of the white card V.

My orderly and I got into our greatcoats and rugs—for it was to be a cold night—and settled into the semblance of two stone figures.

When the last faint flush following sunset had died away, the jungle grew very dark and intensely quiet. A few stars showed themselves over the head of the hill that reared up blackly into the vault of the sky far above us. Down in the valley behind night-birds called at rare intervals. In the *machán* however all was still. Not a sound came from the hillsides.

About half an hour after this a distant rustle was heard up-hill. Then it stopped. A few minutes later Abbas Khan touched my foot. Some heavy animal was coming quite boldly down the hillside. Then came a faint deep breath close under the tree in which we were sitting! My heart thumped heavily. I opened my mouth to breathe less noisily.

There was something moving stealthily near the foot of our tree; but only the faintest of sounds came when a stone turned slowly. We were right between the animal and the spot where the corpse lay bound to its sapling. Would it pass under us and give me a chance on the patch of bran? Hours seemed to pass!

A stick cracked in quite another direction on the other side of the grisly "kill." Very slowly I turned myself in that direction, and strained my eyes on to the faintly yellow strip of bran with that mis-shapen dark blotch in the centre of it.

All movement appeared to have ceased. Probably the panther was sitting, waiting, watching, and would presently creep forward to seek his abominable food.

In this state we sat on for an apparently immense period of time. I noted that the Pleiades, instead of hanging over the dark crest of the Chór Pahar, were now high above my head. A large green-coloured star had just risen over the trees in the distance. I slipped a supporting hand under my doubled-up and aching knee, gently altered its position, and sat on patiently.

Was the corpse down there moving? No! Yes, it was, though. How *beastly!* As I intently watched it, it seemed to roll over! I could, in my fancy, see its dull white eyes gleaming in the starlight, the head raised despairingly to watch, helplessly, the approach of its destroyer.

I began to think of Forsyth's story of "Padam Singh and the man-eater;" of the half-eaten corpse that raised its dead hands to point out the *shikári* shivering in his tree; and how those hands had to be pegged to the ground before the tiger would return to the kill.

A small sound, as of tiny teeth, made itself audible in the stillness of night; a little champing of minute jaws, and then a little squeak, and the eating ceased.

Some mongoose, or jungle-cat, was at the corpse! With a shudder of disgust I turned slowly back to my original position.

Very faint noises came and went in the surrounding jungle; some dried twig or leaf falling to the ground would set the pulses beating expectantly. I was awaiting a creeping object to show itself on the light-coloured patch of bran. Would it come?

Was that a slight dragging sound in the grass? The beast that had come down the hillside *must* have been the panther! Some indistinct and faint—very faint—noises persuaded me that the creature was wandering round us in the dark surrounding jungle. I had heard it under our tree. Perhaps it was sitting somewhere near, watching, feline fashion, ere crawling up to complete its meal.

I was very drowsy. Perhaps I had been asleep for a moment or two. This would not do. Yet it was sleepy . . . awfully sleepy . . . work.

Suddenly behind me came a shock, a gasp of terror; the tree rocked; there was a scraping sound; my orderly had disappeared; and then I heard a soft thud at the foot of the tree. Bang! bang! went both barrels of my gun into the air, and I raised a tremendous shouting, instinctively grasping the situation. Before I could reload, something simply rushed up the tree and fell across my legs into the *machán*, right across the muzzle of the gun. It was the Pathan! Had I been reloaded, nothing could have saved him—I had snapped both triggers against his chest, making sure it was the panther!

The poor fellow was trembling in every limb—as well he might. For a few moments we were both too dazed to speak, but I had reloaded the gun, shoved my loaded rifle into his hands, and we sat facing the only accessible side of the *machán*. Behind us the hillside descended so steeply that no living creature could invade us from that direction.

After a while we heard the crackle of leaves at a considerable distance in the jungle; and then a barking deer or *khákar* set up a sudden and incessant barking, that became fainter and fainter as the little creature retreated down the glen—probably before the panther, which was apparently going off that way.

We now took a couple of the poles forming the flooring of the *machán*, and tied them with the orderly's *pagri* so as to form a slight barrier to any second attack on our exposed side.

I then held a whispered consultation with him. He had escaped without a scratch! His story was that he was nodding drowsily, when something struck and caught both his legs below the knee, and dragged him out of his perch! As he fell, he turned, and gripped a limb of the tree, but was slipping down, with an immense weight on his legs, till his hands came to a fork of the trunk. Here he held on with all his strength; his right gaiter was ripped clean off, the beast let go its clutch, he heard its claws tearing the soft bark, and then it dropped to the ground. Next instant he had somehow regained our shelter!

Although the first attack of this fearless brute had failed, and our position had been strengthened, our feelings may well be imagined! It was pitch dark in the shadow of the trees. I touched the open face of my watch. The hands felt to be indicating one o'clock in the morning. There were still four-and-a half hours of night before us, during which we were liable to be stalked—practically helpless ourselves, but clearly apparent to every sense of this practised, creeping murderer.

Once more the hours dragged on in silence.

Two large owls set up a most horrible low moaning among the trees to the right. The air became damp and very cold.

Morning could not be far off. A faint breeze rustled the tree-tops, and some bamboos creaked uneasily.

Until now not a sound had been heard to indicate the return of the panther, but at last I fancied that the faintest sound of breathing had been borne to my ears. Every sense was instantly at acutest tension. My orderly was breathing through his nose. I leant slowly back, and, pressing his knee, uttered a faint sh—sh!

The topmost branches of a neighbouring *salai* tree quivered. Was it the wind? No; the air was now quite still.

There was something shaking that tree. Its branches moved again—just the tips that were outlined against the faintly luminous sky.

What with the cold and the suspense, I seemed to be shaking the whole *machán*. My throat was painfully dry. The effort to swallow made a fearful noise. I wanted to cough.

Something whitish or greyish seemed to be climbing close to the trunk of the *salai* tree: it moved!

"*Máro!*" breathed the Pathan.

I gently, slowly, raised the gun to my shoulder, shaking with anxiety, and straining my eyes in the darkness.

Nothing could now be seen. It must have been imagination!

The tree quivered again; a faintly whitish patch was very, very slowly elongating itself, and becoming more distinct. I got it well between the ears of my night-sight . . . . .

Bang!

As the sound of the shot went rolling and reverberating through the hills, something sprang lightly off through the grass.

* * * * *

Dawn was surely breaking? Objects stood out more distinctly, and the faintest greenish hue appeared in the sky. The dark outline of the old woman's cadaver became clearer: its upraised hand with the stiffened fingers seemed stretched out in mute appeal against the indignity of the cord that bound it to the tree. Just a hand, a glistening, bedewed head and trunk, and, lower down--Ugh !

The faint crow of a jungle-cock came across the grey depths of the valley. Dawn had come, and the man-eater had escaped again.

* * * * *

About six weeks later, I was coming down from the hills on my way home from an unsuccessful search for sámbar ; having ordered my mare to Belkhera. As Abbas Khan and I descended the foot-hills and approached the village, we became aware of some unusual stir among the huts, from which there arose a ceaseless screaming—some death, no doubt. I had placed my foot in the stirrup, and was vaulting into the saddle, when a Korku came running up. Once more had the panther taken toll of Belkhera!

A buffalo-herd had been seized, while grazing his cattle near the little river, not far from the village. The buffaloes had driven off the brute, and the man had been rescued ; only however to expire in the village, whither he had been borne. The panther had retreated into the hills.

I asked to see the victim of this latest outrage, and was led down the central "street" of the Korku village. The cowherd was lying on a *charpai*, just as he had died ; some vein in the neck had been severed ; and, in spite of a rough bandage, a dark patch of blood was congealing on the ground under the string bedstead. There were the usual deep holes in the throat and on the nape of the neck, and—the Belkhera man-eater's mark was there ! A long strip of skin and hair had been torn off and hung from the dead man's scalp!

All this time the female relatives of the victim were making the most dreadful, and—to their mind—highly commendable noise as they sat around. One could scarcely make one's self heard; so I retreated to a distance to enquire more fully into the circumstances of this last attack—the boldest of all. The *patêl* of the village suggested that I should once more make use of the body of the panther's victim. "The whole neighbourhood was terrorized," said he, "and the villagers dared not enter the *ramnah* for grass, save in compact parties. Their very means of existence was threatened. The *sahib* must really rid them of this scourge!"

To this, however, there was an impediment: the relatives of the dead man would not permit the body to be removed.

I sat down and waited, while a fearful pandemonium of altercation ensued, through which I could make out the shrill voices of the female relations haggling over a question of *backsheesh*.

Finally it was settled that I might have the use of their corpse until dark: after that nothing would induce them to permit it to remain out—the *shêr* might return and eat of it!

We walked up the river bank and reached the scene of the catastrophe. The body of the cow-herd was laid down just where he had been caught, and I prepared a hiding-place in which to watch until dark, when the villagers were to turn out, with drums and torches, and take the corpse away.

But now events took an unexpected turn, as they not infrequently do where panthers are concerned. It was fated that the end of this notorious evil-doer should be brought about in a singularly tame and commonplace manner.

My orderly rushed up and informed me that the panther had *not* gone off into the hills. He had found its tracks leading into a little patch of scrub and *samálu* bush in the river-bed; and, "ringing" this covert, could find no traces of exit. Therefore the panther might be there! At any rate, a silent beat could do no harm.

The village was only a few hundred yards away; and a goodly body of beaters was shortly ready, all armed with bamboo *láthis*. I posted myself on the river bank about a hundred yards up-stream, and the beat began.

A few seconds later a large panther walked quietly out of a cactus bush, and sat down directly below me, looking back over his shoulder. My rifle was raised, and next moment the man-eater of Belkhera had paid the penalty of his crimes.

Stood, pricking my ears.

ON THE COTTON PLAINS.

My earliest recollections are of a yellow, grassy, undulating, waste country, studded with low thorn bushes, in the shade of one of which lay my mother, as I nestled at her side.

The sun had just risen, and shone warmly on my callow hide; in the distance, on the confines of a vast plain, lay a long purple line of hills; the ceaseless drone and buzz of insects filled the air with a drowsy murmur; a flock of cranes passed high overhead, their harsh cries mellowed by distance, as they winged their wedge-shaped flight towards the cultivated country, where the green of the *rabi* crops faded into the blue distance. A feeling of joy, of exuberant youth, flowed through my young veins, as I rose to my feet, and stretched my long ungainly limbs in the glad sunshine; then, executing a blithe gambol and sidelong jump, stood, pricking my ears at the song of a villager driving his yoke of oxen to the plough.

My mother lay with drooping ears, lazily flicking the flies from her haunch, her full dark eyes ever and anon roaming dreamily over the wide expanse of fallow before her. Ah! It was a good country that! Rich fields, good company, and few of the worries of life which fall to the share of the buck whose lines Fate casts in less remote pastures. Any antelope possessing a fairly developed bump of caution should, in that district, grow to green old age, and yet never hear the whistle of bullet or crack of rifle.

Of course it was not such a paradise as held no alarms, for that very moment a strange odour filled my nostrils, and my mother started up, with twitching nose and cocked ears, as two lank grey forms halted suddenly, a field's length away, in an open space in the low scrub. A moment later I was flying after her, as she leaped scudding across the plain, bounding into the air at every few strides. Oh! the exhilaration of that first wild rush over the flying brown earth! We left the scrub jungle far behind, and, crossing a wide dry *nála* at reduced speed, on a sudden wheeled and halted, and I trotted with dilated nostrils and cocked tail to my mother's side. She bent a swift look of pride on me.

"*Shábásh*, little one, the fleetest and sturdiest of all I have borne! Did skulking wolf delude himself with thoughts of an easy prey?" So saying, she led the way towards a large herd of our kind, who were scattered over open ground, not far from a field of tall green cotton; some lying drowsily ruminating, others capriciously grazing or moving slowly about, while one or two does gazed penetratingly down wind. On the edge of the cotton field stood one of whom I had not yet seen the like. Whereas we were sombre yellow-brown creatures, this one was glossy black—black with pure white belly and throat. Moreover, long, gnarled, spiral horns sprung from his head, and ended in sharp points, and, as he turned and paced with lordly mien towards us, his horns laid back over his haunches, nose disdainfully in air, and tail curled up over his back in the arrogance of his pride, I knew that I looked on the lord of the herd—the finest of our race.

As he passed us by superciliously, my mother whispered—"Your father, my dear, a fine fellow doubtless, but foolish, headstrong, and reckless, as are most of his sex. What he would do, or how he would fare without us, his wives, to keep a watch on prowling enemies, I know not. Look at

The lord of the herd.

him now!"—this as my parent dashed out from the herd and rounded up a skittishly inclined young doe, driving her back to us, his sharp horns lowered in feigned attack. "Thus my first lord died. He left us, to fasten a quarrel on a stranger, but in some inexplicable manner their horns seemed to interlace, and in a twinkling three *Párdis* sprang from hiding, and captured him while madly struggling to break the mysterious bonds."

"And the stranger, mother?" I bleated.

"Beware of such strangers," she grunted.

We were a large community at that time, and, when on the move to the evening feeding-grounds, our scattered line might have stretched over the breadth of two fields. As for the cries of the night watchers, perched on their tall *machâns*, they fell on deaf ears—who yet denied us our bellyful save to move us on to some neighbour's field?

The high crops fell, and were gathered; the great stacks of *kadbi* rose round every village; and we roamed over wide plains, stretching uninterrupted save for some round-topped mango grove, or the dark line of trees marking the place where a village rose round its ancient mud *gharri*. Chill dawn would find us grouped in some gram field, the sharp acid rime of which appeals to the salt-craving inherent in us; or belly deep in the broad belts of pale green wheat.

And so the seasons passed.

The dry weather came with its fiery sun, when we, antelope, collected nearer the sandy bed of the river, winding its now thin stream from pool to pool. Then the rainy season; when other herds joined ours, from the level black cotton-soil tracts, and we ranged in our gathered hundreds on the drier rising grounds, all save the bucks standing out conspicuously against the dark wet earth, as some gleam of sunlight caught our yellow skins.

Never shall I forget a day succeeding a heavy fall of rain, when I had lingered behind my mother (I was not now so tied to her side), and found myself separated from her by an expanse of tenacious wet soil. As I stood undecided, there came a laboured panting, and a yell of excouragement, as a village dog, urged on by his owner, snatched fiercely at my flank! With a bound I escaped him, and toiled frantically over the soft mud, into which my sharp feet sank deeply. Again I felt, with despair, the hot breath on my haunch—when suddenly the ground became harder, I drew away from my pursuer, and, gaining the grassy slope of a rising ground, finally shook him off, baffled, in spite of his oiled feet; he now halted with lolling tongue, and, turning, slunk back whence he came.

With the rain the crops rose, and in a few weeks the plains were clothed in green *jawári* and wide fields of cotton, save for the ground reserved for the later sowings of wheat and gram—*jawári* that soon reared its great stalks high above the heads of the workers in the fields; that formed a pleasant covert for us, who now wandered in small and scattered bands, scarce troubling to change our quarters, so abundant and accessible was our food. But with the *jawári* came the *Bhois*. Cunningly disposing their tall nets along the edge and angles of the high millet, they would endeavour to move a herd of antelope so as to entangle them in a *cul-de-sac;* and their patience and skill were nearly always rewarded by some foolish one of our number.

The first time I was introduced to this danger was when my sprouting horns were only a few inches in length. We were all lying amid the stems of a wide field of *jawári*, the thick green heads of which sheltered us from the peculiarly intense sun of late September. It had been very still; when a slight breeze set the tall corn whispering, and brought on its breath the strange acrid odour which I had noticed as being peculiar to men. So pronounced was it that I instinctively sprang up, and was followed by the whole herd, which, after a moment's hesitation, moved off through the thick covert.

In the best of company, I of course brought up the rear of the herd, together with several youngsters of my own age; behind us, as befitted him, paced the lord and master buck—ever the last to fly from danger. Our timid vanguard of watchful does had almost reached the edge of the *jawári* patch, when a sudden flurry arose, and they leaped, bounding and bucking, in all directions. As I followed the lead of my excellent mamma, in whose sound judgment I had perfect faith, I saw my sterner parent trot straight on, with a curl of his lip. *He* was not going to share the universal panic—and on he went.

Then a sudden yell burst out behind him, and he gave one mighty leap out of the field, struck something yielding, intangible, and yet arresting, and came a tremendous cropper, firmly entangled in a long net, as a chorus of shouts rose from the netters. As I darted after the herd, which had escaped to right and left, I have dim recollection of a furious thrashing of hoofs and a grunting, gurgling bellow, followed by much loud guffawing and elated chattering. I don't think they killed him just then. They usually make their victims walk home with them. It is such a nuisance to carry them you see, and matters can be simplified by sewing up the victim's eyelids!

It was not many hours after this that we caught sight of a fine buck gazing fixedly at us in the distance, as we all stood packed together in an open bit of ploughed land.

He paced in our direction, then halted and stared again at a respectful distance, for I may mention that my late parent had a pretty wide notoriety for savage exclusiveness. After following behind us awhile, this buck ventured on closer inspection, and, somehow tumbling to the hang of things, began to assert authority. He actually had the effrontery to chase me from my mother's side and catch me a dig in the ribs. Toward the other youngsters his bearing was superciliously indifferent.

Life thus proceeded without much to mark its progress, save that my horns grew apace, and that the new master of the herd watched me with an ever-increasing ferocity; till, one day, he fell to the muzzle-loader of a native *shikari*. We had strayed incautiously near a *worli*, or landmark, when there came a flash and a bang, and my enemy sank to the ground, as the figure of a Bhil rose from behind the smoke, and ran towards him. As we fled leaping over the fields, there arose that same old gurgling bellow; and that was the last of my father's successor.

Two days after this, a very fine buck took charge of us; and the first hour of office in his new capacity was devoted to driving me from the herd with which I had been connected from my infancy. He succeeded, although I was stubborn; and I at length departed, in dudgeon, with a slight horn wound in my flank. I may remark that my unnatural mother viewed me thus driven forth without apparent concern—another youngster now trotted by her side. Wandering morosely over the moonlit plain, I fell in with three other bucklets of my age, and on comparing notes we found that our condition was identical: each had the same story to tell, and we agreed to join our fortunes and face the world together. During the next few months others in the same plight joined us; thrust forth to seek our fortunes, a fellow-feeling drew us together.

In the course of our wanderings we had left the old country far behind, and one day found ourselves approaching a long line of trees that marked the straight undeviating stretch of a trunk road. It was a glorious cold weather morning. The air was cold and crisp. White rime lay on the yet misty fields, and the road, with its shading line of acacias, stretched away east to the dim grey horizon, where the early beams of the sun shot up into the clear green sky from behind a far cloud bank.

As we moved about, nibbling a frond of fern-like gram here and there, a distant rumbling arose, and a thin curtain of dust among the trees; then the cheerful jingling of chains and harness, as a Battery of artillery came along at a smart trot opposite us. In obedience to a long-drawn-out word of command, they slowed to a walk and passed along the smooth road, the early sun glancing from steel and chain. Further on a short halt was made, and, seizing something from a syce, a figure left the road and came towards us. As we stared at the novel sight on the road, little puffs of smoke arose among the men and a hum of voices. The khaki-clad figure was getting near. I alone had heard of the dreaded *sahib*, and was well into my stride before the first bullet buzzed angrily over our heads off a stone. Then there came a second, and behind me a dull "plop;" and one of our number pitched on his head and lay kicking feebly.

None of us waited to see any more after that!

Nightfall found us again in the neighbourhood of the road, which, like the villages of the plain, possesses a strong attraction for us when night has cast her cold dark mantle over the land.

Perhaps it would be the tinkle of bullock carts; or the flicker of a roadside fire, lit by belated villagers returning from a distant market; or the steady *rub-a-dub-dub* of a village tom-tom rising on the still air. It is comforting, when the night comes down, to gather nearer the goings of man; and few of us lie far afield during the hours of dark.

I had picked up some useful wrinkles while a youngster with the herd, and now every day brought its experience. We learnt what to shun, and what was harmless. Bullock carts laden with chattering natives might pass and repass us closely; but let one inch of a suspicious or skulking body show itself for an instant, and we were off.

One afternoon a fine buck joined us, youngsters, which is unusual—but a long scar showed fresh on his haunch. And a sulky beast he was!

We had occupied the centre of an extensive cotton field that afternoon, and were most of us standing about, too lazy save for a chance nibble at the young leaves of the cotton plants. All to be seen of our morose friend were the points of his long horns, which protruded from the *paláti* stalks.

A figure emerged from behind some *babul* trees and strolled casually and confidently in our direction. It was certainly not a villager, but its advance was so careless, so artlessly guileless, that it had approached fairly close, and was passing on, when something prompted our long-horned acquaintance to rise and display all his black and white glory, as with proudly poised head he regarded the intruder in astonishment. I now recognised the figure of a *sahib*, and led a swift flight, the big buck bringing up the rear; when again came that dreaded sharp crack, and the laggard gave a lurch, but, pulling himself together, turned at right angles, and limped swiftly down the furrows of the cotton, a broken foreleg swinging crimson splashes against the brown stalks. And thus we separated. This episode afforded me a fresh insight into our enemies' wiles.

Some time after this I annexed a herd of does in a curiously accidental manner.

One morning, having become separated from our little *côterie* of bucklets, I had to canter from a village dog, and, further on, emerged from a palm-fringed *nala* to find myself almost among a herd of eight does, owned by a buck not much bigger than myself. Halting suddenly, I gazed at them; then, noticing a cousin among the does, took a few steps forward to greet her—when the master of the herd pushed his way up to me in a most offensive way.

Although his mien was threatening, and the pose of his thick neck extremely choleric, I put a stiff upper lip and firmly curled-up tail on the situation; and awaited his attack. When a couple of paces off he halted, and we stared at each other, legs braced well up and eyepits distended: then he quivered with rage; and, licking his lips, fixed me with a glare, advanced a step or two with studied deliberation, suddenly lowered his horns, and rushed fiercely at me.

I met his charge with firm resistance, and our heads came together with a crack! It was now a question of sheer weight and strength; and, bracing my muscular hams, I yielded not an inch. After some prolonged but ineffectual efforts on the part of my antagonist, he suddenly bounded back in surprise and annoyance; and we again stood facing each other, nostrils dilated, and flanks heaving. Again and again he attacked me, with the same result, to his increasing chagrin. Round and round he fenced, and shoved, and slipped; at length, being extremely short of wind, he halted to think, and, having pondered, was moving back to the herd with what dignity he could manage.

But I had not quite done with him yet, and he only just saved his bacon as I engaged him and forced him back: then with a fierce effort I bore him to his knees, and, as he leaped back, exposing his side, made a rapid rush, and a despairing grunt left his panting throat as my horns took him in the flank.

After this it was a mere pursuit! He never faced me again, as I chevied him over the fields. Then, the fire of conquest burning in my eye, I left him disconsolately gazing from a respectful distance, and stepped proudly towards my does.

When the moon rose late that night, it disclosed the dethroned one still following us; but by morning he had disappeared.

I was now the master of a herd—the ambition of every right-minded buck—and life passed, unmarked by episode, except when I had to fight for my property, or when I added to its numbers. Some two years must have passed thus; and by this time I was, I flatter myself, one of the finest bucks in the country-side. My horns were over 24 inches in length, and were strong and thick; my colour a dark brown-grey, for I am of the caste that never assumes the intense black of the smaller breed—and my bulk and weight have stood me in good stead.

The country where I found myself finally settled is within fifteen miles of a small military station which lies nearer the range of hills to the north, and it is visited now and again by *sahibs*. Thus far I had escaped being fired at, by observing the simple rules which every wideawake buck should have at his command; but of late times I too have had my experiences in this line. For the guidance of other bucks I should observe that one should be particularly wide-awake on Thursdays and Sundays—it is on such days that most of my narrow shaves have occurred. They have been so many now that I can recollect few of the circumstances connected with them.

One day I saw a *sahib* standing in the distance. He wore a white hat with a spotted blue *pagri*, and was accompanied by a native in khaki, with whom he was in deep consultation. I was so tickled that I did not take particular care of myself, and the apparition approached: then, after turning once more anxiously to the native, whom I distinctly heard say "*Ap ki khushi*," it bent its back, and, assuming a stealthy gait, crept towards me. It had not gone far when it suddenly remembered something, and, retracing its uncomfortable way, took something from the native and put it with a loud click in the rifle.

Then it resumed its broken-backed approach. Fascinated by this weird method of "stalking," I stared and stared, till the figure rose and fumbled with its gun: then, as it was possible that it might be pointed somewhere near me when it exploded, I moved off.

Bang! and a fragment of an express bullet, ricochetting off the hard ground, rushed shrilly by me. Bang! and another bullet whispered high over my head; and in the distance a line of women, picking cotton, stood up with frightened faces. I glanced back. My sportsman was gazing sadly after me! I have seen him do so many a time; and, later, I came to know him well. Many a dull half hour has he enlivened! I look for his white *topi* on Thursdays and Saturdays as a relief to the monotony of my existence. Once he brought a very fat *sahib* with him, who wounded me; but I got away, and am all right now.

My last adventure was of a different type. One Thursday I was making across a field some way behind my does, when a slight movement caught my eye; it was the *topi* of a *sahib*, and he was lying behind a little mound. Of course I was off at my best pace, until I had put 300 yards between us : this I always considered perfect safety, so I wheeled, and stood to have another look.

Something shone dully behind the mound for an instant, then tipped suddenly up, and, simultaneously, "chip!" came a slight report—a mere crack—and a searing pain cut along the lower edge of my belly. It was only a graze; but the frightful force with which the bullet twanged off the ground, far beyond me, with a peculiar high-pitched pinging sound, and the absence of the usual smoke from behind the mound, told me of a new destructive force, and one to be terribly feared.

I am getting on in years now, and, I suppose, in spite of my watchful does, shall some day fall to the *sahib* with that strange new rifle. And a worthy spoil shall I make. A 25-inch head ; a fine glossy coat, which I have defended unscarred through hundreds of hard-fought fights ; a buck worth bagging!

And, if I fall, may it be fairly ! Stalk me fairly, *Sahib!* Don't come skulking after me in a bullock cart ; don't wait for me by the tank in the hot weather; and, should my head ever grace your walls, do not forget the many days of quiet sport I have afforded you on my wide rich plains, the glamour of which will surely return to you, even amidst the stirring memories of more exciting days.

Shoot none of my immature brethren, *Sahib!* If you must kill for food, take a few of my yeld-does ; I can spare them—else, how think you will the country raise bucks like me?

A NIGHT BY A JUNGLE POOL.

Evening shadows were lengthening apace, and the last mellow shafts of the declining sun bathed the jungly hill-side in a warm glow, and threw into relief the heavy heads of the scattered mango trees under which we passed—a silent party of four—as we wound in file down the little wood-cutter's path, through the long yellow spear-grass, leading to the already hazy bed of the stream, some hundreds of feet below.

It was past seven o'clock, and an hour since I had left camp, with the intention of passing the night of the full moon at a solitary pool, deep in the heart of a great ravine, several miles from any other water, and, in this parching Indian hot weather, the last resource as a drinking-place of all the game within a long distance.

The ravine into which we were descending forms the head-waters of a large tributary of the Tapti river, and is a deep and fiercely raging torrent in the rainy weather. Like most of its neighbours, it has a short course over more or less flat-topped plateaux from whose edge it plunges over a precipice of black basalt into a deep glen winding a couple of thousand feet below, in a tangle of miasmatic vegetation. Shrinking up quickly through the cold season months, the commencement of the hot weather sees but a few scattered pools in all its mountain course, and a couple of months more of fierce sun exhausts all moisture, save a solitary puddle or two in such spots as are favoured by peculiar geological conditions for the retention of water.

All that now remains of the verdure of the rainy season is a mass of dead scorched creepers, festooning the bare trunks and leafless branches of forest trees, only a few of which throw out a thick head of sappy young leaves at this period.

The general appearance of these jungles is that of English woods in October—thin on the steep exposed slopes of now parched and beaten-down spear-grass, dense and thicketty in the ravines seaming their sides.

Along the dry boulder-strewn bed of the stream rises a fringe of larger, taller trees, opening into little occasional bays or natural clearings; and the entire forest is carpeted, often knee-deep, with the great dried and fallen leaves of the teak and other trees. In such ground not a step may be taken in silence. On the other hand, game which might otherwise have escaped notice betrays itself here by the loud crackling of the leaves.

In those parts game is scarce and wary, and to anyone who would condemn me as a poacher, I would recommend a few days in the dense and hard-to-work jungles of which I speak. If you cannot come to your game, why not let it come to you, which is after all the *raison d'être* of beating or driving; besides this, there is a certain great charm in a night vigil, such as I hope to describe, understood that you don't smoke heavily, or open sodas with a noisy gurgling every half hour, and then go to sleep condemning it all as a fraud.

We had taken the precaution of "stopping" this pool for the past two nights, by the simple expedient of a couple of jungle men and a smouldering cowdung fire placed a hundred yards or so up the glen. My Korkus reported that on the second night they had spent most of their time in a tree, as a tiger had shown extreme impatience at being baulked of his water, and had prowled round and round within a short distance of the pool, giving vent to his disappointment in low growls.

A jungle pool.

I thought I knew this tiger—a shy, wily game-killer—who had evaded many a carefully devised beat, and who had been the cause of much bad language and disappointment for the past two years at least.

But here we are! An abrupt descent over large piled-up boulders, and we are soon at the water's edge, which lies below a flat out-cropping ledge of black trap-rock; sand along the north side, and the steep fall of a precipitous bank lining the far shore. Here, some fifteen feet up, is our hide, on the summit of a jumble of great rocks, and hedged around with *jamún* bushes—unnoticeable and natural to a degree. My orderly called my attention to the fact that a herd of sámbar had been down during the day, since the Korkus had left in the morning. They had not been able to withstand further the claims of a fierce thirst; although they are able to let a couple of days at least elapse between drinks. The sámbar is very partial to water however, especially for the sake of a good wallow in the mire. There were also traces of other animals, pigs, and, strangely enough, a bear. He must have been hard up to stir after the hot sun had risen. Then of course there were numerous marks of the little four-horned antelope and barking deer. These nearly always choose noontide to slake their thirst, tripping with daintily-picked and fearful footsteps to the cool damp sand that fringes the forest pool. We examined the ground carefully for the tiger's marks, so as to try to obtain a hint from which direction to expect him, but the hard withered grass and fallen leaves afforded no information.

As the last glow of dying day fades from the peaks above us, the night chorus of goatsuckers strike up their refrain of "Chuckoo—chuckoo—chuckoo!" and many small birds come and sip, and flit about, rejoicing that the torrid fervour of the day is past. Abbas Khan and I mount to our hiding-place, and the Korkus, having deposited their burdens, and bearing their little gourd water-bottles, disappear up-hill, where we long hear their feet crackling the great dry teak leaves, in the warm still air.

The rug is spread, havresack and water *chágal* put ready to hand, rifles and binoculars disposed handily, a few extra cartridges laid in that little niche in the black rock—and we are ready. What a charm is in this delicious quiet, this heavy scented air, and the curious cries of the jungle breaking the profound silence! The little barbet has changed his day "coppersmith" note for the no less monotonous and everlasting nocturnal one of "Ouic—kur-kur!" and, as the shadows deepen, a large fluffy mass sails noiselessly overhead, and settles on the gaunt arm of a dead tree; answering a distant call by a deep "Whoo!"

I was lost in a reverie, watching the orange disc of the full moon lift over a shoulder of the hills, when the extreme right-hand corner of my eye caught a grey shadow hesitatingly approaching among some rocks in the dry bed of the stream, and the glasses revealed a hyæna, nosing about near the place where we had come down off the hill. He then stood, cocking his strange pointed ears in our direction for some time, but finally limped up right under our rock—a fine big fellow, with a good coat. By leaning over we might have almost touched him with a stick. After drinking he went off down-stream.

Later, a little barking deer came rustling in the teak leaves on the far side of the *nála*, and, down to the edge of the water; and another, further off, moving here and there, kept up his funny little yap of "Aow! * * * Aow!" Higher rose the moon in a perfectly cloudless sky, and the gentle breaths of air died away until every stick and blade of grass stood out sharp and clear in the brilliant light. Small bats wheeled and circled with soft whirring wings over the dark pool, ever and anon kissing the glassy surface in a downward swoop. Why is it that moonlight should throw such mystery over the woods! The slightest sound appears to be a loud and startling uproar, and the occasional scratching indulged in by Abbas Khan as if it would be sufficient warning to all animals for miles.

Curious small noises come and go in the dry leaves, and two tiny owls cause quite a stir, as they softly alight on a slender teak pole, which has a few huge dried leaves attached to its topmost twigs.

The mind too is gently influenced by the quiet scene, and wonders how there can be such things as rage and strife. Why should life not glide thus peacefully on, without jar, in calm beatitude!

The ear catches a far distant gentle stirring in the carpeting of dry teak leaves, now dying away, and then again increasing, coming nearer, stopping, recommencing. The sounds come from the lower portion of that long steep spur which runs from the little level vale of yellow grass right up to the soft mauve distance of crag-encircled plateaux far above us.

The colours of the sleeping landscape, though restricted to blues, greys, and palest yellow, are still marvellously diverse in tone: there the rich soft blue-black of some deep ravine: here the sharp dark branches of a gnarled *tiwas* tree in high relief against a pale background of long withered grass.

The crackling of leaves is more pronounced now, and the binoculars are raised to the dark line of forest where it touches the grass land. Nothing shows for many long minutes.

At length a tall black object is spied moving slowly forward, and after a while it steps into a patch of moonlight, which falls through the twisted boughs, and appears to view—a fine old sámbar stag, with newly-sprouted horns in velvet. A tall *salai* tree is before him, and here he pauses and raises his muzzle ; then, leaning sidewise, scrapes his rough hide luxuriously against the bark.

Tiring of this exercise, the stately measured walk is recommenced, and he feeds slowly off, over a little glade, and gradually disappears in the labyrinth of ghostly yellow trunks. He is probably one of those who drank at our pool to-day, and so is indifferent to water for the next forty-eight hours or thereabouts, though he may turn up in the hour before dawn for a roll and mud-bath.

The sound of his wandering steps in the leaves dies gradually away, and all is again still, save for the eternal "Chuckoo—chuckoo !" of the nightjars, and their prolonged cry of "Hoo—hoo—hoo!" as they flit and sail from tree to tree, rock to rock.

One of the most exciting bits of this night work is the waiting to see what it is that for the last half hour has been moving towards the pool through the tell-tale leaves, and which now emerges, and halts—a dark shapeless mass—on the edge of the jungle.

Perhaps it were hardly interesting to record how several sounders of hog—boar, sow, and many little squeakers—approached, wallowed, drank, and finally trotted off, grunting satisfaction, to where their favourite roots were to be had for the grubbing ; how a pair of jackals arrived, and while one danced a remarkably fantastic fandango in a sand-hole, how its mate discovered some brooding danger and, the signal given, how the pair disappeared, with many a suspicious halt and backward stare—all this in the effulgence of a full tropic moon.

I took out my note-book, and pencilled little notes. I smoked gently ; for I hold that—except under certain circumstances of position and wind—when tobacco smoke can be detected, the natural perfume of he who smokes not would be no less noticeable.

Many a night had I passed in this *al fresco* manner ; but never a one when all so combined to please, and when I had such chances of observing unsuspicious wild creatures.

I was lying back on the bed of boughs, grass, comfortable rug and cushion, when a long cold trailing thing passed over my hand, and away from under my hips, leaving the hairs of my head in a state of electric separation. When the slight rustling had receded well into some rocks, I again drew breath, and quickly removed my haversack of cold roast fowl and other delicacies to another spot. Whether of a deadly species or not, I object to snakes hunting for *murghi* in my pockets !

It was now well past 2 a.m. and I felt drowsy, especially as the tuneful breathing of my faithless disciple sounded like a lullaby in my ears.

Perhaps an hour or so had passed in this borderland of dreams, when a sound struck on my ears that instantly roused us both ; it was the sudden, sharp, rending, trumpet sound of a sámbar's bell. *Dhánk!* There it came again, from up the glen, and continued at intervals, apparently retreating slowly for some minutes, when all was again quiet ; then another bark, louder and much nearer, and the crashing of leaves and jungle, as the sámbar apparently moved rapidly up-hill.

Pulses beat quicker now in keen anticipation, for this kind of thing has but one meaning.

Two figures, dark and stiff, peered over the lip of the rock, the glint of moonlight on a double-barrelled ·577. There came the deepest of guttural sighs from the big, black boulder under the far clump of bamboo.

The moon shone on, and the watch ticked loudly in my pocket, and we waited—weary work, with all senses at highest pressure.

Five minutes must have passed thus.

Ah !—a stone turned then—and now the moon's rays fall on the white face and chest of a tiger, as he moves out of the blackness, and comes gently forward : a rather small and lightly made brute, but with twice the grace and elegance of the beef-eater of the plains.

He comes to a sudden halt, moving his head slowly from side to side. Perhaps a slight human taint reached him, but it apparently escapes notice, for, pausing but a little while, he passes straight to the water ; the powerful shoulder-blades work under his glossy coat as he crouches like a great cat ; and down goes his head to lap.

Gently, ever so gently, the rifle comes to the shoulder, and the white card V on the muzzle stands out well in the moonlight.

A sudden star of bright sparks, a struggling and a rolling, and then a "*Woof!*" as bang goes the left barrel at a vanishing streak of faint grey which flashes up over the dark rocks and is gone.

Caution and quiet were now unnecessary, and as we discussed the *pros* and *cons* of a hit or miss, I treated myself to a well-merited whisky and soda, and turned in for a snooze. I slept till awakened by the words repeated in Hindustani : "*Hazur*, the fate of the tiger has come to pass !"—my orderly being, as befitted a pious Moslem, a firm believer in *kismat*—and, sitting up with the fresh breeze of dawn fanning my check, felt rather grubby after the long warm hours of night in this close ravine. The men were washing their mouths, noisy native fashion, in the far pool, and grey jungle-cocks called defiance from every side. Little parties of them and of the sombre spur-fowl pattered in the leaves round the head of the pool.

Sitting thus, a movement in the limbs of a tall tree beyond the *nála* attracted my attention, and shortly two dark lithe objects appeared, chasing each other up and down the long branches, against the beautiful green flush of the young day. At length they scurried up to the top-most twig, whence one, detaching itself, sailed with a steady downward flight straight over my head, and, curving upwards again like a hawk, alighted softly on the gnarled trunk of a *kowa* tree ; its mate, answering its curiously harsh cry, followed suit, and, as they disappeared in the grey twilight, it struck me that I had lost a chance of adding a flying squirrel to my collection. Their flight was wonderfully easy and graceful, and they must have covered about fifty yards clear from tree to tree.

A sluice in the clear water, and a bite of food was followed by the matutinal cigarette, as the hair and splashes of blood on the boulders were examined ; and then a start was made.

The tracks led up-hill into an extremely thickly-jungled little *khora*. We passed a spot where the tiger had rolled in agony, while his erratic course and the bits of white hair from his chest on any stumps or rocks in his way showed us all was well. As the men picked up the easily read trail, I kept a sharp look out ahead, rifle at the ready ; and so we crept along, under some bushes, round a rock here, through a tangle of small bamboos there, until at last there he lay on his side, thirty yards away, apparently quite dead.

Turning silently to the men I motioned the Korkus back, tipped a wink to Abbas Khan, and took the little white patch under the forearm. Over the smoke a huge tawny form rose up, looked in our direction, and then all was a chaos of gleaming teeth, viciously laid back ears, and flying leaves, as we darted behind a thick tree. Round he came; rolling, falling, rising, doing his best to get at us, when another bullet caught him in the back—and all was over.

When the shivering Korkus had come off their trees, we turned the tiger over, and saw that last night's bullet had struck full in the chest, but, owing to my raised position, had merely run along not far below the skin. It was subsequently found lodged below the stomach. To my surprise he measured nine feet as he lay.

An hour later, as I passed slowly up the precipitous spur leading to the plateau and camp, and took a breather ere climbing the little mural precipice which skirts the flat tops of these hills, my eye fell with grateful recollections on the glint of the little pool, now a thousand feet below in the yet dark glen, which had afforded me one of the pleasantest nights of my life.

BY TAMARIND AND MHOWA.

Although all the signs of an Indian "hot weather" surround us, the sun is not yet high enough to assert his stern authority, and long shadows still lie across the stretch of withered jungle-grass which now clothes the deserted fields surrounding the ruins of Pipalda.

On that knoll once stood the village, under its shady tamarind trees. The great trees are still there, but the crumbled mud walls and the track of the path leading past the old *mhowa* tree to the water-hole in the neighbouring *nála*, whence the inhabitants drew their scanty summer supply of the precious fluid, have long since disappeared; for it is many years since Pipalda, together with three or four other hamlets, was declared *ujar*, deserted, to make way for the growth of this little *bandi*, or forest reserve, some eight or nine square miles in extent, set apart by a paternal Government for the supply of grass and small timber to the surrounding cultivated tracts.

These little *bandis* lie scattered about a certain district not very far from—Nagpur shall we say—and in years past have yielded the most extraordinary amount of game, chiefly tigers and spotted deer, for the sheltering of which they are ideally adapted.

Whether they will ever recover from the terrible famine year of 1900—when the *ungulata* actually invaded villages in search of fodder and water, and were knocked on the head in great numbers by the famishing country-people—remains to be seen, and appears doubtful; but in days not so very long ago they formed a kind of sportsman's paradise.

Composed for the most part of waist-high lemon-grass, studded with copsewood, amid which here and there rises the handsome, oak-like, sweet-flowering *mhowa*, these reserves are usually traversed by a sandy *nála*, in which will be found one or two perennial pools. These winding watercourses are fringed by a strip of the larger woodland trees, such as the mango, *kowa*, banyan, *anjan*, etc. ; and the ground is, for the greater part, a dead flat, rendering it no difficult matter for one unacquainted with its few natural features to lose his way, although not seriously, yet in a manner sufficiently exhausting under an Indian summer sun.

Fairly level ground, shade, water, the proximity of some cultvation, and the usually undisturbed quiet of their solitude, render these small forest blocks quite exceptionally suited to the requirements of the graceful chital, and of truly wondrous numbers of hog, which, in their turn, serve to attract the felines that prey on them. As a rule, at least a couple of tigers and a family or two of panthers were to be found in each of those *bandis*.

The writer will long remember the first early morning stroll he took in one of those delightful bits of woodland. We were engaged in visiting a distant corner of the forest, where two of our tiger-baits had been tied out the previous evening, and after a cup of coffee had left camp, on foot, at the earliest flush of the "false dawn." That it is *hot* in those parts during April and May cannot be denied, and the fierce midday hours sadly sap the strength of the exotic exile; but, at this early dawn, newly-aroused nature enjoys the coolest of all the twenty-four hours, and a light dew has fallen, giving a fresh appearance to the parched surroundings.

The Indian hot-weather season has a somewhat similar effect on the country-side to that of autumn frosts in England. There the excess of cold, here the excess of heat, strips most trees of their foliage, and withers the grass, leaving a few evergreens here and there among wide stretches of bare-twigged coppices; and the heat-haze of India produces an effect not unlike that seen in frosty woods at home, when a blood-red sun is rising through misty vistas of leafless trees—an example of the truth of the adage "extremes meet."

Such is the general appearance of the jungle this morning.

Camp is pitched not far from a small village, in a plot of garden land. The fresh, newly-grown foliage of large tamarind trees shades our little 80-lb. tents. Hard by there is a fine old masonry well, with the inevitable *mót*, or water-raising apparatus. Unless engaged in a beat for tiger, the hot hours of the day—and it is blistering hot now between 9 a.m. and 4 p.m.—are usually passed in camp.

Tents—especially the modest shelter of the wandering *shikári*—are of course unbearable at these hours; but by erecting a *mandwa*, or thickly thatched roof on tall uprights, the camp table and bed may be set in the breeze, hot though it be, and the time passed in scanty attire, not unpleasantly, with a siesta thrown in to compensate for early and late hours. There may be the old jungle diary in which to jot down some interesting experience—the sketch book—private correspondence—a novel—the photographic apparatus. Meanwhile the bullocks pace slowly at their allotted task at the well, and the heavily rising leather water-bag discharges its cool contents with a soothing gush into the reservoir, and from it along grass-fringed channels to irrigate the little plots of summer vegetables.

An old man sleepily drives the bullocks, crooning a monotonous air the while, and urging them with occasional eldritch yells.

I suppose most of us are aware of the existence of a certain demon of mischief that haunts our daily life. I mean the small household gnome who is directly responsible for many of our petty worries—who hides the penknife, or cigar-case, or book which we have for a moment put down, and is very fond of match-boxes. I made a distinct score off him at this camp.

I was shooting entirely with a ·303 magazine sporting rifle at the time, my new ·400 bore cordite rifle having failed to arrive from England to date ; and I had sold my ·577 and another blunderbuss type of obsolete artillery to buy that same ·400. I was, therefore, temporarily dependent entirely on my one barrel.

The "pull-off" of the little rifle had become a trifle heavier than I like, so, urged doubtless by my particular familiar fiend, I stripped the action. Having re-adjusted some matters, I was engaged in replacing the sear spring, which actuates both the trigger and the catch holding the magazine. At this moment my companion was startled from slumber by a loud expletive. The spring had snapped!

* * * * *

I can see the little camp under the big tamarinds now, myself sitting gazing out on the heat-shimmering jungle, with that tiny broken bit of steel in my palm. Wild plans chased each other through my head, each to be discarded in turn. Here I was in the heart of India, *weeks* away from new springs, and not overmuch leave to get through. For the want of that little bit of steel, my tigers would roam all round camp at their ease. I pictured my companion's return, laden with trophies, while I sat in camp alone, or blew out the choke of my beautiful gun with ill-fitting and wobbly-flighted spherical balls. Over it all rose the thin sardonic chuckle of the household gnome!

An hour later my orderly, his knees tucked into my pony's ribs, was fleeing east to the least distant railway station, near which were sundry workshops. However, the buffer spring of a locomotive was scarcely calculated to allay my trouble—which continued.

My despairing gaze fell on the open rifle-case. An old spare "cocking-piece," with its long spiral striker-spring, lay therein. Now spiral springs *can* be cut with a sharp screw driver sometimes; they are also capable of uniting two given points nearly as well as a V—shaped spring. Melted alum will firmly unite separate pieces of metal, especially if aided by a "frapping" of common or garden thread.

I stole a glance, drooping my left eyelid slightly the while, at my household troll. He was dejectedly springing, squirrel-like, round the bole of a tree.

Half an hour later my scantily-clothed companion protruded a red and astounded countenance through the flap of his tent, and as the Lee-Metford bolt clicked merrily a second time, and I "snapped" the repaired lock again and again in my glee, a faint howl from the tamarind leaves intimated the complete rout of a discomfited elf. Strange to relate, the rifle so repaired gave perfect satisfaction during the remainder of that trip, accounting for bears, panthers, and tigers.

To return to the jungles of Pipalda—

Crossing the fallow ground beyond the village, we passed the burnt strip of the "fire-line," and entered the reserve by a rough cart-track, along which we moved for some distance in soft, cotton-soled silence.

After a while we became aware of movement in the grass and bushes alongside, and came to a halt. An excursion through the yellow grass disclosed a huge sounder of hog. Of all sizes were they, from heavy boars to squeakers, wandering and rustling gently homewards towards the deeper jungle, their line stretching at least a hundred and fifty yards in extent. After watching one splendid old boar, with the prism binoculars, which brought his formidable head almost within touching distance, we gently withdrew and regained the track.

The light is growing rapidly now, and a fringe of green trees not far ahead marks the main *ndla.*

As we arrive on its steep banks there is a sharp grating whistle—"Phrew!" and a hind chital darts up the far side, and disappears in long grass.

We stand there, gazing up-stream and down. The plaintive cry of a distant peacock echoes through the quiet woods.

We drop on to the smooth sand of the watercourse. No crackling leaves under foot here; and in perfect silence one may wander along its winding reaches. Damply refreshingly cool it is under the arching trees, as we brush past green *jámún* and tamarisk coverts that fill portions of the dry stream-bed. A koel's mellow fluting resounds from the boughs overhead, gilded now by the low rays of the newly-risen sun. There is a corner in the sandy way just ahead of us; turned cautiously, it reveals a vista of sylvan beauty. In the deep shade of the opposite bank lies one of those occasional pools, and on the moist sand of its margin—one instant only is the picture limned on the retina before the keen-eyed birds take swift alarm—groups a bevy of sombre peahens, their magnificent mate preening the burnished armour of his

A corner in the sandy way

plumage, as he stands on a little sand bank, with the early sunlight playing on him in a miracle of blended colour!

And what is that movement far down the dim distance?—a chital. A stag too!—slowly crossing from bank to bank. More of them! Cannot we steal nearer?—to observe, not to slay, for the jungle must remain undisturbed till we encompass that tiger's undoing. Wait till the whole herd—there must be at least forty or fifty deer—cross and ascend the other bank; then steal down this silent, sandy floor, and creep up its sloping sides.

As we raise our heads over the tall red grasses, there rises before us the drooping foliage of the big tamarinds of deserted Pipalda. There is the old *mhowa* tree, its lately fruit-stripped branches flecked with the transparent gold of budding leaves, and, nearer us, knee deep in the coarse grasses of the little clearing, moves the herd of spotted deer in its capricious ways.

The chital have now reached their home, having no doubt lately made their way into the *bandi* from a nocturnal visit to the open fields outside. These old village sites are always attractive to the *ungulata*, and are a sure find for chital throughout the day, until the cool of evening tempts them from the shade to wander slowly through the forest towards their nightly feeding grounds. Then it is that the silence of the dark hours is broken by the braying of the stags or sharp whistling of the hinds.

Here, then, is the herd at home, as yet unconscious of our presence; and far may one travel to match so fair a sight. It would be superfluous to recall the oft-penned claim of that perfect stag to first place among all the graceful family *Cervidæ*. He possesses it without a doubt, beyond all cavil, as he stands there, unconsciously posing as a faultless picture of colouring and grace of form—those lines of a beautiful shapely frame—the light brown muzzle and dark eyes—the rich deep russet of that snow-flecked hide, and those long, beaded horns, sweeping back in a curve, and terminating in shining polished tips—certainly the most beautiful of the deer tribe!

And his surroundings? While falling little short of the beauties of an English park land, they are those of nature, free and untrammelled: enclosed by no ring fence; guarded by no trespass notice—and all ours!

But something has warned the sharp instinct of a hind that all is not as it should be—some sense of brooding danger—a fitful curl of betraying breeze. "Phrew!" sounds the warning signal—"Phrew!—Phrew!" and in an instant there is a quick flashing of dappled hides.

The herd is gone! Beyond the knoll of Pipalda a distant glint proclaims the line taken by our stag. He will not go far however; and, sad to relate, we shall certainly return to secure that splendid pair of horns.

While their watering habits vary slightly, according to the situation of the necessary fluid, chital may be said to drink twice a day—at dawn, and about sunset.

If covert is nigh, whence a sudden deadly spring may bring a feline foe, their approach to water is an extraordinary sight. The writer had spent a moonlit night in a tree, sitting up for a tiger, and was awaiting the arival of his men from camp ere descending to earth. All night long the chital stags had been braying, and polishing their antlers against trees in the surrounding woods, and now, with the first green flush of dawn, a large body of spotted deer, ever gregarious, gathered hesitatingly on the bank above the pool, which lay almost directly below our *machán*.

That perfect stag.

At last a wary old hind slowly descended the steep bank, lifting cautious feet with a comical high-stepping action; and halted half way down.

Suddenly she whistled, and bolted up the bank; and the whole herd darted out of sight into the jungle.

After some time they slowly collected again. This time the hind got as far as the sandy bed of the little river, when she sounded another alarm—and off they all went a second time.

Returning once more, the whole scene was re-enacted, with this exception, that as several deer had now got close to the pool, there was a bigger and more complete stampede when the warning whistle went.

At length, either having tired of false alarms, or being satisfied that these their efforts to force a lurking enemy to disclose his position would have met with success had he been there, the herd descended the bank in earnest, and crowded to the water's edge; but the timid creatures spent nearly all their time in lowering their heads and sharply raising them again, while several false alarms and partial stampedes occurred. The final scene came certainly before all could possibly have quenched their thirst; and this time a frantic, helter-skelter retreat, accompanied by a chorus of barks and whistles, scattered the herd for good.

Their alarm was no ill-founded one, for a family of three tigers prowled this river-bed, and one had passed this very pool during the preceding night; while tigers' pugs were thickly imprinted in the moist sand, and the whitening bones of many a chital lay in the grass around.

The coverts in those small detached *bandis*, like that of Pipalda, so few and so easly worked, and an animal so easily located by an examination of the one or two rare pools still left in the parched jungle, that tigers were usually bagged there without much difficulty. Sometimes it would be one's fortune to come across a tiger and shoot him practically single-handed, without the aid of an army of beaters ; or the beast might be found on or near his "kill" by the energetic sportsman who had taken the trouble to personally visit his baits in the very early morning.

Such bits of sport when they come are very welcome ; and there is a freshness about them that is often absent from the stereotyped tiger-beat.

On this particular morning, it will be remembered, we had left the herd of spotted deer near Pipalda, and continued our ramble to examine the buffalo-calves tied out overnight.

And so we pass on down-stream, towards the spot where our first *hela* was left yesterday evening—to await his fate. Round that corner, and under that banyan tree, was it not? Yes. There he is, regarding us in the distance with a bubaline stare. The poor little beast emits a little grunting squeak of welcome as he sees us approaching. The pile of fodder placed at his disposal last night has nearly disappeared, so he has not lacked occupation. One of the men unlooses the cords round his fetlock, and drives him off in the direction of the nearest pool, while we continue on our way.

A few hundred yards further on we stop. Look at that!—the fresh and deeply indented four toes and a pad of a tiger. A big one, too! He came off the bank there, and down on to the sand. His tracks are seen leading far along the river-bed in a long dotted line ; and we follow them. Capricious beast, he walked now in the centre, now under the high bank, now over a soft mound of shingle, leaving great shallow depressions in it, or, on favourable soil, the clearly-impressed square "pug" of the big male.

Now we are approaching the second bait, and delight to see the steady tracks leading straight on in its direction. Almost as if we had been actual eye-witnesses can we picture *his* sudden halt last night, as he turned that corner, and saw the poor little buff tethered there before him. So we, too, cautiously turn the corner in that winding water-course!

The *hela* is gone! The bait taken!

A couple of patient inquisitive crows are perched, not far from where he was tied. As we gaze, there is a distant "Caw!" and a third is seen flying low through the trees to join them. Save for this there is a grim death-like tillness. We stare from a distance.

See! That rope that confined the little buffalo's hind leg; it hangs, broken, from the root to which he was fastened. There is the trail of a heavy body dragged along the sand and away round the corner of a little branch *nála*. This, as we know from our inspection of the surroundings yesterday evening, leads only a hundred yards or so into the grassy jungle, and terminates in a *cul-de-sac*. There is no thicker covert in all this *bandi* than that formed by the low tamarisks which fill this little branch ravine; but it is of small extent, and a few well-directed stones would search it thoroughly.

One of the crows now leaves his perch, and flies farther up the deep-cut offshoot, curving up to and settling on a convenient bough. Then down go his head and tail, and "Caw!" comes his voice. No need for human speech, friend *corvus*. Well do we know what you would say!

No hunter has been here before us this year, so, perhaps, the slayer of our buffalo is unsophisticated enough to be lying up near his "kill."

We retire behind our sheltering corner and think it out. Shall we go back to camp, and arrange for a regular beat, with sufficient men to ensure the successful driving out of the tiger? Or are we justified in making the most of the opportunity as it presents itself? Two of our own men and three villagers accompany us—only five beaters in all. But no "stops" are required here.

At last we settle that a quiet little beat is advisable. It will not disturb the tiger if he has moved on elsewhere. My orderly has a watch. It is compared with ours; and careful plans are explained to him. At a fixed moment—allowing a generous margin of time for unforeseen contingencies—he is to extend his men on both banks of the *cul-de-sac*, up which they are to walk slowly, quietly talking, and chopping a tree at intervals.

The old fellow reflectively wags his head, to imply approval. It is not the first time he has played this game.

We leave the men and retrace our steps for some distance. Then we climb the bank, and, detouring in the dry grass, in due time approach cautiously that tree that we marked ere setting out. Every step must be considered now, for, if the tiger is where we hope he is, he will not yet have settled for a siesta, and is sure to take alarm at the least suspicious sound. Slowly, gently then, through the tinder dry leaves.

There is no proper tree to roost in here. Even if there was, it would be inadvisable to climb into it, for the deep hollow to which that crow called our attention is not much more than fifty yards away, and we might rise within the range of vision of him who lies therein! Here however are several stout, close-set saplings and a thorny bush. Behind these we shall be hidden and to a large extent sheltered. If the beast does break, he will pass within about forty yards of us, *going away*.

Yes. This spot will do.

Look at the wrist-watch. Five minutes to wait. See that the "cut-off" of the little rifle is open, the magazine full, and a cartridge still in the chamber. Gently lift away that dry teak leaf. There is a brooding silence, broke by the far away mewing of a peacock—Pe-*haun!*—Pe-*haun!*—Pe-*haun!*

A deep sigh does not much relieve the feeling of tension, which is becoming distressing!

Suddenly through the still woods resounds a distant Tok!—Tok!—Tok! Those were blows with the back of an axe on a dead tree. Faintly sound the voices of the men. There goes the axe again! And another Tok!—Tok! They are getting slowly closer; but as yet there is not the ghost of a sign from the *nála*. We should not wonder if, after all, it contained nothing but the carcase of our poor *hela*.

There comes one of the crows; another behind him. They fly up and alight nearer us. "Caw—caw! Ke-aw!"

The rifle is at the ready; thumb on the safety-bolt ready to press it back. Still nothing appears.

The men must be quite close now. By Jove! There's a figure hastily climbing a tree!

A small bird comes fluttering out of a bush rather to our right, and attracts sudden attention. No. It is nothing. Our eyes return to the edge of the——

In some extraordinary way there is a tiger standing there, close in front of us—broadside on!

"*Chick!*" goes the safety-bolt.

It *is* a tiger! But for the life of us we cannot tell how big, how marked, or any other particulars. Our eyes are enchained by his splendid *tout-ensémble*, until, next moment, he is moving forward, across us, at a slow, leisurely walk.

He is passing now—past—well past—wait another moment—a little more—now——

"*Bang!*"

"*Woof!*"

*   *   *   *   *

The tiger has disappeared in the grass. There is a sudden crying of peafowl all around, as the report of the shot dies away in the jungle; then that too is quieted. Still we continue standing intently there.

After a while there comes the voice of old Abbas Khan shouting from a low tree—

"He's gone on towards the big *nála*."

"Can you see him?" I call.

"No!"

"Then send a man up higher."

A dusky figure is seen climbing. Shortly comes an excited voice—"There he is! See! There he is! Lying down beyond the big *kowa* tree"—and the old orderly goes clambering up after the first climber.

"Have you got the glasses?" we yell.

"What?"

"*Glasses.*"

"They are (here)."

"Use them then, and see if he is breathing."

We cautiously make our way towards his tree, and arriving near it address the old fellow, who is standing up aloft, affectionately embracing a branch, and with eyes glued to the powerful prism binoculars.

"Is he dead?"

"He does not move!"

"Where is he lying?"

"In that grass, that red grass, close to the little *chirónji* tree."

"How far?"

"Perchance it is a hundred paces."

There is a point of vantage among some big rocks rather to our right front, and we are soon on them, within about sixty yards of the *chirónji* tree. But nothing is visible.

"Is he breathing?" we call back in a low tone.

"I cannot tell" comes the reply.

We creep a little nearer, still among tall rocks; there are stones handy, and soon they are flying through the air.

"He is dead!" cries the old man after a while. "A stone rolled on top of him!"

There is a handy tree, with easy boughs, a short way farther on, and soon we are in it, rifle in hand. Thirty yards off, in the grass, lies something black and white, and quite still. We climb a little higher, and stare hard. Then we climb down.

There is a bush still farther on. We peer carefully round it.

His tail is towards us: his head is turned away. And the pose of that head is the pose of death. Nevertheless, for a space, we stand watching, rifle to shoulder.

We stoop, and fumble for a big stone. Then, rifle held ready in the left hand, we cast that stone over the tall grass, on to the brindled hide. Thud!

Next moment the jungle echoes to a cheerful cry—

"Whoo--whoop!" Come along; it's all right!

* * * * *

It is to be doubted whether a greater herd of *Cervus axis* occupied so comparatively confined limits as in those little *bandis* at the period described.

One evening we saw a herd leave the forest for the open fields surrounding it, in which were counted no less than eleven big stags, while the total number of deer was computed at one hundred and fifty, and comprised many smaller "brockets."

Heads of from 34 to 35 inches in length were almost common in those jungles, 37½ being the biggest pair of horns secured.

A stroll through the coppices and grassy rides of the Pipalda jungle in its palmy old days was a wonderful experience to one most of whose *shikár* has been obtained only too literally at the wringing sweat of his brow.

The marvellous abundance of game—the rush of the twinkling legs and spotted hides through the underwood (they never went farther than a quarter of a mile ere pulling up)—and the certainty that one's quarry was *not* a dreamy myth, whatever might be the difficulty of working up to and picking out the biggest stag—this, added to the beauties of that enchanting retired woodland, all combined to form an impression that time can never efface.

UNDER THE JÁMÚNS.

Let not the reader indulge in fond fancies of the delicious and succulent fruit hanging in all its lusciousness on a sun-bathed old wall in distant England, nor yet conjure up visions of the vale of far Kashmir: these plums are but the small black fruit of the Indian *jámún* (*Eugenia jambulana*); and they grow in lavish profusion, astringent, rough, and alum-like to the cultivated palate, on the larger trees that mingle with groves of mango and *mhowa* on the highest plateaux of the Southern Satpuras. The *jámún* displays its prodigal harvest just before the commencement of the monsoon rains, and at this season its shady green boughs are to be seen hanging heavy-laden with the well-known berries, that are about the size and colour of English damsons. A few of the better favoured trees bear fruit that is quite passably sweet, and almost free from astringent taste; and these are resorted to by the Indian black bear and his apparently near relative the aboriginal Korku.

Both Korkus and bears have, before the fruiting of the *jámún*, been regaling themselves on the fallen jungle mangoes, and, before that again, on the rich flowering of the *mhowa* tree, not to mention the *sakhriya*—a queer, sweet-flavoured, whitish berry, which grows in myriads on a prickly bush partaking of the nature of a creeping bramble; and their palates are tickled by the distinct change in diet now afforded by *Eugenia jambulana*. From the deep glens and ravines that sink away sheer from the plateaux-tops of this portion of the Satpuras, our friends the bears come climbing up night after night. They leave their shambling ways marked clear in the dust of the forest road and of jungle-paths; they snuffle and grunt merrily all night under the sweetest trees, blow themselves out enormously, and shuffle away before dawn into the almost inaccessible fastnesses that surround the open park land on top of these hills. Gradually attracted by Nature's wondrous profusion of pleasant diet, there may be found many bears within a radius of a mile or so; but the cover is so dense, the sea of jungle, rock, cliff, bamboo, and giant creepers so difficult of search, that almost the only way of getting a shot at *Bhálu* is to wait dinner for him.

Well do I recall one night that I forced myself, an unwelcome and uninvited guest, on the *Bhálu's* supper-party. I had, while riding home the previous day, discovered a splendid tree of sweet *jámúns*. Rising in my stirrups, I had had quite a decent feed, pulling down the laden branches and then filling my pockets with fruit to munch on the homeward way. I was just departing when I noticed fresh signs of many bears in the vicinity of the tree, and at that moment a little black Korku came along the forest-path.

"Bears!" said he in reply to my query, scratching a sturdy leg with the other horny toe. "Bears! What's that? Never heard of such things. Never knew of anything called a bear. From my youth up I never yet——."

But my cane was crooked round his neck, and I guided him and his uncomfortable grin below that tree. "See!" I urged, "O thou wicked brother-in-law of many bears! Behold! (indicating documentary evidence under the *jámún* tree). Who did that, eh?"

"*O Maharaj!*" he grinned widely, "I see. Yes! How shall I tell lies to your presence? Nightly do they come since the moon was small. Nightly do they suck and wrangle. There's my hut up there, beyond the clearing and the *kutki* field, and I hear and know it all!"

"Then let there be a *chárpai* here half an hour before sundown," quoth I, "and bark-ropes too, against my return; and a suitable reward shall be thine!"

* * * * *

Towards evening I was riding back to the rendezvous. To my left ascended a mountain shoulder, out of which was carved the tortuous little road I followed: to my right there yawned a huge *khóra* of misty depth. At its bottom lay tiny patches of green tall mango groves in the bed of the stream, near the one water-hole that I knew of there. The great Kámdar *khóra!* Nineteen hundred feet deep, and a mile across. From its depths came the faint whoops of *langúrs* at play, and the distant calls of grey jungle-cocks. The sun was declining to rest far beyond the stretching lower ranges of the Me'lghát. The road made some agonising twists, skipped across a narrow, sharp backed *col*, with sheer, bare, yellow-grassed *couloirs* falling precipitously to right and left, and toiled up a long spur to the top of the plateau where grew my *júmún* tree.

My man had preceded me, with rug and food, and the Korku, having fulfilled his promise of the morning, stood there, with a friend to help him fix the *machán*.

There were two large plum trees, about twenty yards apart, and between them grew an *aola* tree. In the latter I caused the string cot to be tied. While this operation was in progress, I and my orderly tore down large quantities of plums, and disposed them temptingly on an open space at a comfortable angle from my tree, and about five yards from the spot where I should be seated, rifle in hand. At last all was ready, and I mounted to my perch and settled everything in a thoroughly comfortable manner—rifle with night-sight at my side, water-bottle hanging conveniently from a bough close to my head, and haversack with light refreshment, *not* of a noisy kind, somewhere handy. The men went away.

It was right at the fag end of the hot weather; and at this elevation—close on 4,000 feet—the breeze was tempered by moisture that presaged a near approach of the monsoon current. The moon was practically full, as she shone through the interstices of the jungle on her way to the zenith. Through a gap in the beautifully rounded foliage of great mango trees, growing hard by the edge of the plateau, one obtained a glimpse of the far-off Tapti valley, still bathed in a reddish mist, or dust-haze, illumined by the after-glow of sunset. Distant tinklings denoted the return home of cattle to the Korku huts some five hundred yards away. The eternal nightjars began to set up their "Chuckoo-chuckoo-chuckoo!" or to sail ghost-like abroad, uttering a peculiar cry that sounds like "Chyeece." Then, somewhere down beyond the edge of the khud, one heard the bark of a wandering *khákar*.

Night-watching in trees is not a form of amusement that appeals to me much now, after a long course of the same—necessitated by the very thick jungles in which most of my *shikár* has been carried out—but the first hour or so of such a vigil, until one gets bored, and especially if animals appear and interest the watcher, never fails to exercise a certain mystic charm. Thick-skulled and unhappy must he be whose perceptions fail to respond to the wooing of our mother Nature in one of her most attractive moods! One is carried away, as it were, to some tremendously distant era, when we all were children of the forest, dependant on the good earth in much more direct fashion than we seem to be now; when the risings of the sun and moon, the passing of clouds, a crackle in the shadow of the trees, a stealthy step in the dark—all seem to have been more intimately bound up with man's very existence. This is the harking back of the soul of man to prehistoric influences!

Time in *macháns* often passes wonderfully quickly. I had looked at my watch, and was surprised to find it past nine o'clock. A jungle path ran along the edge of the little clearing in which stood my trees, and down this came a flitting shape, halted, tripped on again to a sound like light clicking of castanets. A *khákar!* But I have never satisfied myself as to whether this sound proceeds from the little creature's tongue or hoofs. Later on, two small animals, civets perhaps, played about under the far *jámún* tree. About midnight I was straining my eyes to make out a large colourless form that followed the same path down which the barking deer had come. It moved steadily, slowly, keeping to the shadows, too deliberate for anything but a tiger or panther. It disappeared gradually towards a neck of land leading to a higher portion of plateau. Shortly after this there was a distant throaty noise, the rattling rough voice common alike to big boars, bears, tigers and panthers, and, growing quickly bigger in the full moonlight, an old bear came rushing helter-skelter past my tree. Trundling rapidly along, he entered the forest beyond, and came to a halt. Not a sound ensued for about a minute. Then he gave a few loud indignant sniffs, and moved away through the rustling dry leaves.

15

It must have been about 2 a.m. that, lying back with eyes half closed, I became aware of a black object approaching once more. I raised myself quietly. On it came in the bright moon's rays, its whitish snout protruding from a mass of shaggy black hair. A bear! On he waddled until ten—seven—five yards separated us; and down went his head to the very heap of plums we had specially arranged for his delectation. There he sucked and slobbered. Oh, such a smacking of lips—long prehensile lips! Oh, so busy; blowing himself out at lightning speed; crunching up the *jámúns*, stones and all; sniffing, sighing, gobbling, grunting!

In my hand I held a borrowed rifle, my own trusty friend not being just at that time available. As I raised the hammer, humouring it with pressure on trigger, it gave out a soft click. *Bhálu* paused an instant. Then he slobbered again. Yes; I had him fair. Making allowance for the hair on his back, the night-sight, clear white under the moon, lay straight on his shoulder. I never felt more confident of bagging my beast; and I took special pains this time, for the tribe of *Bhálu* had not long since put me in their debt—I owed a fatal grudge. Very slowly I pressed that trigger. *Bang!*

A lot of nasty white smoke hung in the way, as I lowered the weapon to gloat over my prey. There was a shuffling noise. *The bear was not there!* A black shadow shot away into the trees with a "gurr—whirr—burr:" there came the sound of stampeding in the leaves; then a "*Whoof!*" as he struck against something hard in his hurry. The bear was gone; and, as he went, more bears rushed away in various directions from the far *jámún* trees. A couple of humping backs went bumping away in the moonlight. All had gone!—and they never returned.

Next morning revealed a tuft of long singed hair near the half-eaten plums, with a fraction of skin attached. Farther up the path led the tracks of a tigress, and they met, or nearly met, those of a bear. Here was the explanation of the hurry of the first visitor to me under the plum trees.

REMINISCENCES OF JUNGLYPUR.

How they come crowding in on us at times—the memories of days gone by; and what more favourable moment than when one lies back on the big stuffed chair in front of a glowing fire of coals, pipe in mouth, one's feet comfortably on the ingle-nook!

The thick curtains are drawn, shutting out the bitter prospect of driving sleet and slushy pavement, where night comes down on the yellow flickering lamps, and at one's elbow the cut-glass bottle and seltzer sparkle benignly.

The thoughts are far afield. Farther than the autumn just past, with its recollections of moor and loch, spinney and fast-rusting bracken; far beyond these chill seas, "somewhere east of Suez"—in fact, away in that "coral stranded" land of strange interest and warring contrasts, that repels with one hand and beckons with the other! There rises before the mind's eye a vision of the little camp under the spreading branches of some giant mango or banyan tree. The golden sunset glow dying in the west, over mighty forest-clad hills, as we fling ourselves into the comfortable chair, and light a good Indian cheroot—not a guinea a hundred here! The hum of voices behind the little 80-lb. tent, where the skins are pegged out, and the rattle of a cleaning-rod hard at work on the good rifle that has contributed to such an excellent day's sport. In the ravine hard by, as the shadows deepen, the hoarse bark of some wandering deer.

Not long ago I happened to be quartered at one of those little old world Stations yet to be found in India, which would have been quite the dullest spot in the whole of this vast peninsula to which a poor exile could be condemned, had it not been for the sport obtainable in its neighbourhood.

To the southward stretched a great flat and fertile plain, the home of countless antelope, and here and there affording good pigsticking; while to the north there rose, sweeping from east to west, as far as the eye could range, the wall-like ramparts of a mountain system in and beyond which, in the old days, lay a famous big game country. The fastnesses of this region were not outside the limits of a day's ride, while many of its wildest glens could be reached within three or four hours.

Famine, native guns, and the proximity of the Cantonments are, each to a certain extent, responsible for a considerable diminution in the numbers of the *fauna* of those hills, which, like the heavy forests that once protected them, have receded to the more inaccessible nooks of hidden glens.

The traveller, passing up the old route taken by Wellesley's force on its victorious dash from Argaon on Gawalgarh, will now disturb no wild-eyed bison. The mountain bull, through whose very bamboo-grown retreats a British Army then forced its arduous passage, has long since withdrawn himself and the steadily contracting numbers of his kind deeper and deeper into the forest depths. Other game animals have followed his example. But there is still a little *shikár* to be had. At intervals—which are becoming fewer and farther between—red-letter days dawn, reminiscences of what one might have expected long ago in those days when *khubber* was not scarce, and the Briton quaffed his "brandy *pawnee*" in the grateful shade of the golden-blossomed pagoda tree.

So, in the hope that an account of some of the good days we enjoyed there may be of interest, I will refer to my *shikár* diary and refresh the memory.

In these times it is worthy of note that a large amount of our sport was enjoyed within a distance of from five to ten miles of the little Cantonments.

There are few localities in any country which, within five miles of one's house, surrounded by all the comforts of civilization, can boast an extensive deer forest, containing, in addition, panthers, bears and smaller game, and, deeper in, tigers.

It is the hills that most attract the sportsman in these parts, perhaps, indeed, all the world over. Sport seems to most of us at its best when followed among their heights. It certainly assumes a more poetic, romantic interest under such circumstances, although the plain possesses many a charm of its own.

Hill *shikár* entails many arduous difficulties to overcome, in addition to the circumvention of the game itself, besides which, in the relaxing climate of the tropics, it includes enjoyment of a more bracing atmosphere and great change of scene to men whose daily avocations are, for the greater part, carried out mid the comparatively uninteresting confines of the level low country.

Here, in this *Ultima Thule*, the proximity of the hills is the making of the place. How greatly they would be missed may easily be realised when the low-trailing monsoon cloud-banks hide them from view, and bring the drear and featureless expanse of the surrounding plains into unpleasant prominence.

Most of our sport here is had by making short expeditions into the hills, mostly of a day, or even of a few hours, snatched often between working hours. The method employed is to obtain the services of some of the Korku hill-men as scouts. These are supposed to wander about within a ten to fifteen mile radius of Cantonments, collecting and sending in news of any sport worth a visit from their employer. The Korku is by no means a born hunter or tracker. In addition, he has become exceedingly lazy, since, paradoxically enough, famine has brought him plenty! But he is the only man to be had locally, and now and then does a useful piece of work—when the spirit moves him. All the hill-folk within reach of Junglypur know that their reward is certain if they happen to mark a beast home, and will only sit and watch it while one of their number fetches the *sahib*. Even this knowledge, and the fact that some neighbour has just made an easy fortune in such a manner, will not however of a necessity tempt them to do likewise when the chance offers. Laziness, pure and unalloyed, is the only reason one can adduce to account for such apathy. Yet they will labour hard enough to collect and carry, for a similar distance, to the Cantonments bazaar, a bundle of firewood weighing half a hundredweight and worth a few annas.

These Korkus are a branch of the aboriginal tribes of prehistoric India, and are of Kolarian stock, although by this time they have a large admixture of more or less Aryan blood among them. Where they have not had much contact with the dwellers of the plains, they show broad, squat, black features, smooth, hairless, thick-lipped faces, and, as a rule, stunted, though hardy and wiry, little frames. When they have not too free intercourse with the superior (?) native of purer Aryan descent, they are extremely honest and truthful, and are at all times characterised by much good nature and a considerable sense of humour.

The Korkuni appears to be frequently of much better physique than her lord and master; and in many instances, especially where an Aryan cross may be suspected, is far from being ill-favoured, with smooth, finely turned, well-developed limbs, and often a surprisingly fair colour. They have also the free and easy carriage of hill-folk.

To see a party of Korku women swinging down some winding mountain path in single file, armlets and anklets jingling barbarically, chattering, joking, laughing and singing, with a bunch of clematis or the flowers of the *champa* stuck artistically behind an ear or garlanding a healthily supple leg or arm, is a refreshing sight after the cowed and unhealthy prudery of their Hindu sisters of the plains.

It is evident that, in common with most hill tribes, the Korkus have a considerable amount of artistic perception; and a dance, performed in their rude wattle-and-daub villages at the time of that Hindu festival the *Holi*, when they go through regular "figures" to the rythmical accompaniment of strange melody and waving peacock-tail switches, astonishes one by the unexpected grace that pervades its every movement.

I cannot say much for the Korku as a *shikári* however, although he is sometimes fairly good on his own ground, that is to say, in the jungles in the vicinity of his home. There was one particular place—the Barhánpur valley—which nearly always held game. Only a five-mile drive from one's bungalow, along an excellent road, it ran up into the hills to the right for about two-and-a-half miles, hemmed in by *salai* and teak scrub-covered hillsides of considerable steepness, the loftiest of which ran up to about 3,400 feet above the sea and, say, 2,200 above the level of the plain. Several precipitous *khóras*, or ravines, joined it from both sides, and in the centre ran a fair-sized stream in the rainy weather, certain pools of which always lasted out the hot season. In spite of the continual presence of grass-cutters from Cantonments, the natural attractions of this pretty little valley were irresistible to the bears, sámbar, nilgae, occasional panthers, and smaller deer which had their homes in its sheltered nooks. Much of the soil was saline, and it was conveniently close to the crops on the plains below.

In the same way that a favourite eddy behind a rock will be found tenanted by a good fish, no matter how often its former finny resident may have been removed, this Barhánpur valley, if not overshot, never failed to attract fresh denizens to take the place of those we killed.

I remember one bitterly chill and misty morning, in the early part of the cold weather, rising at 5 a.m., lighting the lamp, and, getting on my bike, a twenty minutes' exhilarating spin along the capital road brought me to the lower foot-hills, and shortly later to the "village"—about half-a-dozen wattle-and-daub huts—of Burhánpur, where my orderly met me with a few Korkus; the rest had been already posted as look-out men.

A sharp walk for about a mile up the dank and chilly bed of the yet misty valley, which was already waking to the shrill cries of the grey jungle-cocks and the mewing of peafowl, landed us at the mouth of one of the side glens—the Am *khóra*—near which a good stag sámbar had been seen the previous day. On a little peak, silhouetted against the flush of coming dawn, I made out the forms of two of the scouts. They had seen nothing however, and we held on up the glen in silence, spreading out through the long dewy spear-grass that clothed the level ground bordering the stony watercourse. From a thicket there suddenly rose the beating of heavy wings, and a loud

"Kok-kok—kok-kok!" as a peacock, scattering the dew in glittering drops, burst forth clamourously, and, rising clear of the trees, sailed ponderously away down the *khóra*, his grand tail streaming behind him, brilliant in the beams of the newly-risen sun.

Here and there up the valley rang the loud "Kuck-kaa-kiya-kuck'm!" of a jungle-cock, and as we reached the spot where he had been shouting his soul out, the wary bird might be seen running swiftly off through the leafless under-wood. Further on we surprised a couple of barking deer. Leaping over the dripping grass, heads low, and round, fat, white-scutted rumps high in air at each bound, they popped into the *nála*, and, hopping up the far bank, stood suddenly, artful little dodgers, just behind some tree trunk or bush; then, with a short hoarse bark, off up-hill again.

The clear fresh morning air resounded with the notes of birds and the screaming of the little rosy-headed parrakeets that swept along the hillsides to settle in a cloud on some favourite tree. By this time we had reached the little pass, or *khind*, by which the stag of which we were in search usually mounted to his day retreat; and I had already began to fear that he must have taken another path this morning, or be already couched, and to inwardly curse the annoyingly nocturnal habits of this fine species of the deer tribe, that made it so difficult to find him after the sun was up, when, simultaneously with some of the men, my eye caught sight of two dark objects on the shadowy side of a little spur, and the glasses showed me two sámbar creeping slowly along and up one of those narrow game-paths so common in these hills. As the rearmost animal passed across an open space, I noted with accelerated pulse that it was the stag, and that the reports of the Korkus as regards the size of his antlers had been in no way exaggerated.

The extremely white and polished tips of his tines proclaimed that he could not have dropped his antlers last season, and, although nothing is more deceptive at a distance than the apparent size of the horns of the rusine type of the *Cervidæ*, I put him down mentally as carrying a 38-inch head at least, for it is only fully-grown stags which have attained to their prime that throw their horns irregularly.

I thoroughly appreciated the good fortune which had, at the very outset of the day, thrown him in my way. For every good stag seen in those regions a surprising amount of hard work and frequent blank days have to be undergone.

I was using a ·303 Lee-Metford carbine, which had not long been in my possession; and I had not yet learnt that with this and similar weapons, it is usually far the better plan to take a long and steady shot in the sitting or prone position than to endeavour to work close up to one's game, and then probably get a snapshot at an animal bolting away or past one in a maze of tree trunks and jungle. So instead of stalking up the spur, which, at a distance of about 200 yards, faced that up which the deer were climbing, I made the mistake of trying to work up the ravine separating them, in order to cut them off or get close in on them. Of course I left the men behind.

It was stiff work, and although I "glimpsed" my game once about 80 yards off, I could not tell which was the stag until they had again moved off and out of sight.

By this time they were evidently uneasy, and were steadily—albeit easily—climbing, instead of loitering on their way. Shortly afterwards, reaching the top of the ridge above us, they disappeared over its brow. "Now," thought I, and a heart-breaking clambering run up an extremely slippery declivity took me to where they had vanished. But when I cautiously raised myself and peeped over the ground in front there was no sign of them. After crossing to the edge of the further slope, and satisfying myself that the deer had really moved off, I sat down and examined the hillsides beyond, and shortly came to the conclusion that there was one line, and one only, which a sámbar would have taken.

Going back a short way, and signalling up the men, who were now fully 500 feet below in the Am *khóra*, I thought out a plan of campaign ; and in due time moved quietly along the ascending ridge for about a quarter of a mile. I then approached the edge once more, and found myself occupying a capital position for a steady shot at anything breaking out of the very likely-looking covert which filled a precipitous *kagár*—a deep cut furrow—seaming the hill-side half way between me and the men, who I could now see were extending down its slopes. From the elevation at which I now sat—about 3,000 feet and, perhaps, 1,800 above the plain—a charming panorama lay unfolded at my feet. Ridge on ridge of queer, knife-edged saddle-backs of the curious trap formation, a warm yellow in the light, with deep purple shadows; from my feet the mountain-side trended steeply down, clad with teak poles, *salai* thickets, and clumps of small bamboo, to the valley, a sister glen to the Am *khóra*, (which now lay at my back), rising again to the level Bánur plateaux, yellow with long spear-grass ; while, beyond the sharply defined chasms and ridges of the hills across the Barhánpur valley, the cone-shaped peak of the Chór Pahár cut the clear blue cold-weather sky—a bold wedge.

Away to my right lay the level blue horizon of the plains, the minute white walls of the magazine and other buildings of Junglypur shining remotely distant in the morning sun, marking the spot where the little Cantonments lay nestling in its embowering groves of trees.

From the higher *ballas*, or flat tops around, came the sharp, strident calls of the hill-loving painted partridge.

As I admired these beautiful surroundings, and drank in the light and invigorating hill air, those white dots, the beaters, were gradually working along towards me. At length they reached and entered the *kagár*, in which I felt that the stag and his hind must have halted. Their distant shouts mingled with the crashing of boulders, which rolled from above went thundering and bounding down-hill. I began to guess at the distance to which the backsight should be raised—when the dark form of the hind issued from a thick coppice. She trotted along the hillside, and halted, her big ears moving to and fro in suspense ; then she began to clamber at a lumbering canter straight towards me. On she came, and then in about a minute there rang out a sharp trumpet note of alarm, and a shower of stones rattled down-hill, as she changed her direction on sighting or winding me, and dashed into the glen below. Then, at last, a crackling of leaves up-hill, and the huge yellow rump of the stag, beyond which rose a grand pair of horns, disappeared behind a mass of bamboo thicket.

Rushing up-hill I was just in time to see him cantering along beyond me on the narrowest of little paths that skirted a steep face of black, basaltic rock.

The first shot missed ; but the second bullet was no sooner despatched than he executed a series of extraordinary leaps, head laid back, and fore feet literally pawing the air, as he rushed over the brow of a tremendous *khud* and disappeared.

With a heavier rifle I doubt whether I should have got along as I did ; but with the little Lee-Metford in my hand, I was able to reach this spot soon enough to see my stag laboriously crossing a spur about 200 yards below me, and as I sat down for a steady shot he halted, nose to the ground.

"*Click!*" The "cut-off" had got closed in my hurry, and had prevented a cartridge rising from the magazine when I reloaded. However, this was instantly remedied, and a second later the sight rested once more on that broad dark back.

This time there was no mistake about it, and the stag, reeling and straining an instant to face the hill, fell on his side and rolled heavily against a tree—dead.

When I reached him I found that the first hit had cut his throat close behind the angle of the jaw, thus accounting for his strange "gambades," while the second had entered his back about the middle, and close to the spine, both being Eley's soft-nosed solid bullets propelled by cordite. His antlers, which were massive and unusually deeply corrugated, gave measurements of 38½ by 39 inches, 9 inches just above the burr, and 7½ round the beam.

I now left some of the men—who were industriously removing from their scanty loin-cloths the vicious black seeds of that annoying vegetable the *kussal*, or spear-grass—to skin the stag and bring in his head; and, the day being yet young, at the advice of a Korku scout, who had seen a bear, descended to cross the main valley.

There was a sharp walk of about a mile-and-a-half before me, and I took one of the little paths made by grass-cutters' ponies, winding down a glen to the main stream, and finally reached a spot known as the Jámún Jhira (or "Plum-tree Spring"), a pretty little sylvan nook, where a shallow pool lay along the flat rocks, whitening them with saline incrustations, and a thread of water trickled tinkling into a jumble of smooth pot-holes below a little waterfall. Hard by, a tiny spring oozed out from under the roots of an ancient tree. Beyond the grey rocks rose the yellow spear-grass, clothing rugged hills that were studded with jungle trees displaying vivid autumnal tints ; while far up the narrow glen there hung the distant bulk of the massive heights of Jhákra. Marks of the nightly visits of deer were fairly plentiful in the soft soil and mud bordering the stream, as well as the bath-like mud-wallow of a big stag, called *lotán* by the jungle-men.

Here I investigated the mysteries of the tiffin-basket, while the men squatted about the rocks for a smoke.

On my tendering a cheroot to the Korkus, great was the interest evinced by these simple fellows. Hearing a volley of laughter and chaff, I glanced up to see that the wag of the party had improved on the native method of sticking the lighted cigar through the fingers and sucking from the hands formed into a bowl; he had quietly appropriated the smoke, as it went the round from hand to hand, and sat demurely puffing it after the manner of the *sahibs*—to the intense amusement of his fellows.

After a short rest at the Jámún Jhira we took the hill again, and, as the bear had been lost sight of, beat a large cup-shaped ravine, called the "Kachanár *khóra*." This took a long time, but did not produce the bear or anything else, so, accompanied by the patel of Barhánpur, I climbed out of this "devil's punch-bowl" by a distinctly ticklish ascent, which necessitated several extremely nasty crawls along the dangerously tilted hillside that swept smoothly down, to end abruptly in a considerable cliff of black basalt.

The beaters went back out of the mouth of the ravine, led by the orderly; while I shortly afterwards arrived at the crest of a knife-like serrated spur and scanned the slopes and gullies spread out beyond.

The patel rolled down a boulder or two, but without result, after which I thought I saw the bright rufous coat of a barking deer on an opposite ridge, and took a long shot at it. It turned out to be a bit of ant-hill, and no deer; but at the sound of the shot a black shaggy mass emerged from a thin bamboo clump below me, 200 yards off, and, hurrying along the steep hillside, halted. A ·303 bullet struck close under him, and sent him off with a startled gasp, down-hill of course, in that headlong fashion a frightened bear affects, while another close shave increased his hurry.

I ran along and down my ridge in time to see him reach the level and, turning sharp to the left, make all haste for the next ravine, his woolly back humping along in comical haste. By this time my haste was also comical; but I reached the level in about even time, leaving the patel well in the rear. It was a most trying half-mile race, for there were several deep-cut ravines to scramble across, and latterly another climb to be faced; but, though reduced to a dog-trot on the flat of my feet, I got along, and sat down rather suddenly on reaching the edge of the *khóra* into which old "*Bhálu*" had disappeared. I then saw, from the configuration of the ground, that the bear would proceed up this narrow glen before slowing down. So rose and wearily trotted upwards to a yet higher point of vantage. As I sat down again there he was—about as nicely "cooked" as myself—limping along the opposite slopes.

His actual progress past or away from me was slow, because of the numerous gullies and little spurs he had to dive into or skirt round, so I had ample time. Raising the 200 yards leaf I let drive. Miss! Try again.

This time a ·303 bullet hissed through his long coat, and starred in white powder from the rock behind; at which he "whoofed" with annoyance, and accelerated his ungainly pace. As he came trundling along over a little-open space, another bullet twanged viciously off the ground just under him. With a roar of rage he started to his hind legs, and made a furious demonstration in the direction of his tormentor. Although I was at least 250 yards away, across a deep chasm, it was wonderful to see how correctly he judged my direction. I now stood up and, letting go another despairing shot as he was rapidly getting away, saw him to my delight throw up his legs, roll over and over, and shoot swiftly out of sight below.

The tension being relieved I cast myself down, panting from my recent exertions; then, regaining my breath, descended to the watercourse. As I clambered down by the aid of tree trunks and creepers, I could have sworn that I heard a Swiss "yödel" up-stream, so I cheerily replied to it—"La-la-la-hi-tu!"—and hastened over the rocks. What was my surprise to hear it a second time, and catch sight of the melancholy, upturned visage of my victim, as that mournful ululation welled from his throat for the last time and echoed down the glen. Then his head dropped, and he curled himself up for the last time.

I have heard other bears chanting their own requiem, but never another that warbled it so weirdly as this.

One of the tiny bullets alone had struck him, fairly amidships, and was found nicely mushroomed against the skin on the far side—a solid, soft-nosed Eley's. His feet were badly torn and bleeding, owing to that rough and hurried journey from the spot where I had first disturbed him.

The men now came up; the soda-water arrived and was very welcome. The bear's legs were tied together with fibrous strips of the bark of the *dhamin* tree, a sapling was felled and run through his legs, and hey presto! "*Bhálu*," borne by half-a-dozen staggering Korkus, emerges from the Machhar *khóra* for the positively last time—"feet first!"

Elated by such a capital morning's sport, I turned westward and beat along the banks of the little river, missing a four-horned antelope that, with its mate, went darting and dodging away through the maze of *salai* stems. Farther on we beat a thickly-wooded terrace running along the side of the now deep sunk watercourse, and, being luckily posted, a lot of peafowl thrashed heavily up in all directions within easy range, and gave a pretty right and left to the gun, the cock closing his wings with a snap, and collapsing limply in mid-air, like a gigantic pheasant.

This wound up the morning's doings, and I was shortly rid of my shooting boots, and running homewards on the bike down the long gentle slope that trends away from the base of the hills. Another hour or so found me engaged at the billiard table in our little Mess, having killed the bear over again at tiffin.

Another day, it was after a long blank morning of hard tramping, when we were returning home, that a man came running after us to say a bear had been marked down. Foot-soreness suddenly vanished, and we quickly reeled off another *kós* to the place where a small dot in the upper branches of a teak tree showed us the watcher patiently marking old "*Bhálu*" down.

"Somewhere in that little scar half way up the opposite hillside" was all the information he could give us. The bear had been seen by these fellows, who had been cutting grass on the hillside, as he went meandering and snuffing his way home from a night's visit to the *bér* trees at the foot of the hill country.

I was afraid that we should be detected if I attempted to surround the little ravine into which he had been marked, and, once disturbed, the thick jungle was all in favour of the beast getting clear away; so, placing men in trees to watch the face of the hill and signal any premature move on "*Bhálu's*" part, I moved off alone and stalked the *nála* long and carefully up-wind. On arriving there I found that by going very cautiously along the bank and peeping over at intervals, it was possible to examine the ravine fairly well; but it appeared to be deserted. Just then a little puff of wind struck my back and, passing on, appeared to rustle the fallen leaves among the boulders in the dry bed of the watercourse. The slight rustling continued. Then, very slowly, one of those big black boulders in the shade of the bank stirred in its bed of dry leaves, and became a bear that moved a step forward and wagged its dirty-white snout from side to side with a puzzled expression.

Crack! went the ·303 from behind the trunk of a sheltering tree, and a tuft of black hair sprang from his back. *Crack!* again, as he sprawled about the *nála* and passed behind a bush. Next moment a black hair trunk, with a whitish sort of label on the front of it, appeared violently struggling up the bank towards me, still in silence. A third time the little rifle spat; and now the hair trunk rolled back amid an awful outcry—"Whoo! whoo! whoo." But the well-known sound is well-nigh indescribable. An attempt at it might be, say, a blend of passionately gurgled yödel and the soulful notes of a dog with an ear for music. A few more ululations of the kind that are, unfortunately, too funny to reach one's heart, and "*Bhálu*" lay still in the *nála* below. Once more had he become a black boulder in its bed of leaves!

The men now arrived, and he who had done the scouting was pouring a stream of voluble abuse over the shaggy hide. I pricked up my ears.

"What's that you say?" I enquired, "abductor of women!"

"Oh yes, *Sahib!* The old blackguard! Doesn't he just? Didn't a bear carry off a woman of our village, and shut her up in a cave all the rainy season!"

"When?"

"Oh, years ago, when I was a *bachcha!*"

"You seem to know a lot about it," said I. "But perhaps the lady was a relative of yours, eh?"

"*Nay, Sahib, ham kaisa*——" but his abashed protestations were drowned in the ill-suppressed cachinnations of the other Korkus, and an explosive and spirituous choking from Lallu, a vagabond old bacchanalian, who acted as my *shikári* at that time.

Bana, or "The Bear," became that luckless fellow's nickname thenceforth. It is curious how widespread is this native notion regarding these ursine amourettes.

One of the funny bits of this morning's work was the look of startled surprise on the face of another sportsman, who had received news of the same bear, but from another source, and had ridden cheerfully six miles out, when he suddenly met "*Bhálu*" coming home in a cart!

To descend to sport of a somewhat tamer kind than that which has been already described, there were plenty of antelope within easy reach of Junglypur.

By taking a tiffin-basket, and spending the morning and afternoon out in the plains, with a mid-day halt under some shady grove of trees, a complete and healthy change was to be had from the dull routine of station life; while a light tent and a slightly more elaborate arrangement of the commissariat and transport enabled one to extend one's range so as to include our one and only snipe and duck ground, which lay some 24 miles to the eastward, and in the vicinity of which the buck were numerous and carried somewhat better heads than was the rule nearer civilization. In those parts a black buck bearing horns over 20 inches in length was considered good, while 22 to 23 inches would be a prize.

Now, we are well aware that antelope shooting is very apt to pall, and is looked down on by some great hunters as a pastime only fit for the babes and sucklings in the *shikári* line. However, in default of nobler game, and if indulged in with a due regard to its peculiarities, without a burning desire to make a large bag in as short a time as possible, this pursuit is capable of affording a great deal of sport and much quiet enjoyment.

Antelope shooting, to give the most pleasing results, should be conducted with a complete disregard for the *size* of the bag, and with an absence of all hurry.

In the country of which I speak there was nothing whatever to prevent a steady shot bagging his dozen buck in a day—that is of course if the sport were to be judged of by quantity and not merely by quality. Except where the herds of antelope had been unduly harrassed by native *shikáris*, the most successful plan was to walk boldly in the direction of or past the buck, edging in quietly, and only taking a shot in the standing position when within easy range, the antelope being so accustomed to the presence of people working in the fields, or passing from village to village of the plain, that the adoption of a confidently casual manner, while showing one's self openly to their watchful gaze, was almost invariably successful with an animal that judges of the harmfulness of an object by the apparent quality of its guile.

Let one attempt a regular stalk however, even with the aid of good cover, and it would be fortunate if some wary doe did not perceive and give timely warning of the impending danger.

The conclusion to be drawn from the above is that, if you desire to make antelope-shooting a real pleasure and a true exercise of skill, there must be no trading on this one weak point of an otherwise extremely wide-awake creature.

Another condition is the use of a light and handy small bore rifle, and the smaller it can be, with due regard to effectiveness, the better. Delicate the sport, delicate also the means thereto. This will make as much difference between buck-*shooting* and buck-*stalking* as that which separates the rude taking of a fish from his element with the snatch-hook and the subtle beguiling of some wary chalk-stream trout by means of delicate tackle and the most cunning presentation of the dry-fly. Besides this, the pursuit of antelope, conducted on such lines, will afford ample scope to all the powers of the greatest glutton for difficult stalking and hard work.

Although antelope show no distrust of the human taint when the owner thereof is in full view, they will be found to behave very differently should he be concealed in any way; and, by the man who takes to stalking pure and simple, after having been in the habit of employing other methods, will be found to display astonishingly keen perception of scent. Indeed, I have known men who have shot plenty of antelope aver that these animals have no apparent scenting power—the reason of this misconception being that buck rely much more on their keen vision to preserve them from the dangerous proximity of human enemies. They will nearly always be found extremely difficult—almost impossible—to "drive," and, by reason of their experiences with native professional netters and snarers, exasperatingly shy of all efforts to guide them towards any given spot, even up-wind, which is the usual course they take in changing ground.

One hears a geat deal about the "fatal curiosity" of all deer. Is it not rather a desire to probe the quality of the suspected danger and avoid imaginary alarms that prompts this so-called inquisitiveness, especially when the object of distrust resembles any of their possible animal foes?

Buck-stalking may not sound particularly interesting to some seasoned *shikáris* but, after a long and difficult approach, when at last one lies behind the sheltering bush or mound of earth, one's efforts are surely amply repaid by a close survey of the interestingly unconscious game, especially when aided by a binocular glass. The amusing antics of the young fawns, the ever suspicious and wakeful mien of a sentinel doe, or the dignified behaviour of the glossy black master of the herd, whom one may even now spare unless the attractions of an unusually fine pair of horns should overcome other promptings—all form a picture of engrossing interest to the man whose soul is not too lofty to descend to such comparative trifles.

A clear, sharp morning in the cold weather season, as the dogcart bowls merrily along the hard white road, passing a country cart or two that their muffled-up drivers turn aside with jingling of bells—swathes of white mist lying along the yellow stubble and the fresh green of the *rabi* crops, and mingling with the smoke of the early fires that rises from the village by the ford—a jackal slinking off across the fallow—the whirr of a startled partridge from the roadside,—the red ball of the sun rising through the mists of dawn to his inexorable work of the day—the halt by the roadside, where we meet the bullock cart, to transfer the lunch-basket—the start across the level far-stretching antelope plains—and then, the morning's sport adjourned, the shade of yonder thick wide-branching old mango tree, lunch, a bottle of nectar-like beer, and a quiet smoke. Does not that recall many a pleasant day in this much-maligned land?

Besides buck, the plains yielded us chinkara and nilgae, that is to say, in the neighbourhood of the lower foot-hills; and the latter being in those regions a very different animal to the typically confidential blue-bull, capital stalking they afforded as they wended their way into the low hills in the grey of the morning after a night spent among the crops of the open country. The beef-loving Mahomedan of the native city and bazars had long since driven most of the nilgae from the ground within easy reach of Cantonments, but a dozen miles or so along the base of the hills, either west or east, brought them within reach of the sportsman.

Of course these large antelope are a perfect scourge to the cultivators, whose fields lie near their haunts and are subject to the depredations of *Portax pictus* or, as he has lately been named, *Boselaphus tragocamelus*. So it was quite a common thing, on cutting one up, to discover a native bullet or slug embedded in its flesh, enclosed in a cyst of hardened gristly tissue. The blue-bull is a strange creature indeed, with his high withers, lean horse-like head, thick crest, drooping quarters and cow-like tail, and very similar in build to many African antelopes. What a trophy he would afford did he only grow horns in accord with his enormous bulk—horns, for instance, like those of the sable antelope of Africa, whom he in many ways resembles!

The range of hills lying to the north of Junglypur were at one time the home of many bison, but, what with the unremitting attention of sportsmen, the insidious and continual attacks of the poaching native, and the enclosing of their haunts within forest reserves, by which the jungles are preserved from the annual conflagrations so beneficial to the grass and other food products of the wild bull, these grand animals have dwindled in numbers till, to prevent their utter extermination, rules have been framed to limit the number allowed to be shot to two bulls per annum. These measures have, it is believed, been beneficial, and although these unburnt, dry, grass-choked reserves can never now support more than a very limited number of gaur, their further destruction has been stayed.

Illustrative of "life's little ironies," I was once out in those hills, about half a day's ride from Cantonments, with a friend who had secured the permission, so difficult to obtain, to shoot one of the bison allowed that year, while I was limited to the sámbur, bears, etc., which were conspicuous by their absence. My companion, after several days' fruitless labour in the search for his one bull, had given it up in despair, and had joined forces with me to have a final beat for sámbar ere leaving the locality. As I sat behind a tree-trunk, near a tiny clearing on the hillside, there came crashing of bamboos and lo! a mighty bison.

Climbing a knoll not fifty yards from where I sat, the great bull emerged on the open, and paced solemnly along, till he got my wind and came to a sudden halt. I had now despatched my orderly, who accompanied me, to swiftly seek K—— and bear him the news that his bull had at last arrived and stopped the way, and only by a most painful effort of self-control restricted myself to "drawing beads" on various vital portions of my *vis-a-vis*.

Not catching sight of me as I sat behind my thick tree-trunk, and imagining I suppose that my disappearing henchman was the only cause of the human taint he had perceived, the bull moved slowly forwards till a distance of only some twenty paces separated us. A fine sight; his noble, solemn countenance crowned by the curly white yellow hair that grew on his forehead between the spreading horns. Suddenly sighting me he again halted and, staring fixedly, snorted sharply. I remained perfectly motionless however, and after a few more whistling snorts, and stamps of his fore foot, he began edging round the tree—which I carefully kept between us. This sort of game went on for some time, the bull never much more than thirty yards away, after which, having described the best part of a circle round me and my tree, he turned away after indulging a prolonged stare, and the ridge of his great dark chocolate coloured back disappeared behind some long grass. Following him, gingerly, I suddenly started back on seeing him again facing me; and, this time, thought that he really meant business. Nothing would have given me greater pleasure than to have knocked him over, but for the feeling that it might be a disappointment to K——, who deserved the shot for which he had worked so hard in vain. I also reflected that a preserved bison had been shot by a sportsman, not very far from here, in order to save his life; and that the plea of self-defence, which he had urged, had been accepted with anything but a good grace. Stifling my natural impulses therefore, I gently retreated, keeping the bull in sight, and longing for the arrival of my companion. The end of it was that the gaur went thundering down a steep hillside towards the main ravine just before K——'s arrival. He was not found again.

Too patent to a panther of experience

There were a good many panthers near Junglypur, chiefly found in the lower foot-hills and in the vicinity of villages; and these were shot in the usual manner, by sitting over a "kill" (either natural, or a bait previously tied up) or, what was much more deadly, by occupying a roofed-in rifle pit, and picketting a goat within about fifteen feet of the loophole. A lonely perch in a tree was however the commonest stratagem, though obviously too patent to deceive a panther of experience!

The element of luck is too powerful a factor however in this tree-roosting, hole-haunting form of amusement, the most successful exponent of the art being a friend of mine, who never even troubled himself to keep silence, but coughed, yawned, and shook the tree with wide leg-stretchings at his ease. In this manner he bagged five panthers, within a few weeks, from the same tree.

The rapidity with which a bold or previously unfired-at panther will sometimes arrive before the watcher's hiding-place is phenomenal. On one occasion, about four o'clock in the afternoon, the writer, having climbed to his perch and seated himself, was busied in arranging the leafy shelter, when the tethered kid, that had been straining at its bonds and yelling after the yet audible footsteps of his retreating men, gave a start, and rigidified into a silent stare. A fine panther stood there, not five yards away, with his upturned greenish-yellow eyes fixed enquiringly on the *machán.*

Another day we were sitting in a tall burgot tree over a tiger's "kill" during the early afternoon. A panther came unconcernedly down the *nála*, heralded by much "tok-tokking" of peafowl, and flung himself down gracefully directly below us. As he was not wanted just then, I amused myself by seeing how far it was possible to go without actually alarming him; and it was not until several biggish pieces of stick had landed flop on his sleek hide that he had appeared to find it uncanny, and moved off as nonchalant as he had arrived.

Then again, one evening, on returning to camp in the jungle, my servant told me that a panther had been seen crossing the forest road into a small dell, where a barking deer now yapped loudly at intervals. Seizing a kid, and hurrying off with it, we had barely time to tie it up and slip behind a bamboo clump when a dry leaf cracked in the jungle, there came a light spring, a momentary struggle, and the head of the marauder rose over his fallen prey—to receive a deadly shot in the neck!

It is the easy success of such few opportunities that lures one into making a patient fool of oneself on the many occasions when luck is out, or the panther wary.

There is one particular ravine near here—the Dhár *khóra*—which is a sure trap for any foolish beast that may elect to occupy quarters therein. This deep glen winds up between tremendously steep hillsides to an abrupt *cul-de-sac* under a five hundred foot high horseshoe-shaped precipice. There is but one way out—that by which the entrance was effected. Now and then a bear, panther, or other creature enters this gloomy ravine, to lie up among the bamboos and boulders under the cliffs; and, if the fact becomes known, it is not very long ere a grinning Korku appears at the *sahib's* quarters with the news.

A large and very cunning panther had been creating havoc with the cattle which are herded during the rains in the Barhánpur valley, of which the Dhar *khóra* is an offset. He would prowl nightly round the zariba in which the cattle were pounded, and, after very long and cautious reconnaissance, about the deathly hour of two in the morning, would select a suitable calf, stealthily leap the thorn hedge, and, before the startled herd was aware of it, crush back with his prey, through some weak spot in the enclosure. Next morning the exasperated herdsman would follow the long dragging trail to some *nála* or nook, where, if small in size, only the head and pedal extremities of the victim would be left: if large, and so affording more than a comfortable bellyful for the spotted tyrant, the unconsumed remains would have been removed with a skill that usually baffled any attempt at discovery. On one occasion a long search revealed the carcase suspended on the branch of a tree far above our heads. The entire fore-part of a plump yearling calf, which could not have weighed less than 140 lbs., had been carried up the sloping trunk of a *taklai* tree that grew on the steep slope of a woody ravine. The smooth, soft, skin-like bark bore a complete record of the panther's engineering feat. He had left the remains of the calf most delicately and ingeniously balanced on a large branch that protruded from the main trunk, some twenty-five feet in air. One fore foot had been adjusted on a small excrescence in the bark, and this gave the carcase a perfect counterpoise. It would have been a difficult task to set three able-bodied men, working in broad daylight, and supplied with ropes.

At last this panther killed a laggard cow close to the mouth of the Dhar *khôra* trap, but lay up elsewhere. Next evening a goat of high vocal attainments was invitingly picketted close to the natural "kill," and I sat up over it.

Not till well after dark on this moonless night did the panther arrive, and then the first intimation of his presence was a little gasp, that was choked into a sigh, as the garotted goat sank to earth. This was followed by a horrid sound, like the sharp ripping open of a carpet bag. Just able to discern the faint white of the brute's chest at that very short range, bang! went a charge of slugs. Silence. A few minutes later a furious tugging commenced, and again the white patch showed dully under the trees. Bang! again without result. After this we went home. During the night—which made the third time of his bold return to the "kill"—the panther polished off both the goat and the remains of the cow, after which feat of gormandizing he left the tracks of his very comfortable and leisurely retreat up—at last—the fatal glen. Informed of this, I drove out next day, and on reaching the Dhar *khóra* found my flat-faced Korkus ready posted for the familiar silent beat. At the very last moment the panther turned sulkily out of the last bit of cover, and slunk off round a corner—for all the world like a cat detected at the cream jug—presenting however no shot, as he turned up among the boulders of a dry watercourse at right angles to the main *nála*.

A stiff climb and détour placed me once more above his second line of retreat, and this time we all felt sure of him. However, the beaters came on slowly and thoroughly, arriving just below my post without any result. This was extraordinary; and an animated exchange of signals was in progress when there came a low whistle from my old orderly far below. He had disturbed the panther, which must have squatted in some hole and let the other men pass right over him.

Now the brute came gliding and leaping up towards me in that peculiarly heavy lumbering way which so often misleads one into under-estimating the panther's pace. By this time the Korkus had climbed out of the watercourse, which at this spot is practically a succession of dry water-shoots, as it falls precipitously from the encircling cliffs to the glen below.

Like a yellow meteor.

Just below me was a small bit of cactus scrub, and in this our spotted friend came to a pause. I took the chance; hitting him, as I afterwards found, in the foot. The left barrel scored a miss, and, by the time fresh cartridges were inserted, he was sprawling up some precipitous rocks with the same deceptive lobbing gait. At the next shot, hard hit, he clung desperately to the smooth surface of a boulder, and fell back some feet; but recovered himself and crawled along horizontally, getting under a little ledge. He had now ascended into the base of the cliff, which hung beetling over us five hundred feet above the ravine, and which, nearer its base, decends in perpendicular basalt scarps, alternating with short precipitous slopes of rubble and rock. Above one of these slopes he now lay in a sort of niche under the sheer rock-face, showing nothing but the end of his tail and the ridge of his back. Seeing that he was now in the hollow of our hands, I climbed some way higher to get a clear view of him; then, with a man holding me firmly behind, got astride a little *salai* tree projecting from the dangerously steep hillside, and balanced self and heavy cordite rifle for the shot. The bullet struck fair on the panther's spine, and out he came, rolling rapidly over and over to the edge of the slope. Next instant he shot over as though impelled by a spring, and, every claw extended, described a beautiful curve in mid-air, to the accompaniment of astonished exclamations from the wondering Korkus. Falling through a clear hundred and fifty feet, like a yellow meteor, he disappeared into the ravine, still revolving; and then there came a distant but sickening thud. My orderly, warned by my cry to "stand from under," very nearly got the carcase on his head! Of course, that panther was as dead as a door nail when I got down to him; and, luckily, his skin had not been damaged in the fall. Sunset was now glowing behind the black cliffs, and the Dhar *khóra* lay already shrouded in cold shadow. After a refresher from the well-worn old tiffin-basket, we walked homewards through the darkening woods, night suddenly casting her star-pricked mantle over the hills as the roosting cries of pea-fowl echoed mournfully abroad. As we passed the *gaoli's* encampment further down the glen, a shout brought the sturdy herdsman from among the already zariba'd kine to view his defunct enemy.—*Wah! He* would trouble the cattle no more, and high time too. But others would take his place. "*Achchha, Sahib!* Roru shall be sent with news if more *gáras* occur—which *Bhagwán* avert!" he mutters to himself—and we pass on. At length the roadside is reached near little Barhánpur, the panther is stowed under the seat, and the good mare, seeming to care nothing for her unwonted passenger, swings us swiftly away down the straight homeward stretch.

At present Junglypur is looking its very best. There has been a good rainfall this year, and there is promise of a splendid cold weather. The wide plains, right up to the base of the hills, are waving with plenteous crops. There is an unusual abundance of animal and bird life. Black buck and chinkara are to be seen within the Station boundaries; pig appear to be plentiful in the *sendhi nálas*, where we hope they will stay after the crops are cut; and all night long, with wakeful shout, the watchers guard their fields from tall *macháns*. Up in the hills, six miles away, it is lovely. As you canter towards them at daybreak, the red rim of the sun, rising over the morning ground mists, throws their sharply chiselled features into strong relief against the deep shadow of their glens and *khôras*. From remotest east to west stretches the long mountain range. A tall succession of golden-pink wall with deep purple fissures. Its peaks and valleys in such a cold clear atmosphere look almost toy-like, miniatures of mountain land, yet the former are nearly 2,500 feet above us, and that little ravine seaming their sides is four miles long. The country rises gradually to the foot-hills, and the crops grow less thickly as we approach them. Some open fallow land succeeds the tall *jawári* fields. There stands a herd of antelope, absurdly tame at this chill hour, as, huddled together, they gaze at the passing rider: the buck, though black, is not possessed of a head sufficiently good to tempt us. The hills begin to throw out long steep spurs; their hard outlines become softened by the jungle now distinguishable on their slopes. The little clump of *mhowa* trees at Belkhéra comes into view a mile or two away. We shall leave our ponies there, and strike up the long glen on foot.

This section of the hills is more rugged, but less densely jungled, than the loftier flat-topped ranges towards the west and interior. In the hot weather it is almost waterless, and the game has then receded to the regular forest country; but at this time of year it provides ideal shelter to animals, such as the sámbar, bear, panther, and smaller game, which seem to prefer it to the now thick green jungles of the forest reserve.

Very plentiful are sámbar this year. The forebodings caused by the havoc which the famine of 1900 undoubtedly caused among them appear to have been too gloomy, for there seems to be a goodly stock of hinds—each with a fawn—and stags are about too, as many peeled trees testify.

We pursue almost the same track up the Belkhéra glen as we did that morning on our way to look up the man-eating panther.

Now we are steadily toiling up the steep thousand feet of the Tor Ghát. When we sit down for a breather half way up, there is borne to the ear, through six miles of clear dry atmosphere, a faint and distant "Tupp!"—"Tupp!" of rifle practice going on at the range far out on the plains below.

The scenery of these hills is well worth a stiff climb. I suppose it is the distance-annihilating atmosphere of India that renders them so comparatively insignificant when viewed from afar, since during the rainy season their summits, standing out above cloudland, assume their truer proportions. The visitor to these regions will be surprised to note the extent and depth of the chasm-like ravines, and the bulk and height of the elevated plateaux that lift their shoulders in all directions. Some of the higher peaks are composed of sharp and splintered basaltic rock, inhabited by troops of *langúr* monkeys. At this season of early December the long grass is still green and luxuriant, its surface matted with the peculiar black bunches of ripening seeds which constitute the highly unpopular "spear-grass," and the sportsman, if he be wise, will wear breeches made of good, new, stiff khaki drill. Later on, the spear-grass seed dries, and the tiny barbs, each of them a seed, drop to the earth. If the dry grass be parted after this has taken place, the surface of the ground under it will be found thickly covered with a soft and furry brown fluff composed of these seeds—a wonderful provision of Nature against their total destruction by fire. When the big grass fires of the hot weather sweep over these tindery expanses, the flame rushes by, merely scorching the upper layers of this fluff; and with the first heavy rain of the monsoon these solitudes are quickly reclothed in green.

The prevailing tree here is the *salai*, the light graceful foliage of which is still unshed, and we may detect, here and there, one of their trunks standing red and frayed—the work of a sámbar stag who has been cleaning the "velvet" off his itching horns against it.

As we climb up slowly out of the deep valley, there stretches out a rolling mountain region that is all our own, wander as we will, hunt as we will, for mile on mile in every direction. Water is now plentiful even up here, and often one stumbles on a *lotán*, or marshy hole, screened by tall red grass, where the big stags "soil" nightly in the mire.

At the northern end of the long Belkhéra glen, and separated by the pass leading from it into the Patoli valley, stand the two Jhákras (*barra* and *chota*), their flat summits rising to a height of 3,500 feet. Far below their northern slopes lie some distant green patches, which are the scattered crops raised by the Korkus of Patoli. To those crops the truculent stag, the watchful hind, and the callow long-limbed fawn descend, together with the shades of night. From his perch in the night-watcher's *machán* the indignant Korku hears the breaking of the succulent heads of *jawari*, as the deer pull them from their stalks: frantically he yells, and whacks his empty kerosine tin: from other fields comes the mournful clacking of more elaborate wooden rattles: the nocturnal marauders beat a hurried retreat, crushing many a long millet stalk to the earth as they go—to resume operations in neighbouring fields. The Korku nods drowsily again, a forlorn, black, blanketted silhouette against the stars: the night wears slowly on, gradually chilling to the dawn. By the first faint harbingers of dawn in the eastern sky a dark shape is seen approaching the lower slopes of the hill. It halts a moment; then a massive pair of antlers show against the pale horizon as it resumes its leisurely way. Half way up the side of Chota

Jhákra, and just above the lower rock scarps, is a very pleasant *lotán*. As the false dawn spreads its green flush abroad, the stag heaves up from this mud wallow, scrapes his mud-plastered sides and grinds his rough horns against the sapling at its brink, and passes slowly on up-hill. Higher still he may be seen rearing himself up on his hind legs against an *aola* tree, or moving about below it picking up the fallen fruit—hard, acid berries; then he saunters out of sight into a jungly hollow beyond. If we follow we shall see him "eating the sunshine," as the Korkus say, basking in the early beams of the sun, perhaps lying down on some open spot, and rising again, once or twice, before pushing his way into that dense patch of long *rausa* grass, under the thick shade, where he will finally settle down in his "form" for the day. In such a lurking place he will lie as close as any hare, his head pressed earthwards as you pass unconsciously by. Here also he will sit tight until the beaters are almost on him, when, with a rush and a bound, he will, specially if an old and wary fellow, break back through the line and be off to some other retreat.

This morning I had intended working the northern slopes of Barra Jhákra, but was met on my way thither by two Korkus, who told me that a stag had been seen, and marked going home up in the spot that I have described—a shallow jungly depression, just below the crest of Chota Jhákra—so I turned aside and took a little path leading to this hill, which was about two miles off. Old Lallu, Jhápu, and serveral Korkus from the village of Bánur had the stag marked down. He was somewhere in that cup-shaped corrie, but they could not exactly say where. It was rather a difficult affair for one rifle, since the stag might take almost any course when roused. As a rule, there are certain routes which game, aroused in certain localities, will take when startled, and these are often known to the jungle-man; however, on this occasion a mistake was made. I took up the best apparent position, posted stops, and the beat began a long way off, round a shoulder of the hill.

I have heard "beating for sámbar" criticised as a most unsportsman-like method—"stalking is the only legitimate means of shooting deer," etc. I am afraid these arm-chair critics know but little of *Cervus unicolor*, the real Simon Pure, as found "at home." There are, of course, rare occasions when these deer may be stalked—I have done it myself; but in ninty-nine cases out of a hundred the thing, in its stricter interpretation, cannot be done once he is in his Central Indian fastnesses. A belated stag may be found at very rare intervals in ground suitable to a real stalk; a stag in horn during the rains may offer a like opportunity; or you *may* hit off and intercept a beast going home in the twilight of the dawn; but these are exceptions to the rule that this cautious nocturnal animal is usually well into his thick jungle by the time it is light enough to see your rifle sights, and, once there, you will rarely move him, so as to get a shot, unless you rouse him with beaters. Then, again, this beating for sambár rarely results in having the deer walked up to your post to be rolled over in inglorious ease: the beaters are merely the finders, the rousers of the game; when that is done the affair has only begun. The stag may take almost any line; the sportsman's business is then to intercept him, cut him off, watch him till he halts, and then creep in on him, etc.—tactics that look very simple on paper, but which cannot be recommended to the lazy or poor-conditioned sportsman, accustomed perhaps to the comparatively confiding habits of spotted deer, swamp deer, etc., whose habits and habitat admit of finding and stalking in the more orthodox way. These peculiarities of sámbar *shikâr* make it sufficiently arduous and exasperating to offer attractions when tamer sport has begun to pall on one. Anything like big bags are practically out of the question ; blank days are conspicuously to the fore ; and since it is peculiarly difficult to make an accurate estimate of the size of the stag's horns, the greatest care has to be exercised to avoid the slaughter of full-grown stags with small heads. The ten hours of a cold-weather day in the bracing air of these hills seem disappointingly short when spent in the pursuit of wary old "Dhánk."

The beat began, as I have said, and, after a while, an excited yelling began, ceased, and I learnt that two stags had broken back. This should have warned us, but the beat was resumed on the same lines. I could see a man here and there, as the beaters came along the woody hill-side ; then they reached the spot I had marked as likely, had almost passed it, when there came a yell of excitement and a crash! Up jumped a big black stag right among the howling Korkus, three hundred yards away, and rushed back through the line ; stood an instant—a perfect picture—with the sunlight glinting from his polished horn tips ; then dived under the trees, showed his yellow rump an instant, and was gone! He had been lying in that patch of long grass, under the thickest shade he could find, and when I examined the placed it was reeking of that peculiar sickly-sweet odour which big stags have at this time of year. This stag left little trace of his retreat, but the lie of the ground pointed to his having gone round the shoulder of the hill towards a big *khóra* which runs up from the lower-lying Barhánpur valley. Some hours were spent in working through the neighbouring depressions on the west side of the hill, and a couple of hinds, a fawn, and a brocket passed below me—all taking the same route down a long spur to this *khóra*. One of the men said he saw a big stag as well, but no trace was found of him. Finally, we descended and tried our luck just above the upper end of the big *khóra*. I was watching, with my glasses, the men in the distance, when there was a sudden commotion, and a stag burst out of a small ravine in front of them, and came running along the slopes, about five hundred yards away, taking a line which would lead him a long way below me. There was nothing to do but to run for it, down a break-neck three or four hundred yards of grassy stony hillside, and cut him off; and I arrived, panting, just as he came racing over a sharp spur through trees and long grass. He swerved suddenly on noticing me, and I then noticed that his horns were half grown and in "velvet," so lowered the rifle, and he disappeared, crashing down through thick jungle, in long heavy bounds.

The men climbed down to me in time, and I then heard that a very large stag, presumably my old friend of Jhákra, had again broken back. He had then been seen slowly making off, at his leisure, towards the spot where he had originally been roused. The stag which I had just seen was his companion, and had no doubt been made use of to cover his retreat by this cunning old beast, who had then sneaked off in the opposite direction. After resting by the nearest pool in the ravine below, and sampling the contents of the tiffin-basket, we returned to Jhákra and tried for the old stag, but without success. The afternoon was now wearing rapidly away, so, turning southwards, we left the big hill, and worked through the cup-like hollows, nearer Barhánpur, for about an hour.

I was proceeding carelessly up one side of a little knoll, on the far side of which toiled the men, when the sharp crack of a twig caused me to glance up, and there, almost perpendicularly above me, and not sixty yards off, stood a monster stag—horns laid back, mane bristling, and tail standing stiffly out! His vital parts were protected, more or less, however, by a maze of branches, the smallest of which might have turned a bullet, and next moment he was off at a lumbering canter: a snapshot was fired at him as he burst across an open space, and a despairing left barrel loosed as the huge black back and yellow rump disappeared with a lurch over the sky-line.

Shoving in fresh cartridges, I tore up after him (as he must cross a certain large open space of grass ere gaining the forest beyond), and looked in vain for his dark shape, which ought now to be crossing the grass; but he had vanished. Moreover, no sound of his retreat could be heard in the coppices to right or left. We were just going to examine the ground for blood, when, close in front, a great horn tossed in the spear-grass, and a choking gasp announced my good fortune at last.

The Korkus would have it that this was our old twice-met friend. If so, then there was certainly luck the third time.

He was a very old and mangy fellow, with long and half healed gashes over his brave old front, and one of his brow tines had been broken near the tip in the late rutting season's encounters. My extremely lucky last shot had caught him far back and high up; but the liver shot is scarcely less quickly fatal than a bullet through the heart, and he had never reached the covert he had sought.

The quivering of an eyelid was sufficient to satisfy my orderly's conscience as, with a muttered "*Bismillah ilkahu Akbar!*" the knife completed the ceremony of *hallal*.

There.........stood a monster stag.

And now the declining sun gave warning that the return journey should be begun. Without a moon it is awkward to be overtaken by night on those rough hillsides, so with a parting injunction against my next visit, and the stag's severed head being borne by one of the men, we hastened towards home along the precipitous, wall-like saddle-backs which separate the Belkhéra and Barhánpur valleys, descended in twilight a narrow rocky path that falls, turning and twisting, down their rugged sides, and at 7 p.m. found the ponies at the village. Four miles or so over a stony cart track by starlight brought us to Cantonments.

In common with most wild tribes the Korku is a timid creature before a stranger, and, on meeting the *sahib* on *shikár* intent, often becomes so secretive that neither wild horses nor even the almighty rupee would drag from him any local knowledge of which he may be possessed. The sportsman will find this secretiveness very baffling; and to what lengths the jungle man is capable of extending it the following narrative will reveal:—

One hot morning in May the writer and a companion had entered the jungle to investigate certain rumours that we had heard as to the presence of a tiger in the Ambadoh ravine. Ambadoh, the 'pool by the Mango tree,' is a delightful little spot in the Junglypur hills and its extremely picturesque glen goes twisting and winding down between steep hillsides to join a large tributary of the distant Tapti. These jungles are, during the summer droughts, very bare, and the white and shrivelled grass exceedingly hot and choking; but here and there a pipal or banyan casts its grateful shade, and, in combination with certain charmingly secluded pools, serves to offer sufficient attraction to wandering felines.

H. and I. passed the mango pool, and went about a couple of miles down-stream, quietly pottering along dry stretches of boulders, and examining sand and dust for the necessary tracks. At a spot where a considerable tributary *nala* joins the main ravine lies a narrow bay of level soil, rather raised above the level of the floods; and here grows much long 'burroo' grass, shaded by a few small new-leaved mhowa trees. Not far from the border of this little 'strath' rises a spreading banyan; in the river bed below lie some delectable pools. Soothed by the sylvan beauties of this spot, H. and I. repaired to the water's edge, and, reclining in the shade, masticated a biscuit, and raised aloft the pleasantly-gurgling water-bottle.

Anon, refreshed, we prowled on, and, about fifty yards further on, regarded with pleasure what we had come to see—the pugs of a tigress; but we failed to mark the prints of some smaller pads, or passed them by as those of hyæna, or other lesser beast of the forest.

Up to this point we had been accompanied by four Korkus, whom we had met on their way to cut bamboos, and had persuaded to come so far with us. These people now desired to be excused, in order to attend to their work, and we having casually inquired in which direction they would now proceed, they had indicated a course uphill and away from the river, leading past the aforesaid banyan tree and 'burroo' grass. So we left them drinking water and squatting on the laterite rocks. Half an hour later H. and I. accompanied by two of my own men had explored about half a mile down-stream, up a stale pug-marked branch *nala* and down again, when I remarked a suddenly thoughtful look on my old orderly's face, as he paused and seemed to listen to some sound—but the incident passed.

Not finding any more tracks down stream, we had turned and were retracing our steps, when we became aware of the four Korkus hurrying down the far bank of the river bed. Surprised at this sudden departure from their original bamboo-cutting expedition, we stopped and called to them; but in a pre-occupied kind of way they continued their course, one of them signalling that this was their path. Now had my old fellow mentioned to me the cause of his previous pause and thought, subsequent events might have turned out very differently, but he did not. 'Chance' was creeping in.

'Suspicion should rest on every departure from the normal.'

It was becoming hot in the deep-sunk ravine, and up we plodded over pebble and sand, past the pug-marked pool (erasing the pugs), past almost the level bay and banyan tree, H. going along the farther bank. By the pool-side I stooped, and scooping up a little water patted it refreshingly over my scanty locks. Then I replaced my sun hat, and ascended a little bank on the higher ground to settle on a spot for our bait that evening.

'Baurrgh-ha-waurrgh-ha-harrgh-a-waugh!'

The deafening noise burst all around me in the vibrating air, stunning and confusing for a couple of seconds, until, elongated and flattened, the form of a tigress grew clear under the banyan tree close to my right front, as she rushed towards me, bellowing, and scattering the dried leaves. Behind her two little brutes of cubs; they also in full song! My 12-bore ball and shot gun flew to my shoulder; the roaring comet came to a sudden halt. Finger on trigger, I took a few steps backward, then more; reached the edge of the bank; darted down it; and, pursued by the same disgusting outcry, made nimblest time across a mass of boulders—in some queer manner managing to watch my rear as I skipped along. Slowing down, I perceived H. making a flank movement in my direction, and joined him on the far bank behind another splendid old banyan tree. The two men were not far off, in a similar position. The roaring having ceased, we ascended our tree, handed up rifles, and reconnoitred.

The tree from which the tigress had made her demonstration was now about one hundred and ten yards away, and when I peered through the forked trunk of our refuge, there lay the tigress—like a big cat by the fire. She had gone back, and was lying in the shade, close to the gnarled trunk of the banyan, in full view. As the shot was not altogether an easy one we agreed to wait a little at least, until a steadier hand would give us a better chance; and so continued to watch the tigress, who every now and then turned her head to look behind her, or to her left, in the direction of our tree. Her cubs she had no doubt sent on before her into the grass. At last, feeling steady, we had almost prepared to fire, when the brute slowly rose to her feet and paced gently forward. Even then the sights were aligned on her shoulder, and the trigger all but pressed, when she turned, and presenting a back view, glided into the long 'burroo.' About half an hour was now spent in trying to discover her new position, but the difficulties of the ground and cover defeated us, and we turned homewards, leaving her to another day, mistress of the situation.

On my next visit, when I approached the spot from a different point and examined it with great care, I left a buffalo calf as bait. Finding the tigress had left the immediate neighbourhood, it was interesting to go over the scene of the previous day's excitement, and it was now seen that, when so suddenly stopped, I had arrived within about twenty-five yards of the family tree, from which the tigress had charged out for about ten yards. It is probably fortunate that instinct warned me *not* to fire on that occasion. As it was, the tigress gained her point, and was content with having covered the retirement of her cubs. As is usual in such very sudden encounters, I carried away only a fleeting glimpse of a tawny stretched-out form, and a memory of a peculiarly dark-red flank.

The experience of another occasion, on which almost the same tactics had been pursued by another family tigress, leads me to believe that it was unlikely that the brute would have followed me up or made good her charge. Had she done so, I should have been forced to turn and shoot her—or try to do so—and it is difficult to say what would have then ensued. My orderlies, who were also armed, retired straight across the river-bed, and from their position could have aided me had the beast come on; but as a most trustworthy man of this class once very nearly shot me when following up a wounded tiger, it is possible that I should have had more to fear from this direction than from the wild beast.

It remains to note that the four Korkus, though of course they deny it, came on the tigress after we left them, and were driven off just as I was. The thoughtful look on my orderly's face was due to the roaring which she had then indulged in; only it was too distant and indistinct, he says, to distinguish at the time; and so he had said nothing about it!

The behaviour of the jungle men in not letting us know of the presence of the tigress was quite in keeping with their character, but it might have resulted in a melancholy incident—for me; for the tigress, having been already excited, was much more likely to 'go for' one on being disturbed a second time at such very close quarters.

During the rainy season—June to September—there is, in our parts, little to be done in the way of *shikár*. The state of the level 'black cotton' soil, which is also covered with tall crops of millet and cotton, precludes enjoyment of sport on the plains. In the distance the hills are seen smothered in dense fogs or driving rain-storms. When the clouds roll temporarily away, they stand out soft-wooded with rolling vegetation, and tinted of a wondrous blue.

Up there, just now, the jungle is extremely dense. The long green grass is, in many places, high over one's head, and soaking wet. Every forest tree and bush is in full leaf. Animals are scattered everywhere, wandering as they will, without restraint as to water or sufficient covert.

Sámbar are practically all in velvet, although here and there some mature old stag may possibly be found in hard horn, which he has not shed as usual during the preceding month of March or early April. To leave the beaten track, or the more open short-grassed plateaux, is to dive into a luxuriant and dense undergrowth, matted and knotted together with heavy foot-tangle and the snaky tendrils of the giant *Bauhinia* creeper; while fallen and rotting tree-trunks, rocks, and holes impede the difficult way, and disgorge battalions of the voracious grey-striped mosquito, who buzzes in his myriads under the dense shade cast by the large umbrella-like leaves of the *taklai*, bastard teak, teak, and other rain-breaking trees.

In the larger teak forests the undergrowth is perhaps a little less dense; but the grass is often much longer.

The huge rough leaves of the teak, flapping and scraping mournfully together in the moisture-laden wind, take the rain-drops with a metallic patter. Great masses of yellowish-white blossom adorn their heavy heads. The woody hillsides rise sheer, their emerald heights concealed in drifting mists, which ever and anon drench the forest in torrential downpours. There is a sound of many waters abroad. In the valley a broad river brattles clear and amber-tinted over its shingly bed. The red muddy flood-time is past, and the once friable earth is again bound firmly down by the monsoon verdure.

Fevers and dysenteries wait on the luckless sportsman who at such a season ventures to tarry long in these wildernesses, the general unhealthiness of which is not dried up until another four or five months have enabled the sun to strip off leafage and get well at the roots of the grass.

The higher plateaux, however, enjoy a very pleasant climate during breaks in the monsoon. Shrouded in dense white vapour (this is at an altitude of close on 4,000 feet), until the mists lift about eight o'clock in the morning, to display grand views of woody mountain scenery, one may prowl the lighter up-lying jungles and open grass land very pleasantly throughout the day in search of casual *shikár*, and in the evening enjoy a fire in the corner of the shooting hut. The woods are full of orchids, wild balsams, moss, ferns, and tinkling streams. It might be a region very remote from India's plains; yet, only a few miles off, down below, our little Cantonment lies sweltering in the muggy atmosphere of one of the hottest provinces in the land.

Large herds of cattle are pastured on these uplands now, and the herdsmen are not averse to furnishing news to the sportsman when a wandering tiger or a leopard takes his toll of them. Other methods being futile at this season, a patient seat in a tree is the only way of bringing the feline to book ; and he may now return to his 'kill' at any time of day, especially when the mist-banks settle down on the woods. The writer has known tigers thus shot at midday, and early in the afternoon. However, as already noted, there is little sport to be had in the rains near our little Junglypur, although a tramp along the open, outlying foot-hills, where the soil is gravelly and the going hard and dry, will repay the wandering rifleman by many a charming stalk at gazelle and antelope.

Localities like this little station of ours, where some pottering sport, as has been described, may be had within a walk or ride of one's quarters, are now few and far between in this deteriorating land.

Poor old 'Junglypur!' In spite of its drawbacks, its admittedly bad climate, its loneliness, some of us will ever have a soft corner for it in our memories.

Many the jolly day spent on its plains, and in its jungly hills, and in its comfortable old-fashioned little Mess, the walls of which bear silent testimony to the sport it has afforded to more than one generation of sportsmen. To us, apparently the last of these, it has given of its best—scarcely comparable with the 'best' of its palmy old days—but something nevertheless.

Tigers, panthers and leopards, bears, bison ; many a fine sámbar—among which may be counted trophies magnificent even in a region where the 'rusa' is at his very best—beside nilgae, barking deer, four-horned antelope, etc., and, in the open country, chinkára and buck in great numbers. Also some pigsticking, and a little small game shooting, the best day, to my recollection, being a yield of a hundred head, including seventy hares.

Stalking Chinkara.

But all this is over now, for Junglypur is numbered with those deserted camps scattered about India, where a few grass-grown plinths, a row or two of once grateful trees, and a forsaken cemetery mark the mournful spot where a colony of the ruling race once lived and died and had its day.

From the carriage window, as the train creeps across the rich level plains of one of India's most fertile provinces, can be seen, flung along the horizon like some purple silken drapery, the distant line of the hills that look down on little Junglypur and the country which gave us many a happy day's sport. Last time I passed that way my eye rested with many pleasant memories on their highest point, that I knew lay close to the little station, where, but for the game it afforded, I should have spent the dullest days of my life.

ROUND THE CAMP FIRE.

The fire-undermined logs suddenly fall together, sending a plume of yellow sparks flying upward against the black night sky. We wrap our cloaks more tightly, and draw up chairs to the blaze, spreading appreciative hands towards the attractive light and warmth.

Behind us stand the white tents, in whose comfortable shelter a good dinner has set us at peace with all the world. Further off, the small fires, over which our attendants are preparing their evening meal, throw a flickering light on the motley equipage of an Indian camp; while above our heads hang the dark hollows of the huge ancient mango trees of M——. Once more have we pitched camp at the old place.

Our last visit was paid during the fiery month of May, and a very different place was M——then. But now it is Christmas week, and one revels in the perfect weather of the winter months in Central India.

Hark! There is the sharp whistle of pinions, as a company of duck wings its swift path through the cold still air, high over the camp. The well-known sound of the pintails conjures up pleasant anticipations of sport to come, with duck and snipe, in the familiar old localities. Over beyond the fire there, in the darkness, lies the dim line of the jungle's edge—a small piece of forest reserve, where, in the good old days, it was no great feat to bag a Christmas tiger, in addition to as many spotted deer as might be required.

Very peacefully quiet is the scene in this cricket-trilling silence of an Indian night, broken at intervals by the distant howling of jackals and the occasional bark of a dog in the neighbouring village. It is round the camp fire, gazing into the glowing embers over a steaming glass of grog, pipe in mouth, that a thawing process promotes the discussion of subjects interesting to the sportsman.

In referring to the past, frequent use is made of the phrase "good old days," as if those were necessarily better times than what we have to put up with now, for it is natural enough to invest past pleasures with a halo of exaggeration, of glory such as may not be achieved in these degenerate days. In some sense this glorification of the past is quite misplaced, and only due to the human tendency to paint past pleasures in none but glowing colours, while regarding the present through dull-tinted glasses; but as a rule this tendency has something tangible behind it, and, in reference to big-game shooting in India, alas! only too clear a justification. There do yet remain some localities which, by reason of their seclusion, difficulty of working, or from their being overlooked by sportsmen, have depreciated only to a small degree; but, as regards the majority of hunting-grounds in this country, the cry of "Ichabod!" is only too well founded.

For many years past the diminution of Indian game has been a subject for remark, and although in some parts of the country efforts have been made to secure the remnant from extermination, and by means of preservation bring the head of game back to something like its former abundance, the greater portion of the country is still being rapidly depleted of its fauna, especially those of the more coveted species; for precautionary measures have as yet been only local, and India generally lacks such laws as would have a really wide-spread result.

Before proceeding further it would be well to consider the causes to which may be attributed this deplorable toll which is being taken of wild life throughout India.

To begin with man, the most formidable of the enemies that wild animals have to fear, we find two different types of hunters in the country.

Firstly, there is the British sportsman—a class which, owing to various reasons, seems at least as numerous as ever, if not more so than before, owing to the larger number of Englishmen now resident in or visiting the country. And of him there are varieties.

Taken in the best sense of the word, the British sportsman, while to a certain extent contributing to the inroads made on wild animals, has apparently little real effect on their numbers. He shoots fairly, and the unwritten laws that regulate his behaviour generally prevent him from taking unfair advantage of game, or affecting its existence by killing females and young of the harmless species.

Unfortunately there are exceptions to this rule; and men are to be found who from no youthful excess of ardour, no indiscretion born of inexperience, can hardly be persuaded to spare when anything living comes within range of their weapons. Such men are found in various classes out here, and are not necessarily restricted to those who can scarcely be expected to know better; they comprise individuals who can plead no shadow of an excuse.

At the same time it is believed that unsportsmanlike habits are on the wane.

A particularly harmful period was that about twenty years ago, when the 'Express' rifle, then in its infancy, suddenly enabled men to inflict far greater loss on wild animals than they had been capable of carrying out with the less accurate weapons of a former day. It is well known that a great deal of unsportsmanlike shooting—mere slaughter indeed—was indulged in then, and up to fairly recent times. The writer is acquainted with a case where two officials, of the old school, spread destruction abroad, in their own district, for many years, with dire effect on the game, especially bison and sámbar, many hundreds of the latter being shot without distinction as to sex or age.

Such practices however have more light let in on them nowadays, so we find in consequence that little havoc of this sort is played with game in the present time.

In the vicinity of colonies of an inferior class of Indo-European, we find a certain amount of promiscuous and harmful shooting indulged in; but it is seldom that these depredations extend further than antelope, pig, etc., for it is difficult for people of this kidney to get into forests to any large extent, or wander far from the railway.

It should be remembered that the question of game-destruction at present under discussion is that of India generally, and is not intended to apply to any more or less confined and favoured parts—such as Kashmir—where, until a recent date, the European sportsman has indeed been a recognizable factor in the diminution of game.

Taking the country as a whole, and speaking generally therefore, it appears to be a well-based assumption that the

British sportsman—so few in comparison with the wide stretches of game-producing country—is not to an appreciable extent to blame for the marked falling off in the numbers of its fauna.

On the other hand, in whichever direction we turn, and however we regard the question, there is abundant evidence that the root of the evil lies in the depredations of native *shikáris*—trappers, snarers, and shooters, but especially shooters. For when we come to sift the means of destruction in the hands of natives, it will be found that trapping, snaring, and the use of bows, arrows, and other rude weapons have existed from time immemorial, whereas the period from which one can place a finger on the marked diminution of game dates from the time when serviceable guns became cheap and easy of purchase by native *shikáris*.

It is they who are the men on the spot. Their numbers vastly exceed those of sportsmen; and although in a given space of time one native *shikári* may kill less than a single Englishman who is out on a shooting excursion, yet the toll taken by the former is a never-ceasing toll. Day in, day out, through all seasons, and from year to year, his hand stays not, and it attacks the fountain-head of animal life—females, immature, and young.

To quote figures obtained from a fairly typical district with which the writer is acquainted, and which is more than half of it hill jungle of a wild character, but where the ways of the native *shikári* are liable to be more keenly watched than in most localities, it is found from an examination of the returns of Government awards paid for wild animals killed during a period of several years that, whereas 14 tigers, 9 panthers, and 11 bears were killed by sportsmen, 31 tigers, 52 panthers, and 42 bears were accounted for by the native. And this in a portion of country which is fairly regularly and constantly hunted by British sportsmen.

When, in addition, we are able to estimate native character, we have not far to go to find that for each one of such dangerous animals slain, a very large number of deer and other harmless creatures must be made away with. The native gunner has a remarkably keen eye to the main chance; and the immediate prospect of what he will gather in on the spot, by the sale of flesh, horns and hides, is far more alluring than that of the problematically few rupees that may filter down to him through the numerous native myrmidons and bloodsuckers that hedge about the offices disbursing the Government award.

Another and very clear proof of the truth of these assertions lies in the well-known fact that during the period immediately following the Indian Mutiny of 1857, when the native gun retired into a remarkably strict condition of *purdah*, game of all descriptions increased to an extraordinary extent.

To enter on a discussion of the classes of natives most to blame would be too lengthy a matter here; but it is fairly certain that, after the village *shikáris*, policemen and forest guards are to a large extent guilty parties. In any scheme to restrict guns, therefore, due consideration should be given to the supervision of these worthies.

In addition to the distressing state of affairs consequent on these depredations,—which are, after all, only natural to the untutored and irresponsible native,—there have been noticed a few cases of organized destruction of game, so thinly disguised that one wonders how it has been left to mere sportsmen visitors to discover their existence—a reflection which is, to put it very mildly, the reverse of complimentary to the district officials, who ought to have known of and taken measures to repress them.

A few years ago it was the lot of the writer to discover an agency for the wholesale slaughter of big game in a certain district.

After tracing it so far as he was able, he brought it to the notice of sportsmen, through the medium of the then leading sporting newspaper on the Calcutta side, as follows :—

EXTERMINATION OF INDIAN GAME.

Yet another appeal to sportsmen to be merciful, and refrain from slaughter, in a leading article, entitled 'The Extermination of Wild Life,' printed in the —— of September 18th, and an appeal that is no doubt a necessary one. Only in the last batch of English newspapers I notice in the columns of *Black and White* the reproduction of a photograph, accompanied by an effusion from 'A Sportsman,' who brags of having *in nine years* killed *eight thousand* head of Indian and Burmese game!

At the same time there are other forces at work, steadily diminishing the game of our Indian plains and forests. The British sportsman is not so entirely to blame as one might be led to think by the number of complaints and hints of butchery laid at his door. In the hope, therefore, that attention may be drawn to the existence of a destructive agency, the effects of which are far deeper and more searching than those of any white man's *shikár*, I shall endeavour to arouse the interest of sportsmen in this direction.

If only some concerted and combined action could be arranged, it might be possible to bring some influence to bear in the proper quarter, so that preventive measures might be taken, as will be suggested hereafter.

Lately I had the pleasure of contributing to the —— an account of a two-months' shooting expedition undertaken this year in a very remote and wild part of peninsular India. In that article I touched on the reasons adduced to account for an enormous diminution of the game of those tracts—a diminution that has taken place within the past thirty years only, and which is certainly not due to the British sportsmen, of whom very few ever visit that country. I described the numbers of rotting bison heads to be found in almost every hamlet, the numbers of local native *shikáris*, and the bands of ruffians that cross over into 'Mardian' from the neighbouring Native State and from British territory. I noted the presence on his regular beats, of the horn-collector.

In the Western Gháts, in Southern India, in the Deccan, and in Central India, I have noted the ever-present native *shikári*; and in all cases it has been the same old tale of the indefatigable destruction of game of both sexes and of all ages—patient, unremitting toll, taken day and night, week in and week out, month after month, and year after year. What wonder then that we are beginning to note the failing numbers of the denizens of plain and jungle! Even the most favoured or jealously preserved ground, yet bearing a goodly stock of game, is bound to suffer in time from the steady drain going on all around.

Very lately I came across a case of organized destruction of game, so astounding in its simplicity, so terribly effective in its action, that it hastened the carrying out of the intention I have had for a long time past to bring up this subject of native *shikáris*.

At the end of last August I visited a range of hills said to hold a fair number of bison. The time was not altogether auspicious; but I was tired of vegetating in my bungalow, and determined to chance the heavy rains and wet that was certain to be my portion. I had never bagged a really good bison, out of three shot in ten years, and was anxious to secure a head that would take a place of honour on my walls beside good specimens of other Indian game. These hills lie close to the river Tapti. They are somewhat remote, and seldom visited by the British sportsman.

A journey of sixty-five miles over jungle tracks, and a very difficult crossing of the Tapti, which was running down after a heavy flood, took me to the ground I had determined to work.

I pitched camp on a knoll overlooking a small Korku hamlet, and sent for the local *shikáris*. There were bison on the higher hills, they said, but they were much scattered now. "Oh, *Sahib*!" said one of them. "If you had only been here in the hot weather, you could have shot *khandis* (large measure) of them down there!" and he indicated a little valley, now green with long swathes of jungle grass. "There was the only water in all the country side, and in the early morning one could count the bison like kine—by tens and by dozens!"

"How many did you shoot?" I enquired.

A cunning look stole over his face as he looked at me sharply, but I was nonchalantly lighting a cheroot, and wore an innocent look. "Oh, two or three!" he allowed; "but others shot more, and a tame buffalo died in the pool; so when the *ban hélas* drank there, they died too! "But they mostly died by eating bullets?" I suggested,—and the old man acquiesced with a sickly smile.

I worked those hills as best I could, but never came on a single mark of bison, and on very few of other game. Three four-horned antelope were all I saw during the week I was out. And now comes the gist of my tale.

I employed two *shikáris*. The old man I had already conversed with I sent off to look for tracks in one direction;

while I and the other, a younger man, used to proceed in another, over the hills.

I had seated myself for a rest on a fallen tree, and asked the *shikári* what was done with any heads he might "pick up."

"Oh, we take them to Ishnaag!" was the reply. "He lives in H——."

Now there was a village of this name not five miles away on the banks of the Tapti, and I had not quite caught the name. "What? That village over there?" I asked.

"Oh, no; not that H——! Ishnaag lives at H——, twenty-five *kós* in that direction," —— and he pointed north.

"Ishnaag?" I said to myself—"Ishnaag?" and then, suddenly, a light broke in on me. I had it! This "Ishnaag" was a taxidermist of whom I had heard, and I remembered his address *was* H——.

That *shikári* was a most ingenuous individual. I was certainly cautious in my method of "pumping" him, and did it little by little, not all at one time, and not evincing very great interest in his replies. He told me all with a delicious candour, and, as I could see absolutely no reason to doubt his assertions, I have no doubts at all of the truth of his disclosures. The pith of our conversation was as follows:—

"What does Ishnaag allow you for the various heads and skins you take to him?"

"For a bison's head Rs. 15; for a sámbar's head Rs. 5; and if it is *khúb zabbar*, a real big one, then perhaps Rs. 7. For a chital head I get less. For a tiger's skin Ishnaag gives Rs. 50, and for a panther's skin Rs. 15. A bear's skin fetches Rs. 4. For a sámbar's skin, male or female, we get from Rs. 5 to Rs. 7."

"How did you get to know of Ishnaag? He lives a long way off," I asked.

"Oh, we get our powder at H——! Besides this, long ago, a messenger came from Ishnaag to all the *shikáris* round about, and told them the prices that would be given. Every one knows Ishnaag. He is our mother and father! He is very kind to us. No trouble about payments, and no bribes to be given, as when one is foolish enough to take a tiger or panther skin to the 'Saddar' for payment of the Government reward. Ishnaag says nothing, and asks no questions; only says 'Bring more soon' and 'Here is your powder and bullets. I have deducted their price from the value of your heads and skins.'"

"And are there many *shikáris* that go to H——?"

"Plenty of them, *Sahib!* All the villages near the *bandi* have *shikáris* of their own, and, besides these jungles, there are good jungles for *shikár* all up there (pointing north). I have met the *shikáris* of those parts at Ishnaag's."

"But the bison remain in the *bandi?*" I suggested, "also most of the other game."

"Oh, that is nothing!" quoth this artless child of the forest, "that is nothing! All one has to do is to give something to the *Jamadar sahib* and to the forester; one rupee or two rupees, or a sámbar's *charsa* (skin), and nobody says anything. Look! It was down there in that valley last year I shot a splendid *héla* (bison). I waited for him coming from the water, and killed him with one bullet. Yes, he ran a few hundred yards, and then I had to shoot him again to make sure. I shoot twelve, fifteen big animals every year. But up north there, a man called 'Lallu' shoots sometimes twenty-five or thirty. He has got a splendid gun, and he never misses!"

On the last day of the expedition I got a severe attack of jungle fever, and the exertion of riding thirty-two miles, and driving twenty-seven more, while under its thrall, aggravated it and brought on a bad attack of dysentery; which until lately prevented me from carrying out my intention of disclosing this terribly destructive system of collecting 'sporting trophies' elaborated by 'Ishnaag.'

I wrote to Ishnaag the other day, asking him whether he had any sporting trophies of bison, sambár, chital, tiger, panther and bear; and, if so, what were the prices thereof, "well stuffed and set up."

His reply, just received, runs thus—

"We have the following at present:—

	Rs.
One tiger skin	300
One ,, ,, ...	200
One black bear	80
One panther	140
One ,, ...	100
One ,, ...	98
One ,, ...	85
One sámbar head (33 inches)	80
One ,, ,, (35 inches)	75
One ,, ,, (30½ inches)	65
One ,, ,, in velvet (29 inches)	60"

Ishnaag, by the way, also writes that he has "some very good specimens of *Boer's* heads" at Rs. 40 to Rs. 50— —which proves that war is war after all, in spite of England's pacific policy in South Africa!

Ishnaag thus appears to make a very fair thing out of his connection with the local *shikáris*. Perhaps it would not be going too far to say that the influence of Ishnaag is felt for a radius of at least fifty miles. As the game within that radius diminishes and disappears, his influence will be felt still farther afield. I cannot say for certain, but there are probably more trophy-collecting agencies, like that of Ishnaag, in other parts of India. The devastation caused by the marketable value thus placed on heads and skins must be enormous.

I am afraid that some forest officers will be quite angry with me when I state that, in my opinion, all the laws and regulations they may make, and all the precautions they may take, short of stationing an English gamekeeper at every forest post (and picking their gamekeeper!) will never prevent poaching in reserved forests by the native *shikári*. It is the gun trade that is at the bottom of all the trouble. Confiscate guns and put a prohibitive tax on powder and caps—especially on caps, for native gun-powder is easily produced locally—and the root of the trouble will be touched.

Except in certain localities, where special indulgence might be accorded, cultivators do not suffer much from the depredations of forest game. If the game of India is to be preserved from certain eventual extinction, guns must be taken away and licenses given only in very exceptional cases. The illegal possession of a gun, especially on the confines of a reserved forest, should be made a very grave offence, and one involving severe punishment. Many of the guns I have seen in the possession of native *shikáris* have been uncommonly serviceable weapons (muzzle-loaders on the percussion system), and accurate up to two and three hundred yards—very nasty weapons indeed behind a mud wall. The question of suppressing guns is no doubt a difficult one. The Native State of Hyderabad in the Deccan is simply full of guns; and it is from Hyder-abad that guns are sold and distributed throughout neighbouring tracts. Something might be done however by getting a tight hold of the trade in percussion caps. All the caps that one sees are imported; and lack of caps means many muskets rendered useless, and so many wild animals saved.

In conclusion might I suggest that the Editor of the ———would earn the lasting gratitude of all sportsmen by organizing among them some concerted movement by which the question may be tackled in the best method. Exhortations to sportsmen are all very well in their way, and in some cases no doubt highly necessary; but they alone, even if we all abjured sport in consequence, could and would have little effect.

Sportsmen are certainly more merciful nowadays.

I know of many cases in the old days, even as late as ten to fifteen years ago, when hind sámbar were invariably shot if they turned up in the beat.

Sir Samuel Baker in his younger days has described the killing of a good many hinds. Forsyth in his 'Highlands of Central India' shoots hinds more than once, to say the least of it,—and not by mistake either.

I honestly do not think that the sportsman of to-day is at the bottom of the diminution of Indian game, nor that he requires (save in exceptional cases) so many exhortations to show mercy. The native *shikári*, egged on by 'Ishnaagses' and the horn-collector, and, deeper down still, the prevalence of so many guns, are to blame, and should be taken in hand ere it is too late.

*   *   *   *   *

Not long after the publication of the above came the following interesting letter:—

"Sir,—With reference to the article which appeared in your issue of the 16th October, regarding the extermination of Indian game, I should like to inform you that while in Bombay the other day I called on a certain co-operative society to make enquiries about the stuffed heads of Indian game exposed for sale on their walls.

"I was informed that there is a considerable demand for such trophies among 'globe-trotters' *and others*, who like to carry away little mementos of the 'fine sport they have enjoyed in this country.'

"On enquiry I discovered that the self-same 'Ishnaag' referred to in that article furnishes most of these sporting trophies.

"I enquired the price of one fairly good sámbar head—execrably set up by the way, and a mere caricature of poor old *Cervus unicolor*—and was informed that it was Rs. 250.

"Kindly compare the following :—

Native *shikári's* price for above head...	Rs.	6
Ishnaag's price	,,	100
Co-operative society's price	,,	250

"Now, if this sort of trophy-collecting is to continue unchecked, why should not I and other sportsmen enter the arena in competition, shoot all the undersized game we come across, stuff the heads ourselves (I'll turn out a better sámbar than Ishnaag any day), and sell direct to globe-trotters *and others*?

"Commercially considered, this would be a profession far superior to those in which many of us are at present engaged."

* * * * *

The result of these disclosures was at first very gratifying. Complaints of a similar nature, and letters discussing the destruction of game, poured in from sportsmen in all parts of India; numerous preventive measures were mooted; and, later, a notice was circulated, inviting sportsmen to give their views on the following lines:—

(1) General observations on the destruction of game.

(2) Any information you may have—precise or approximate estimates—any instances you can give thereof.

(3) The cause.

(4) The remedy. Suggestions as to greater restrictions, the issue of licenses, the actual weapons that should be licensed for protection, any observations on the sale of arms and ammunition to natives, close seasons, penalties for offences, &c.

(5) Traders in pelts, trophies, plumes, etc., their influence on the decrease of game.

(6) Any other remarks bearing on the subject.

To this a large number of replies were received and tabulated, and at length the movement seemed to have acquired sufficient momentum to carry it towards success, when an untoward occurrence removed the guiding hand of a well-known resident of Calcutta, and resulted in the indefinite postponement of the plan of campaign.

At this stage the matter still rests. When it will revive is matter for conjecture.

The subject of game preservation measures of a general (and at once effective) nature throughout India is one beset with many difficulties, which are not apparent until the matter is looked into rather closely. It involves some important issues; so important indeed that any too sudden approach might result in the shy birds we sportsmen are endeavouring to stalk being startled into such a flight as would take them for some time beyond our reach. So, until some practicable line of approach can be found, or our game may have shifted into some more stalkable position, a policy of masterly inactivity would appear to be indicated.

Much however can be effected meanwhile by those in local authority, who have the interests of game preservation at heart, if they will keep a watchful eye on the issue of licenses and make sharp examples of poaching offences.

Before leaving the subject of game destruction, with this indication of the tap-root of the evil, it may be useful to endeavour to foresee what effect is likely to follow the promulgation of such excellent game regulations as have lately been issued in Western India.

It is obvious that these laws, if strictly obeyed, should entirely prevent poaching, for they at every point confront the deadly methods of the native poacher. But will it be possible to enforce them everywhere, or, in some localities, ever enforce them at all? Many of the more remote areas in this country are difficult to control, the inhabitants being quick to combine against their rulers, or to turn the workings of the law to their own ends; finding, in the case of subordinate officials, that new rules only open up fresh avenues to extortion and blackmail from their uncomplaining brethren.

Without efficient supervision, therefore, even the best devised laws have small effect, there being in bureaucratic methods a tendency to issue ukases and await the result with folded hands.

But it is perhaps ungenerous to look the gift horse in the mouth; and sportsmen should be grateful for such a good beginning. The pity of all this necessity for game regulations is that under them Indian sport will to a certain extent lose its wild free character—a legacy left to sportsmen of the future by the apathy of those who failed to take proper measures in time.

Famine is, alas! a game destroyer with which it is out of our power to deal.

A further consideration of the game destroyers of India brings us to those great pests of the jungle—the wild dogs.

Decrease in the numbers of game, such as deer, etc., would lead one to infer that a corresponding falling off might be expected in those predatory animals directly dependent on them for food and existence; yet there is little doubt that the numbers of the wild dog (*Cyon*, or *Cuon rutilans*) have largely increased of late years, while their usual habits of retirement and shyness before the face of man also seem to have undergone a change. Even within the experience of the writer, the wild dog, once almost a *rara avis*, has become far too common.

One has only to note the effect of an incursion of these deadly little hunters into a game-bearing section of country to realize their power. Let but the scent of a few wandering *Cyons* arise in such haunts, and, as if by magic, every other creature scatters and disappears. Not only is there a rapid exodus of the *bovidæ* and *cervidæ*, but even the terror-striking feline himself—tiger and panther alike—seems to receive an urgent call to other localities far removed from the disturbing presence of the red dogs.

The writer once had an opportunity of witnessing a case of one such sudden *débacle*. He had made an excursion from his standing camp to verify reports received of a tiger which was killing in some distant coverts, and had set off on his ride one hot afternoon. It was towards the cool of evening that the track, which had been passing through a bleak succession of bare rocky hills, suddenly descended to a secluded valley full of the kind of covert beloved of spotted deer. Forced to the surface by horizontal beds of hard laterite, where the little stream turned close in under the hill, a succession of small shallow pools gladdened the eye down a vista of waist-high grass and scattered woodland. As we passed along its mile or so of length, this charming oasis seemed to be literally alive with *chital*, whose dappled hides could be seen in all directions as the deer went leaping off; or halted to gaze fixedly at the intruder in all their graceful beauty.

Marking at least one stag as worth returning for later, we loitered on our way, charmed with the beautiful sight.

The night was spent at a village. Next morning it was found that the tiger, which only the day before had killed a cow in the vicinity, had completely disappeared, as also the remains of his kill, owing, so local news ran, to the arrival of a pack of *cyons*.

At almost the same hour next evening, therefore, we entered the *chital* valley on our return journey.

To our astonishment it was completely deserted, and wore that appearance, unmistakable to an accustomed eye, of utter desolation and absence of animal life.

This was extraordinary; so my man and I separated, and rode in search through the grassy hollows that only twenty-four hours since had teemed with spotted deer. It was as if yesterday we had beheld some fairy vision, some illusory caprice of the brain.

But soon were we to become aware of the reason of the solitude so swiftly fallen on this favoured spot.

As we approach the line of pools, what is that dark red beast—and another—standing by the water's edge, while yet more emerge from the grassy covert around?

Rich, deep red coats; sharp snouts; rounded prick ears; thick brushes, tipped with black. It is the red dogs—the terrorizers of the jungle—the raiders—the poachers!

The Poachers.

Out of the saddle sharp, and pluck the little rifle from its bucket. Then quickly down behind that long grass. As we raise our heads cautiously behind this little tree, the dogs can be seen boldly regarding us.

Bang!—over rolls one; and they turn and hasten off. Bang! again; and another twists sidewise into the jungle, where he is soon found and disposed of.

In the distance the survivors can be heard as they move off, uttering their strange almost bird-like call—"Phew! Phew!" a call that is remarkably similar to that of the *chital* hind when she seeks her wandered fawn.

On another occasion I was prowling the jungles bordering the Sípna river one morning in late February. Rain had fallen the previous night, and as I entered a beautiful sequestered glen running at right angles to the main valley, my attention was attracted by a number of vultures sailing towards a point half a mile away; whence also came the raucous cawing of crows. Making my way through the now sodden and silent leaves—what a change from the crackling and rustling of other days!—and the long dripping grass, which exhaled a pleasant herb-like scent, I at length arrived at and peered over a little knoll. Below me lay a little open clearing by the rocky bed of the stream; a tiny cascade fell into the head of a cool green pool; and on the flat rocks around it lay a pack of wild dogs.

I wriggled a little nearer, and watched this interesting group from a distance of about thirty yards. Half sunk in the water reddened by his blood lay the carcase of a young sámbar, while his murderers reposed in various easy attitudes around. A couple of them, not yet fully gorged, tugged at a leg projecting above the water, and every now and then made a furious charge, leaping and snapping, among a crowd of expectant vultures. Bits of flesh lay here and there on the rocks by their satisfied owners. Whether it was the change in tone of the cawing of *Corvus*, ever watchful on the tree on the bank, a slant of betraying wind, or an instinctive feeling of impending danger, I do not know, but, after about five minutes, there was a sudden stampede in my direction; so calling to my orderly to use the ·577 with the best possible effect on the brutes, the sharp crack of the ·303 sounded the death-knell of one of the rascals, and another escaped hard hit. I regret to say that the ·577 did not have a look in at all, for I should have liked to exterminate the whole gang.

While skinning the wild dog, a couple of Korkus arrived and asked to be permitted to take away all that remained of the sámbar. From these jungle-men I gathered that they, in common with the crow and vulture, were very frequently supplied with meat by these marauding packs.

Although counting myself lucky at having had this glimpse into the inner life of the jungle, I should have liked still better to have been in at the death. It must have been a fine sight—the failing deer making, with the instinct of his race, for the last resource (water), the fierce attack of the hungry dogs, and the final struggle in the pool. A scene well worthy of the brush.

Again the scene is changed. I am walking up the old Belkhéra glen. The way lies up the damp stony bed of the stream, between short steep scarps that enclose it on either hand. Just before turning off to ascend the valley side, up the abominably steep Tórghát, I heard something moving up-hill, and, after a while, spied the horns of a young stag sámbar showing now and then above the long grass. He was creeping quietly along the hillside, and I watched him for a time, wondering where he was going, this particular spot being an unusual one in which to find sámbar.

On turning my head, as a movement caught my eye, a wild dog quietly walked into the bed of the *nála*, and stood gazing in the direction the stag had taken, while another emerged from behind a rock, 'nosing' slowly along. I should have liked to watch their movements, but was so exposed to view that the dogs must see me next moment; so fired at once, knocking over the nearer of the two. As I did so, a third bounded away to my left. The one I had hit dragged itself up the bank and into some grass, where it was found dead.

While examining it, the other dogs were heard calling to each other in some neighbouring ravines; so I tried to copy their curious whistling note as best I could. To my surprise one of the dogs returned. He came trotting enquiringly back along the bed of the stream, stopping suddenly as he caught sight of my hat; and I missed him as he turned and ran. However that was not a bad morning's work, for no fewer than ten pups were removed from the female I had shot, together with a large quantity of freshly bolted meat, some scraps of sámbar hide, and the complete fore pads of a hare!

The sportsman should never lose an opportunity of destroying wild dogs, even at the expense of disturbing other game which he may be following at the time. If some wholesale method of getting rid of these deadly vermin could be devised, the now attenuated herds of deer and other creatures on whom they prey would have some chance of regaining their former abundance.

As yet the only useful method seems to be that of raising the amount of the Government award for their destruction, and issuing special forest licenses to trustworthy native *shikáris* for this purpose—a plan which is already being tried in some places.

It may be argued by some that the interest in game preservation displayed by sportsmen has its origin in selfish motives, and that they would not exert themselves much in the matter if it did not affect their own sport. In acknowledging that such considerations influence one to a certain extent, in addition to the desire, which all lovers of Nature have, of staying the ruthless depopulation of a country, these are not the only pleas in favour of putting a stop to the present waste of jungle life.

The effect that apparently insignificant matters often exercise on large issues should not be lost sight of.

If India, in the not very distant future, is to become depleted of her game, and so hold out fewer inducements to young men of sporting proclivities, she may cease to attract to her public services many recruits of a most desirable type. In addition to this, it would be a calamity if this country, which has so long offered such advantages to men of keen hunting instincts but small means, should cease to occupy its position as one of the finest training-grounds for English sportsmen and soldiers. The advantages of *shikár* for the soldier is a theme that may be rather oversung by enthusiasts; but it cannot be denied that it is a distinctly useful taste for him to indulge, assisting to develope, as it does, many other qualities besides those of hunting, tracking, and an 'eye for country.'

It must have been noticed that the Englishman, in his passion for games and athletic exercises, is tending evermore towards those which are carried out in a confined space. There is a place for most things, and our choice of games is usually good; but to find men bound exclusively to the cramping limits of, say, a racquet-court's four walls, when there is easy access to an almost limitless expanse of free open country around, affording almost every opportunity for the use of horse, gun, rifle, or spear, seems to imply a lack of versatility, and is disappointing to some of us.

There may be, indeed there are numerous reasonable causes of this tendency to exercise one's self after the manner of the squirrel in its cage ; but it is not difficult to trace its results—especially in the case of the soldier-officer.

Such and other considerations cannot fail to advance the plea for the preservation of Indian game.

⁂ ⁂ ⁂ ⁂ ⁂ ⁂

To pass to other *shikár* subjects, there is a topic of considerable interest of which the writer was reminded the other day on meeting a friend who had lately returned from an expedition to certain jungles not unknown to fame as the resort of big game.

Although good shots and keen *shikáris*, he and his equally youthful companion had succeeded in securing only one tiger ; whereas their bag of bears, leopards, and deer was quite a good one.

In the course of conversation my friend discussed, with some pardonable heat, the suspicions he had formed with regard to the reasons of failure with the tigers ; and having a vivid recollection of similar experiences ourselves, we found ourselves able not only to confirm his suspicions, but to suggest other causes, which, as, it subsequently transpired, fitted his case with remarkable accuracy.

These young men had long and eagerly planned this particular trip; and having, as they thought, arranged preliminaries satisfactorily, after much trouble, they had set out with not ill-founded anticipations of a roseate hue. Reaching their shooting-ground at a very considerable expenditure of their slender means, and not a little patience by the way, they had, although not actual novices in tiger *shikár*, gone through an immense amount of hard work to no purpose; which had finally resulted in the incapacitating of one of them by jungle fever. Although almost all their available time (two months) had been spent in working for tigers, they had only succeeded in shooting one—and that one by mere chance. On the other hand, as regards less noble game, hard work had met with its reward. That tigers were there is proved by the fact that a week or two later, a local official—a man of no experience in *shikár*—following almost in their footsteps, had shot seven, while the total number of these animals killed in that district during the same year amounted to over twenty.

Some of his experiences, angrily related by the disappointed sportsman, were of an extremely diverting nature, though in no wise unfamiliar to those acquainted with Oriental subtleties. But, divested of their humourous wrapping, these are pills at the swallowing of which the Englishman makes a very wry face; and at such pernicious influences as they reveal, his gorge rises in indignation and disgust.

Accustomed to a mode of dealing at least fair and square, we are peculiarly liable to be deceived by the easy hypocrisy that, generally speaking, comes so naturally to the Eastern mind; so, although the following matter is the reflection of no novel experience, it may have its use in resetting the edge of one's memory, or serving as a hint to those whose 'tender, trustful years' may render them prone to appraise their Aryan brethren—and some others —by their own standards.

In order to appreciate the following remarks, it should be remembered that the tiger—that magnificent brute the lustre of whose halo even the most fulsome panegyric cannot dull, to whose pursuit even the jaded, blasé sportsman returns with a never-failing interest—is a creature of remarkably open modes of life. Under favourable circumstances his probable line of action can be previously determined with almost monotonous certainty, especially by those jungle-men or local native *shikáris* whose acquaintance with a particular beast may almost partake of the nature of personal acquaintance; while on most occasions, although one may be unable to encompass his undoing, a practical certainty can be made of ensuring his flight to other haunts—in other words, of frightening him away.

It is this power of a clever *shikári* to take the tiger, with a little arrangement, in the hollow of his hand, that unfortunately makes it possible for the pampered guest or courted globe-trotter to recline at his ease in a comfortable *machán* (plush-lined and otherwise sumptuously fitted in some instances!), set down his half finished champagne cup at a touch from his attendant, and, with the 'well-bred gesture of ineffable boredom' beloved of lady novelists, murder the splendid brute that has been guided within easy range of his post by an army of fawning parasites, aided, in their turn, by the plucky unarmed beaters assembled to cater for the "sport" of the "*Burra Saheb!*"

Meanwhile the hard-working resident *shikári*—of small means probably—who, right or wrong, regards the denizens of the jungles as rather his, by virtue of the life he has given to the service of the country, can, on meeting with a crafty underhand opposition, only chew his bitter mortification and vow to desert the pursuit of the 'royal beast' for that of game, which is only the prize of him who works hard for it—a vow which is quickly forgotten as the fascination of tiger *shikár* returns in all its inevitable force!

And so it goes on; from the by no means overdrawn picture of the favoured guest downwards. The tiger bears his price on his head; and on the payment of that price, be it in coin or in kind, he usually goes to the highest bidder—all of which detracts from the value of his pursuit as compared with those forms of hunting into which pecuniary considerations do not enter to such a degrading extent, and throws a considerable amount of doubt over the claim to good sportsmanship laid by the man who has 'slain his hundred tigers.'

To continue our theme.

As a rule the Indian mind seems to attain its greatest brilliance when engaged in the congenial occupation of *khat-pat*—the petty intriguing and childish cunning that derives its power from its very weakness and apparent insignificance. Here indeed is something that the Oriental thoroughly understands, for the sake of which he readily deserts his usual condition of apathy, and on which he enters with a perverted zest that in a better cause would command our admiration, applying thereto all the wile of a brain the workings, the inconsequence, the vagaries of which are often incomprehensible to Western ideas.

In addition, the Indian, even of lowly degree, is no mean student of human nature, and is keenly alive to the benefits that may accrue to him by the judicious conciliation of those set in authority over him. We find, therefore, that he is an instrument that can be played on with remarkable success by quite an ordinary performer.

Keeping in view the direction of these preliminary observations, let us imagine some Indian 'district' which contains good hunting-grounds giving shelter to a typical fauna, including tigers, and that in such a district an 'outsider' desires to indulge his fondness for sport. Now it is possible that he may imagine that all his difficulties end with the receipt of permission to shoot in those jungles; but, if he is wise, he will recognize that there are a few preliminaries to settle before arriving at this consummation.

It may be that all of the district officials are keen on shooting; and this is certain to complicate matters, and make the case the most difficult of all for our 'outsider' to tackle; for there is no avoiding the fact that the officials administering a district in various capacities are usually in a position to bring pressure to bear on refractory subjects at their will, while the inhabitants are practically bound to observe their wishes in such matters as are here treated of.

Or it may be that none of them care for the pleasures of the jungle; and here the path would appear more smooth,—which however depends on a variety of other circumstances.

Let us however take a simple case—from which those more involved may be inferred by the reader—and assume that of the four or five district officials, the Deputy Commissioner is the only one keen on tiger-shooting.

Although it depends on several factors, it may be taken for granted that a Deputy Commissioner has the power to make himself, within certain wide limits, absolute autocrat of the country he administers.

In such a position he forms a point on which the attention of his native subordinates is focussed, and is the centre (sometimes unconsciously) of a keen struggle for advancement of an official, commercial, or private nature. There is a continual effort to enlist his sympathies, to gain his ear, to obtain by his fancied favours some apparently trivial advantage; and it may be imagined therefrom that few points of his character escape notice. What, then, more natural than that those who are able should lose no opportunity of ministering to his taste for sport, should he possess such, nor hesitate to employ any means that they imagine may aid them to gain his favour by so doing.

From this it is not difficult to infer the effect on the sport of the 'outsider' should the Deputy Commissioner show the least tendency to look askance at men making shooting excursions into his domain; nor indeed the crushing results of an active dog-in-the-manger policy (happily rare) when he actually sets impeding machinery in motion.

At the same time those who theorize to the effect that district officials have no more right to the game than have men from a distance, are apt to forget the workings of human nature. It is not unnatural for these officials to imagine that they have a kind of prior claim. And if, as is done in some districts, an area of reasonable size be set apart for their sport, few of us would complain. Unfortunately it seems easier to some natures to grant the 'outsider' permission to enter their imaginary preserves, and then assume an attitude which is only too easily read by obsequious native underlings.

To what lengths such practices have been known to proceed may be seen in the case of a certain jealous official, who was in the habit of issuing two differently coloured forms of *permit-de-chasse*. A pink card appropriately signified to forest and other minions that the efforts of the holder were to meet with a rosy success, while a plain white passport was a tacit indication of the blankness of the unfortunate recipient's prospects!

So much for the more depraved side of the question. Let us now take the more usual case of the district official of open-handed generosity who, though keen himself, wishes to share sport fairly with visitors. Here again, alas! we experience the deceitfulness of this land of our exile; for the mere fact of the "*Dipty Sahib*" being fond of shooting erects a formidable stumbling-block in the path of our 'outsider.' Even against his orders, his dusky subordinates, appreciatively scenting some fancied subtlety, redouble their efforts on his behalf; and his kindly intentions are likely to be frustrated by the very people he may have deputed to help the stranger that is within his gates.

Some years ago a good fellow of this description had invited a young subaltern to join him in his annual tiger-shoot; but do what he would to place his guest in the most favourable positions, the tiger was invariably driven up to the post which he himself had taken up.

Realizing at length that tigers were assets apparently too valuable to his *shikári* to be thrown away on a youthful and unknown visitor, the host bethought himself of a stratagem.

"Now then, Daghabáz Khan!" said he to the astute individual who occupied a position analogous to that of head keeper, "this won't do! The *Chota Sahib* is not getting any sport. Put him in the best position again, will you, *and see that the tiger goes to him this time!*"

"*Sahib!*" replied the Oriental, with a perfectly acted appearance of injured innocence. "Have I not been doing so all along, according to your honour's commands?

And yet (*Allah* witnesseth !), what can do! The animal *will* go to your honour! Yet if the *Chota Sahib* will this time take *this* post"—indicating what was in this particular beat undoubtedly the only route for a driven tiger—"perchance his luck may turn."

Some time after the subaltern had occupied his perch and heard the head *shikári* move off, he was startled by a low whistle from the jungle behind him; and behold! his host, finger on lip and twinkle in eye, making signals to him to descend.

"Just exchange positions with me, my dear fellow," he heard him say, "and mind you go quietly, for the old man has left a 'stop' in a tree not far away!"

The change was duly effected; and this time all went as it should—except indeed for Daghabáz Khan.

The beaters approached. The tiger appeared. But, strange to relate, he had failed to take his natural line; and he halted, as if actuated by clock-work, right under the tree where the Deputy Commissioner should have been—but was not!

Hardly had the echoes of two rapid shots died away, and been succeeded by the re-assuring note of the *sahib's* whistle, than Daghabáz Khan was to be seen standing submissively beneath the successful sportman's *machán*.

"*Hazúr!*" he began smugly, "I did my best. But the luck of the *Chota Sahib* must indeed be evil, for, as your honour sees, the tiger——"

"Don't mention it, Daghabáz Khan!" came from aloft, the confounding accents of the delighted *Chota Sahib* himself. "Verily art thou the prince of *shikáris;* and, for this my success to-day, will I bestow on thee a testimonial transcending in its flattering terms all those already in thy possession!"

We now begin to see some of the difficulties likely to beset the path of the undesired visitor on tigers intent.

Although it is very tempting, the writer feels that too much space has already been devoted to this subject to allow of further anecdote exemplifying the working of the wiles employed. The reader is therefore referred to the Appendix, to the obscurity of which the disclosure of these depravities is relegated.

Most of the dodges therein revealed were picked up by the writer sadly, regretfully, one by one, as they were traced to one Jhoot Singh, a handsome, apostle-featured *shikári* of Rájpút descent, once deputed to accompany his camp after the manner of the confidential gillie who leads the deluded guest into a Scottish deer forest with tacit instructions to 'show' a few stags.

Gifted with a most prepossessing exterior, and a cool stout heart, such a past master of the arts of humbug and chicane was Jhoot Singh that it was not until a year or two later that his true character transpired, when, bit by bit, the puzzle of his subtleties was pieced together. So clever had he been that a handsome 'douceur' had changed hands on the occasion of our parting—which was accompanied by expressions of mutual esteem.

The manner of Jhoot Singh's exposure was thus. The writer had met the very "*Dipty Sahib*" who had then been in charge of that district—a man of a somewhat jealous quick-tempered nature—and he had been so goaded by a delicate reference to the success that the writer had forced, in spite of the thinly-veiled opposition of his native subordinates, that he could not resist a jeer at our estimation of Jhoot Singh's character; and so gave away, in the rash heat of his pique, not only the real nature of that worthy, but also the fact that he himself was well acquainted with the object of his mission in our camp!

An amusing correspondence, published in the *Times of India* in December 1900, concerning certain Christmas shooting camps, seems to indicate that such jealousies are not necessarily restricted to any particular locality.

India being the last country in which such degeneracy of habit may be safely indulged in by public officials, it is incumbent on the shooting public to apply what antidotes they can, and lose no opportunity of assisting such fallen countrymen to recognize and correct the narrow-minded ways into which they have fallen, owing no doubt to a too long and intimate contact with native idiosyncrasies. But the means employed in dealing with these fortunately rare cases will necessarily have to be as subtle as the evil it is intended to counteract.

*** *** *** ***

Within the last five years a notable change has taken place in the big-game sportsman's weapons, which suggests a subject too interesting to pass by without some brief notice.

This is the passing of the black powder rifle, both of the 'Express' and large bore type, and the genesis of the cordite rifle of medium bore.

Up to about ten years ago sportsmen used either the large bore rifle (or ball gun) or the express rifle, both with black powder. About that period it was discovered that the new military small-bore rifles possessed wonderful powers, when used with a suitable bullet, and these rifles so deservedly engaged the enthusiasm of many sportsmen that they emerged triumphantly from all kinds of troubles occasioned by faulty, smokeless 'powders' and unsuitable bullets. As was natural, however, these rifles were soon tried beyond their powers and out of their own particular sphere. In some cases they exceeded their admirers' most sanguine hopes; in a good many others they led to very dire accidents on account of their general lack of knocking-down power.

So there grew a demand for weapons possessing similar advantages but of larger bore and greater power.

The outcome of this was the medium bore cordite rifle, which has now become so popular.

It is worthy of note that the evolution of this type of sporting rifle is due to the skill and enterprise of a firm of London rifle-makers then supposed to occupy a somewhat second-rate position; the 'leading' firms meanwhile apparently regarding its efforts with complacent humour. Their attitude however was altered when it was seen that such weapons had come to stay, and possessed qualities that rendered existing sporting rifles obsolete. So soon therefore as was compatible with an effort to keep up the prestige of the older weapons awhile, in order to avoid a 'slump' in their value, the 'leading' firms began to follow their pioneer's lead, and to turn out new rifles, differing by a few hundredths of an inch in the diameter of the bore—for the sake of an appearance of 'originality,' or in order to make a speciality of their own cartridges!

So rapidly did some manufacturers take up and turn out the new cordite rifles that they failed to pay proper attention to their peculiarities; and this resulted in some cases of failure and even of disaster to the breech or barrel—all of which re-acted unfavourably on sportsmen, especially those of conservative ideas, who looked askance at such dangerous arms.

In addition, there occurred a few cases of sportsmen coming to grief, owing to the alleged failure of the new weapons to 'stop' dangerous game.

Although this was to a certain extent due to the carelessness of the sportsmen themselves, in not taking the trouble to use a suitable bullet, it was in some cases also attributable to the makers, who had failed to supply ammunition suited to the circumstances.

The medium bore cordite rifle being a weapon of an 'all-round' type, suitable for use against heavy thick-skinned game as well as animals of a lighter and soft-skinned type, it is necessary to use at least two kinds of bullets in it—(1) *penetrative*, which is represented by the solid nickel-covered bullet, and (2) *expanding*, which are of various types (soft-nosed—'peg'—hollow-pointed—'capped'—split, etc.) The latter, moreover, include bullets of greater and lesser degrees of expansive power, to which may be added the still lighter expansive bullet for use on the smaller harmless animals.

From these various kinds of bullets the manufacturer as well as the sportsmen should be able to choose a projectile suited to the work it is intended to do; and if they misuse a too penetrative bullet on a charging lion, or a too expansive one against the head of an elephant, they must take the consequences.

That manufacturers are often as much to blame as sportsmen in this connection is proved by the absurd advertisements one sees describing the powers of some of these new rifles. There is so much effort made to prove that they possess greater penetration and striking power than the old black powder weapons that, manufacturer leading sportsman astray, they both forget that there is other game beside pachyderms, and fall into such absurdities as guaging a rifle's usefulness by its power to punch holes in an armour plate! And so the tale proceeds. Off goes the hunter, armed with some theoretical paragon of a rifle guaranteed to penetrate so many inches of steel plate—but of which he knows uncommonly little—certain of its marvellous effect against all and every kind of big game, and imagining that all he has to do is to press trigger, when the doomed animal will (to use a favourite phrase) 'fall as if struck by lightning!'

But when the inevitable catastrophe arrives, no allowance is made for the fact that, on occasions, nothing in the way of fire-arms appears capable of "stopping" an animal unless struck in brain or spine; so, condemned out of hand, without a thought as to the real reason, nothing can then be too bad for the wretched weapon!

Many men have been disappointed with these new rifles when making trial of them on antelope, etc. They expect so much of these weapons that it is disappointing to find that, in such cases, their killing power does not seem to be much advance on the old "Express." But they should not be disheartened until they have given the cordite rifle a trial against heavy game, when its extraordinary power, meeting with the requisite resistance, will be fully developed.

The many advantages of the medium-bore cordite rifle are too well known to require repetition. Its disadvantages seem apparent in but one direction—its somewhat excessive weight when made in the double-barrelled form.

Single-barrelled rifles of this type are not of all-round use, while in them recoil is unpleasantly increased. Magazine rifles of this class have been attempted, but hitherto seem to have been only dangerous failures.

That the new weapons, when properly constructed, can be perfectly satisfactory under Indian conditions is proved by the fact that the writer, in practice and in *shikár*, has fired over six hundred rounds from his (a ·400—55—400. hammerless, top-snap action) under all climatic conditions of the plains of India, using it with perfect results against almost every kind of game there to be found. The breech action and barrels are as true and tight as when received from the makers (in 1899), and the weapon, except for slight wear to the browning, is not to be known from a new and unused weapon.

Although it is possible to utterly neglect and mishandle a black powder rifle without actually courting disaster thereby, the cordite rifle cannot be so treated with impunity. Its care may be entrusted to no native servant ; its owner must be prepared to repay its excellence by his personal unremitting attention ; and it is necessary for him to have some knowledge of its peculiarities.

The following may be useful to some of those who possess or think of owning cordite rifles :—

(1) Purchase (direct if possible) from a reliable firm.

(2) Avoid light rifles.

(3) Carefully enquire whether the rifle has been tested with ammunition under conditions of temperature up to maximum solar heat of India.

(4) Get ammunition from the makers direct, or through their special agents.

(5) Familiarize yourself with every detail of your rifle.

(6) Make its condition your personal care. Rust or heavy-settled fouling will send up pressures rapidly.

(7) Before loading, be particularly careful to remove all oil from (i) the cartridge, (ii) the bore, and (iii) the chamber, all of which, if left oily, might give increased pressure.

(8) Do not *unnecessarily* expose your ammunition to great heat, although it is a fact that cordite resumes its normal condition when re-cooled.

To sum up the matter of the Indian sportsman's battery is a matter of difficulty, as among men of differing views different ideas naturally prevail, and even when these are sifted it is difficult to particularise.

The result of some years' experience, however, which the writer and friends whom he has consulted have had with various rifles, has been examined and an average struck. The weapons coming under notice have been as follows :—

8-bore rifle, 10-bore and 12-bore 'Paradox,' 12-bore rifle, ·577 magnum (Sam. Baker pattern) rifle, ·500 magnum rifle (440 grain bullet), ·500 express, ·450 cordite (Rigby's) rifle, ·400 cordite (Jeffery's) rifle, ·303, Mauser ·275, and Mannlicher ·256.

From the above the consensus of opinion is that no satisfactory truly all-round rifle yet exists; after that, a choice of weapons rests largely with the sportsman himself. Allowing that a smokeless propellant is in all ways superior to black powder, the rest is a question of a man's build and physique. *If he can handle it*, the bigger the bore the better for close jungle work. For ponderous game the medium bore cordite rifle comes in first favourite. For dangerous soft-skinned game, at close ranges, the ball and shot gun of the Paradox type, not smaller than 12-bore. For long sporting range shooting at harmless game, on hill or plain, the ·303, as giving rather better killing power than the smaller bores. In these three we have succeeded in reducing to the minimum a long list of favourite weapons.

Except for use on ponderous game, with the proper bullet, the high velocity rifle appears to have almost too high a velocity for sporting purposes. Throughout a considerable experience it has been noted that, although actually conveying less *damage* to the animal struck, the slower travelling ordinary express bullet—and, in still greater degree, the Paradox bullet—*knocks down* an animal; whereas the cordite rifle appears rather to numb its victim with the extraordinary velocity of its projectile, which seems to lose knocking-down power in an impact which is so sudden and penetrative.

There seems to be less chance of an animal eventually getting away when hit by a high velocity rifle; but the slower travelling bullet rolls a beast over, at least temporarily, and enables one to put in more shooting before it can regain its legs. Dynamics appear to bear out our argument. It is the knock-down push or blow that is so useful in that short second of time when a man may be reached by a brute thirsting for his blood; and that this is best conveyed by a handy ball and shot gun seems incontestable. What we *do* require now is a reliable *smokeless* powder for use behind the Paradox ball, for the smoke produced by black powder is awful, especially in a damp atmosphere; and this seems to have been at length produced, and recently pronounced a success.

*** *** *** *** ***

A difficulty is sometimes experienced by sportsmen in temporarily treating and preserving from injury the skins of tigers and other animals shot; the usual practice in India being to peg out the skin in the shade, and dry it with the aid of wood ashes, alum, or other astringents and alkalies. After such drying the skin becomes extremely stiff, and has to be carried about in that condition, unavoidably receiving injuries that may jeopardize its appearance on being finally cured. Such troubles, as well as those of 'pickling barrels' and other devices, may be avoided by employing a *chamár* or *dhór* (native leather workers and curers). These men are to be found in almost any bazaar, and are quite willing to accompany a shooting expedition for a small monthly remuneration. Their methods vary, and they should not be allowed to work except under superintendence; but the following system is one that they thoroughly understand, while it is very simple, non-poisonous, and will cure skins perfectly without having the least injurious effect, as is produced by the use of lime and like deleterious substances.

First day.—As soon as possible after the beast has been shot, the *dhór* should set to work, and the skin should be carefully removed, special care being taken that the ears, paws and lips are thoroughly turned inside out and skinned right down to the tips.

The *dhór* then 'shaves' the skin with his currier's knife (*kúrpi*), removing all vestiges of fleshy matter. He then rubs in, very thoroughly, powdered alum six parts to saltpetre one part, until the skin is saturated with the mixture, when a little will remain unabsorbed on the surface.

Fresh buttermilk (procurable in most localities) is now poured on the skin, sparingly, and rubbed in; and the skin is then turned inwards, flesh-side to flesh-side, and its surfaces thoroughly rubbed together, until the buttermilk has penetrated into the pelt. (About three large tumblerfuls of buttermilk are sufficient for each such application in the case of a tiger skin.)

The skin is then brought neatly together, flesh-side to flesh-side, folded up fairly tightly, and put away for 24 hours. In this state it may be carried about, provided it is not exposed to the sun's rays or to too great heat.

Second day.—The skin will be found to have swelled and thickened, and the 'dressing' will have completely penetrated it, oozing freely through the hair side.

The skin is then unfolded, again shaved, again dressed with the aforementioned alum, nitre, and buttermilk, and put away for another 24 hours.

Third day.—The skin is unfolded, and thoroughly dried *in the sun*, until as hard as a board; which has the effect of tightening it, and preventing subsequent slipping of the hair.

Fourth day.—The skin is softened in water, again shaved, given its final application of dressing, and folded up for the last time.

Fifth day.—The skin is unfolded, shaved, and dried *in the shade.* The leather will now be quite white, and fairly soft.

To render it quite pliable, the *dhór* may fold and roll it together, and, placing it between some soft substance, such as sacking, beat it continuously with a mallet or smooth rounded billet of wood.

The advantages of the above process are that skins so treated retain unsullied their clear pure white and other colouring. This curing process can be carried out on the march, 'pegging out' (which is not very desirable) can be avoided, and the skins may be carried with perfect safety and in a very small space.

Until 'aired' in the sun, skins thus cured have an odour not exactly unpleasant but very pungent, which effectually safeguards them from the attacks of animals or insects; but an application of turpentine will now do no harm.

*** *** *** ***

Should the sportsman wish to provide himself with the wherewithal of treating wounds, especially those inflicted by felines, which are rendered so dangerous by the invariably septic condition of their claws and teeth, the following may be found useful:—

A strong glass syringe, a pair of forceps, some antiseptic lint and cotton wool, borax and iodoform powder, and a bottle of tabloids of perchloride of mercury.

The latter when dissolved in water, strength 1 in 1000, makes the surest antiseptic lotion when used in the syringe. Carbolic and other *oil* should be avoided.

*** *** *** *** ***

To men accustomed to hunt in bracing temperate and cold climates only, the camp of an Indian *shikári* would perhaps appear unnecessarily, even absurdly luxurious. The hardy hunter from the North-West of America, for instance, used to 'roughing it' with pack and 'billy,' might feel inclined to scoff at the appurtenances of his fellow-sportsman in the East.

But in the hot and enervating jungles of India billy-boiling and roughing it will not do; which is proved by the fact that there are no white labourers in this country. No white man can, for any length of time, undergo physical labour in India under a labourer's conditions.

Out here, even at the least unhealthy time of year, a few scratch meals or insufficiently and badly cooked food may soon result in dysentery; while the exertion of hard work under an Indian sun, if uncompensated for by rest, good palatable food, and a little reasonable stimulant, would as surely lay our hunter, however strong, open to the debilitating attacks of an ever-lurking malaria.

Plenty of hard work awaits the man who would ensure successful *shikár* in India ; but the heavy extra strain to his constitution, caused by the heat, peculiarly intense sun, and relaxing foreign climate, must be compensated for by a reasonable amount of comfort and attendance on his return to camp—which is fortunately easily arranged in a country of cheap servants and carriage—or most unhappy results may follow.

IN THE SÁL FORESTS.

> "The best laid schemes o'mice and men
> Gang aft a-gley.
> And lea'e us nought but grief and pain
> For promised joy."

So said the ploughman-bard a hundred and more years ago; and, with a trifling modification, so thought we on our return from a distant shooting-ground of India not long since. Tired and weary of the worries and drawbacks connected with sporting expeditions undertaken in the more accessible districts, attracted by the novelty of exploration, and fired by the entries in the diaries of one who had travelled, shot, and administered the country some forty years before, I persuaded a kindred spirit to join me in that enterprise.

It cannot be denied that we had certain warnings; but what of them! For the last eight years and more had I not gloated over the old diaries, pored over the well-known maps, dreamt of the sportsman's paradise at last to be realized? And at length was not the auspicious time come?

"Shot out!" Was it? we knew something worth two of that. Those diaries! Even remote pastures change in thirty-five years, but the change could not be so great after all. I would be well content with one quarter as much sport as that recorded in the neat old-fashioned hand-writing within those musty covers.

And so the grand expedition started. The middle of the month of March saw a little wisp of dust crossing the blazing and parched face of the country, some hundred and eighty miles by rail and dâk from our starting point. As it drew nearer, the tinkling of bells and rumbling of wheels indicated a species of travelling caravan, and shortly four *ringhis* jolted past in dust and glare. In the first there reclined a *sahib*, a man of parts, as the complaining wooden axles plainly testified; next came your humble servant, deriving certain consolations from a cunningly-disposed horse-hair mattress and a large cheroot; *ringhis* numbers three and four contained various packages and bundles, surmounted respectively by lusty Karámat Khán—as much as could be seen of him through a voluminous *rúmál*—and by a bilious-looking and long-suffering individual named Chinnaswamy. A 'squawk' of protest, half smothered in the dust, seemed to suggest that the latter had found a tolerably comfortable seat on the hen-coop.

And so we rumbled on.

Night succeeded day, and day night; but still the word was 'forward.' Bullocks were changed; carts collapsed, and were mended; mango groves were dimly aware of nightly phantoms that paused to masticate a meal by the flicker of a hasty fire; the change of drivers made itself known, even in the slumbrous hours, by the varying peculiarities of individual 'savours.' The feathery tamarind tree knew us by the empty "army ration" tin; the broiling stretch of sand and trickle of shrunken stream by the staccato objurgations of the frenzied *gári-wála*. On the third day dawn found us in the midst of a mighty forest, and hard by a forest post and hut. A short while previously a bull bison had found an unusual kind of grave in a well a few hundred yards away. "What was the water like?" we asked. "Well," replied the custodian, "perhaps the *sahibs* might not like it, but it's very sweet!" Some ten miles more of the densest jungle and bamboo thickets found us nearing the end of our one hundred miles of journey by *ringhi*, when suddenly the conveyance occupied by the well-nourished 'man of parts' gave way. There was not very far to fall however, and the entire axle-tree having been detached, a teak pole from the jungle and a few blows of an adze furnished the necessary repairs.

We found our horses at the appointed village, near which the entire population was occupied in capturing the fish that were suffocating in the turbid puddle which represented what must once have been a large tank; and after a short rest, a ride of fifteen miles took us to our first camp. Hot baths and a good square meal served to dissipate the highly uncomfortable memories of our long forced march, and in the evening we strolled down to the river bank and regarded, on the far shore, the land of promise that we had come so far to enjoy.

Next morning we continued our marching, and found all the kit and carts delayed at the crossing of the river—splashing slowly through the warm shallow ford, or labouring in the hot deep sand. The crossing was diagonal, and three hours passed ere the last cart was forced with yells and shouts up the far bank and entered the promised land. Riding on, the thin jungle changed to trees of larger size, many green and fresh-looking. In some shallow valleys were the now hard-baked traces of rice cultivation on a rough and ready plan; and in many places we saw the impressions of the feet of the wild buffaloes that in the rainy season wander over this tract. Of course we at once fell into the common error of imagining many marks meant many buffs. We had not yet learned that one small herd of these ponderous creatures will cover the whole country-side with marks in a very few days and nights.

More marching brought us to the river again, having now crossed the big elbow or bend in its course. The country now grew more interesting. The villages were inhabited by Máriahs, the wild tribes that people the uplands of Márdian across the river, and were entirely novel. Well-built thatched cottages, each separated from its fellow, stockaded compounds, and very neat bamboo fencing enclosing each little establishment. On our arrival at our half-way place, by name 'Vayanar,' we were escorted to a little building in the centre of the village, and prayed to seat ourselves, while one well-built young Máriah beat ferociously on a large *tom-tom* suspended from the rafters.

This little house, open on all sides, was evidently the Town Hall and Theatre of Varieties combined. Weird-looking carved wood maces and clubs, for dancing purposes, so we were told, reposed among the rafters. Besides this, we heard later on that these 'Town Halls' are considered by the young Máriahs of both sexes as the 'abode of love'—places where—*pace* Robert Burns—the youthful, modest, loving Máriahs—

> "In other's arms breathe out the tender tale,
> Beneath the big *tom-tom* that scents the evening gale."

The Máriah language is very pleasing to the ear, being very liquid, with curious soft gutturals and clicks of the tongue.

The men wear very little clothing, a thin strip of cloth, suspended from a string tied round the waist, passing between the legs from front to back, and a kind of *kamarband* wrapped round and round the waist, with the end hanging down in front. The rich Máriah does not sink his treasure in more clothes than these; but he goes in for a large and varied assortment of beads, and has the lobes and outer edges of his ears perforated to an alarming extent, and hung all round with a perfect bushel of brass rings.

A small-sized postage stamp would be a most effective substitute for the clothing of many of these weird people, but rings and beads they *must* have. A really 'rich' Máriah simply coruscates with glass and tinsel ornamentation, especially, as I have said, in the region of the ears; while a village dandy will affect a 'gem' or two bound over the forehead. Their physique is good, though most are small; and rarely is a dark-coloured Máriah seen. Their skins are wonderfully fair, in some cases as light in tint as that of a fair Brahman.

The women appear to wear even less, if possible, than the men, and are not loaded with beads, etc. Instead of this they are much tattooed all over. Extraordinary patterns are engraved on their faces, in some cases causing the most ludicrous exaggerations of expression. They are apparently extremely timid, and the sight of a horse—a mythical creature to them—sends the poor things darting off like deer into their great protector—the dense jungle. In the villages however they will walk past quite close without evincing any nervousness. My kodak films failed me, and so, to my regret, I have no snapshots of these ladies.

The Máriahs are distinctly interesting therefore, and we soon discovered that they possessed sterling qualities of honesty and truthfulness, while their willingly given services were a pleasure to receive. Aborigines they may be, but they are very different to the aborigine of whom one forms a mental picture.

Of the Indian buffalo there are two varieties, which differ slightly enough as to have received at the hands of the naturalist the separable designations *speiroceros* and *macroceros.* Sprung from a common stock, environment has had its usual effect, and, though practically identical, the two varieties display slight differences of horn-structure and habit, which are apparent enough to the ordinary observer.

Bos Bubalus macroceros is the long-horned species found throughout the Brahmaputra Valley, the Terai, and the Sundarbans. He it is who boasts the finer head, and is the subject of so many tales of ferocity and unprovoked attack amid the close and impenetrable mazes of his swampy retreats in the abovenamed parts of North-Eastern India. Of this creature we find record of a single horn in the British Museum measuring 78½ inches. If we allow one foot for the breadth of skull across the forehead, this gives a total 'sportsman's measurement' from tip to tip of 169 inches, or over 14 feet!

Speiroceros, meaning curly-horned, is the variety inhabiting the southern and eastern portions of the Central Provinces and neighbouring wild tracts of country.

Macroceros carries a head usually considerably longer than his congener of more southerly habitat—especially in the case of the cows—and his horns are generally straighter; while that of *speiroceros* has an appearance of greater stoutness of build, and the horn is often set on at a rather different angle. That the buffalo is essentially a reed-haunting jungle-boring old pachyderm it needs but little perspicacity to discern. Those great plough-like diverging horns, sweeping back in easy curve, were plainly intended by Nature to divide the hampering tangle of his jungly grassy home, as well as to assert his authority over a ponderous and placid harem, and guard him from treacherous foes. It is not therefore the decreasing necessity for such use in the thinner jungles of the Central Provinces, the increasing need for lighter armament on those more open plains, that finds the buffalo of Lower India equipped with horns different to those of his northern relative?

Then, again, the habits of the two varieties are dissimilar. While those of the swamp-haunting *Bubalus* easily suggest themselves, they are in no way an indication of the mode of life pursued by our more compact and active friend of southern habitat. *Speiroceros* is a great wanderer, solitary bulls, or a bull or two in company—usually a big fellow, accompanied by a 'fag,' so to speak—making very long journeys under cover of darkness, and travelling from one line of river to another, often over considerably elevated intervening country. The herds of cows and calves, sometimes accompanied by young bulls, are found as a rule in certain fixed localities, according to the season of the year; but they too are apt to disappear completely and rapidly if alarmed or otherwise set travelling; and, although they prefer an easy line of country devoid of hills, will climb considerable heights to gain their objective beyond. The hunter, therefore, must be prepared for astonishingly lengthy days of tracking; and he should avoid going on any but the freshest of tracks, and those at or near dawn, or he may find himself in for journeys of a duration quite outside ordinary calculation.

One of the greatest charms of buffalo *shikár*, in the grass and *sál* jungles of the part of India now referred to, is the tracking; which is often so easy as to offer no insuperable difficulties to the average sportsman. Although he cannot hope to rival those wonderful perceptions of the wild man, who lives all his life in the closest intimacy with Nature, it is astonishing how proficient he may become with a little practice. Of course the climate is against us to start with, and that is no doubt why so many are content to moon along in the wake of their trackers, coming to the front only when the game has been found.

The best time of year for a trip after the buffalo of these parts is undoubtedly at the *mirrig*, cr earliest rains, although there are certain grave disadvantages which often preclude one from taking advantage of this time of year, such as, to take but one of them, the difficulty of returning to civilization once the flood-gates of the monsoon are fully opened and rivers brimming full. When the first showers fall, sending the released tiger, bear, deer and other wild animals wandering far and wide without anxiety as to water and shade, the buffalo ceases his peregrinations of the open season, and, sometimes re-united in considerable herds, affects the comfortable life on open grass and glade land. Far from the river he may be. What matter! There are now innumerable pools and marshy depressions in this region that resound to the luxurious squelching of his huge wallowing carcase and the profound blowing and puffing of a monster at ease. This is the season of his loves. Here and there the soft clayey ground will be found ploughed and furrowed in all directions. Perhaps a ponderous strife uprooted those young saplings. In the distance a low deep note brings us to a sudden halt; the trees are all adrip with the last short shower ; and as the early sun touches the jungle it glitters with millions of faceted gems.

At the end of a long grassy ride a shower of diamonds falls sparkling down, and a tree-top is seen quivering—which can scarcely be the breeze. Wait! Hark! Did you hear that splashing and that "click-clack?" What is it but the huge hoofs of our *Bubalus*, sucking at the mire as he slowly paces forward. And then a great grey-blue side! Another, all red and glistening from the mire-puddled soil—and see! the earth soft and noiseless for us the creeping enemy, leafy covert all abroad, a steady settled wind; we shall have no difficulty in approaching almost near enough to pluck a hair from those huge sides, and, unless tempted by an extraordinary length of horn, may spare at the last moment.

Such is the pursuit of *speiroceros* under the most favourable circumstances; but here again, although he has now abated his nocturnal habits and long expeditions, we must choose his track with care, and, above all, shoot hard and straight. Once crossed and intermingled with the scurryings of a frightened herd, the tracks of the great bull may be lost for ever; and that is beyond the art of Máriah or Gónd.

But most of us will doubtless pursue our bull in the open season, during the summer heats, when that malarious jungle, filled with feverish exhalations and microbes of unknown venom, has been dried by a rigorous sun into the semblance of salubrity for the European traveller.

The position of these wilds the writer would not object to give here were Indian game less on the decrease. They lay there forty years ago. Of which time I possess a diary then describing them—truly a hunter's paradise, to be read of with beating heart and watering mouth. They lie there now—Ichabod! to be mourned over; their day gone by, desolate, crossed at intervals by some rare, shy, phenomenally astute descendants of the once great herds, now practically extinct by reason of murrain, drought, and, deadlier still, incursions of gun-bearing natives and gun-running merchants from that horrible country lying to the west, across the big river, where, at an even earlier date, most of the *ungulata* had become but a memory.

But the country itself has not changed much. In the western portions the ordinary dry central Indian forest covers its undulating features and clothes its rugged hills; but to the eastward the *sdl* forests begin, their western limit strangely marked, so that a bird's eye view shows their green line cutting north and south as if their plantation had been arranged by human agency instead of by Nature herself. The reason of this abrupt termination on a north and south line may be known to the expert forester; but my companion and I, although we examined the geological features of the country, were unable to account for it. Hence, for hundreds of miles eastward, the highly gregarious *sál* spreads its glossy green, almost to the entire exclusion of other timber, except where there are tracts capped by trap or basaltic rock, where of course the characteristic *salai* and stunted teak of this formation re-asserts itself. From east to west of this country passes the river, leaving mountain ranges on each hand, through which it has worn an arduous granite-bound course to join the greater river on the west. Its higher waters pass over an upland plain for many miles somewhat sluggishly till they plunge over a fine fall stretching right across its bed in the abrupt manner we see in the falls of the Congo and Zambesi. Hence it seeks a lower level with much greater rapidity, partaking of the nature of a highland stream. Indeed its rapids and pools irresistibly remind the traveller of a Scottish salmon river. When the writer viewed his companion, salmon-rod in hand, industriously beguiling the wily *mahasir*, heard the rush of the waters as they tumultuously entered a broad deep pool, and, above their roar, the musical screaming of the winch, he shut his eyes to the vivid green of the *sál* forests around him, and to the piercing rays of the declining tropic sun, and, with but a small stretch of the imagination, was back amid youthful scenes by banks of Ness or tumbling Awe. While encamped by its shores that river was an ever-pleasant feature of our trip. Those enforced and weary days of waiting, that the big game hunter knows so well, were to us all too short. Rod in hand, the hours, even under a broiling sun, passed rapidly away. *Mahasir*, our old friend *Barbus tor*, inhabited each thundering run and oily depth of that enchanting stream ; and bold sometimes, coy usually, strangely full of guile for an inmate of so virgin a river, by turns rewarded and deluded us. The amount of good fresh tackle we left in that rocky eastern stream was astounding. Never, I ween, had the spirit of those waters reaped such a harvest of spoons, traces, swivels, spinning tackle and line--not to speak of a top-joint one disastrous afternoon !

Long shall we remember those rushing rapids ; the granite sided islets with their drooping boughs and ferns ; the great solemn *sál* forest through which the jungle river ran towards the setting sun ; and, when floating silently home to camp, down some placid reach, the indescribable charm of a scene unique, I fancy, in the 'plains' of India ! The very birds, the riverside vegetation, the shape of the violet-shadowed hills, were strange and unknown before. Numbers of the large black and red 'Malabar' squirrel played among the trees ; a cuckoo of entirely novel voice sent his four delightful notes echoing along the woody shores ; our little boatmen conversed shyly in strange and dulcet speech. Rod, rifle, and gun would be forgotten, laid aside, in that warm sunset glow reflected from water as serene as the sky it pictured ; then in the distance, round some rocky bamboo-feathered promontory, we would sight our little encampment overlooking the river-bank, and, gliding nearer, note our modest table and chairs set on some cunningly chosen eminence rising from the smooth yellow sand of a water-lapped shore.

It had cost us many an arduous march to penetrate to those—to Europeans—almost virgin jungles; long days in blistering Central Province heat; and struggles across country devoid of any but the wildest tracks, where baggage carts had to be lifted over immovable trunks of fallen forest giants, or a way cleared in the thick green undergrowth. And at last here we were, nearly two hundred miles from the nearest railway, in the very midst of the country described in the faded yellow pages of the diaries kept by him who had explored these solitudes nearly forty years ago.

To give an idea of the height to which our hopes had risen before we found what havoc a few years of native guns had wrought, I cannot do better than give a few extracts from his records :—

"*April* 13*th*, 1868.—Went to the pond beyond the river, and sat down in the open to await dawn. Four buffs, one I think a bull, came up, drank, and walked off. Too dusk to see. When it became light enough I went on their tracks and came on eight buffs. Tried to circumvent them, but they took a different route to that I had expected. Got on their tracks again, and unfortunately when in very thick jungle one of the cows spied us, and off they went! Followed on in the direction they had taken. Saw some *gaona*, or red deer. Going up the side of a small hill I threw two men on opposite sides of a ravine in case of bears.

"On reaching the top found high grass all about, and was looking about when up sprang a fine bull bison and dashed off. I had a snap shot and fired too high; but as I fired he threw up his head and gave a moan. I followed the tracks and found that he soon stopped running. After going about half a mile I put him up out of a *nála*, and saw by the slow way he went up the opposite side that he was badly hit. Fired two shots as he went away, both of which took effect. I then tracked him by his blood for a full mile with great difficulty, as his track was barely perceptible. At last in some thin jungle up he got, and went away hard again. Hitting him with a ball from the big rifle (muzzle-loader), he walked into the open and stood looking very sick below a big *mhowa* tree. At last he sat down, this last run having done for him, for although he got up and looked very mischievous, he fortunately had not a charge left in him, or at one time it would have been ugly work. Going up behind him the first ball from the small rifle had no effect, but at one from the big single-barrel he slept with his fathers. A very fine bull indeed, not aged, but with very fine horns. Cut off his head and tail and walked home.

"Went out in the evening after chital, of which there are very large numbers here to the south of the river and falls. At some distance from the village shot two fine spotted bucks and could have got more."

"*April 16th*—Sent off kit to M——gaon, and went out at 3 a.m. to the pond again. As I approached it heard a herd of buffaloes run off through the mud. At dawn I took up the tracks. After a while we sighted a herd in another direction, and they turned out to be bison. We went round a long way to circumvent them, and came plump on another herd that were walking away to the hills. Unfortunately they saw us, and off they all went; so I let them pass, and went on the tracks of the herd first seen, but failed. After this I returned to the second herd, and at last came on them sitting on the side of a hill. Wounded the bull badly, but he got off after a long day, and towards evening I returned to the river and my *shikaris* boiled me a little rice. This and plenty of I—— water was my repast."

"*April 18th.*—Went out south of M——gaon. After going some distance spied a herd of bison. Had some trouble with them, and to my disgust bagged a cow. All the cows here are big and very dark coloured, and it is difficult to pick out the bull. Came on some red deer and bowled one over, which gave us all a run before it was secured. On the way home saw some buffs, but did not go after them. Marked the spot for to-morrow or next day."

"*April 19th.*—Went out after the buffs, but getting seedy had to return home early in the day."

"*April 20th.*—Went out and had a long day, feeling seedy all the time, but bagged a fine bull-buff."

"*April 23rd.*—Went out in the evening, and about sunset came on an immense bull-buff—a solitary fellow. Got up to within eighty yards, but being shaky with fever was nervous, and hit him too high up. The bull made off with his head up, and getting into the open stood looking about him. Crept up and gave him two more shots—but bad ones—being incapacitated by this infernal fever. Being late and far from home I turned back."

"*April 24th.*—Went out for the big bull. Came on him suddenly, after going a long way, but did not get a fair shot. Two miles further on came on him standing in the jungle. Hit him, but he went off slowly. Having been out all day, I returned to camp, six miles, in the evening, getting home very late."

"*April 25th.*—Got again on the bull's tracks, and near Anantpur came on the place where he had been lying down. Beyond this his tracks led to water, and then back into the same stunted *Shorea robusta* (*sál*) jungle. All of a sudden

Buffaloes in *sal* forest.

the tracker started back. I went in front and saw the buff lying, as I thought, dead. I stepped back and looked at him from another point of view. 'Oh,' says Boodoo, 'he's dead!' I made a noise. Still no movement. I thought of firing into him as he lay, but unfortunately did not, making a 'cluck' with my tongue instead. Up sprang the buff and darted off at no end of a pace. We followed. I was so astonished that it was some little time before I could fire, and then the ball did not seem to have any effect. I ran some distance and then getting on my horse kept the bull in sight. He stopped on seeing me, and *came at me*, but I easily trotted out of his way. This run blew him, and he wheezed badly as he went off. The bull then disappared. Boodoo said he had gone back. We then went round the nasty thick jungle, and we couldn't see well into it. I then thought of going in on horseback and seeing if I could find the bull. I did so. It was very windy and very hot. At last I heard a rustle, and, looking up, saw the brute coming down on us. I was walking towards him, and he was in full rush at me. I wheeled round my horse, he also, being frightened, aiding me in doing so, and so hoped to escape; but before my horse got off the bull reached him, and, butting, threw him forward on his knees! The good beast did not fall however, but recovered himself, and with one vigorous kick behind dashed forward and brought himself and his master out of the scrimmage safe. At one moment I had thought it was all up with both of us. I lost my hat. The bull was then followed up and finally bagged. In the afternoon a bear came rushing along at a great pace; but I bowled him over, and when my gun and rifle were both empty another came."

"*April 28th.*—When towards M——gaon saw two sámbar, but no shot. Farther on came on a herd of ten buffaloes, out of which I bagged a very fine big cow. Coming home had a long shot at a *gáona*, or red deer. Saw five more of these fine animals in the *sál* jungle near camp.

"Went out in the afternoon. The jungle to the east of this village appears a very likely place for sport. First we saw a bull buffalo, who however spied us first, before we saw him, and made off. As it was getting dusk we did not follow him. Came on a few bison grazing, but was frustrated in my attempt at near approach by a very wary cow. Took a longish shot, and as I fired they all made off, and close to them a large herd of buffaloes. There were also some red deer or "Barasingha" in the long grass. Nearer the village shot a "four-horned deer."

To give more than these few extracts might prove wearisome. The writer of them describes more sport with buffaloes, bison, tigers, bears, and red deer, during the early rains that followed—the *mirrig*, of which mention has previously been made. His notes show what a splendid head of game that country once supported. As the country itself is now no whit more cultivated and but little more opened-up than in those old times, this is a particularly clear case of the horrible havoc wrought by the native gunner. Many a tale the writer could unfold concerning the ravages of the poacher and the enormities of the horn merchant in those tracts.

As regards the danger of hunting the wild buffalo of those parts, sportsmen appear to be somewhat divided in opinion. The writer of the diaries above referred to only once found himself in a position of danger, and that in the days of muzzle-loading weapons; and although particular buffaloes are noted to have shown considerable malice in the way of butting trees and making blind attacks on other inanimate objects when wounded, the majority seem to have acted similarly to those of which we ourselves had experience, showing the greatest anxiety to escape their puny antagonist and remove their enormous frames from his Lilliputian attack. However, some years ago, a sportsman met his death, in those very jungles, from the horns of a bull that he had wounded. The story runs that he had gone out one morning on the tracks of a big bull which he had hit the previous evening. He was armed with a heavy black-powder rifle—probably an 8-bore—and coming on the bull lying down in an open glade, he approached perilously near, in order to finish it off; and was charged. The bull is said to have chased him to a tree, round which the unfortunate man dodged, and on each side of which he then seized his pursuer's spreading horns. In such unequal strife the *Bubalus* and his opponent did not struggle long. The sportsman was tossed easily aside, and then terribly gored, one great horn completely penetrating his body. When the bull left him his retainers rushed up, but their master was beyond all aid. He ejaculated the one word "Water!" and was dead before their eyes.

Such calamities shock the keen *shikari*, and a narrow escape may teach him greater caution; but it is rare that these deter him from again embarking on his engrossing pursuit.

The jungle again exercises its compelling fascination; the mind's eye pictures its delights; the rifle—old friend—emerges from its case, caressed once more of fond hands; Time, healer of scars, physical and mental, does his appointed work; and Nature leads the wanderer once more to her beloved solitudes. At first the hunter returned may start and handle his weapon sharply at a rustle in the bushes; a sudden clamour, or, more still, the harsh voice of a wild beast, may momentarily unnerve him; but gradually he will, with a smile, return to the old ways, and his experiences of the past become but additional jungle lore to enrich the memory.

But this is wandering from our *speiroceros!* Yet, after all, what is it that exercises that unfailing attraction that his hobby possesses for the true follower of Nimrod? Not the bare collection of trophies; not the satisfying of a mere hunting instinct indeed. No; it is something more than that; something that appeals even to a mind insensible to Nature's beauties, to her charms when sought in the forest or on the mountain-side. It is the partial return to man's pristine wild life, in a land where the artificialities of civilization have not yet greatly affected the pursuit of game. It is that broad free feeling; the ability to throw out a wide-sweeping arm and say to oneself, "This is all mine to rove!"; and, besides this, the various interests to be found in the country, its people, its fauna, and their habits.

When I and my companion reached our land of promise, we found ourselves sadly hampered by lack of local knowledge and by our total ignorance of the habits of the buffalo of those regions. The river, split up in many places into gurgling channels that traversed a perfect maze of luxuriant vegetation, smothering innumerable islets in its embrace and hiding deep dark recesses full of dark fern and moss, led us at once astray. All that we had read on the subject of buffaloes—from Assam and the Terai—as well as Forsyth's remarks on the Sambalpur country—led us to believe that if our great game were to be found here, it would be among these almost impenetrable islets. Thus we wasted time. The shy inhabitants—extremely retiring little creatures, true denizens of the forest, and timid as the wild beasts themselves—were extraordinarily secretive, and our own men were as much at a loss as ourselves. At this juncture we were delivered from our perplexity by Amir Ali, a Mahomedan shopkeeper, who lived in a considerable village, the capital, as it were, of the surrounding wild country. This individual was brought to our camp by our men one evening, and in the course of a very short conversation we managed to pick up valuable hints as to the habits and present whereabouts of our ponderous quarry.

During an all-too-short sojourn of two months in those delightful wilds, we found that, with the exception of a wandering tiger at rare intervals and a few small bison, with, say, a bear here and there, and a very few sámbar and chital, the country was denuded of all game, save a few scattered herds of wild buffaloes. The mournful prognostications indulged in many years previously by our predecessor of the diaries had turned out only too true. Those keen hunters, the little jungle-men, aided by gun-running friends from over the border, had done their work; and the 'Márdian' country was swept of its game, save the hardy and dangerous *Bubalus*, attacks on whom were not lightly undertaken by their tiny foes.

To roam that magnificent natural game preserve was a melancholy occupation. Monkeys and peacocks were almost the only inhabitants of those grand *sál* jungles. Scarce a barking deer or four-horned antelope leapt the rotting fallen timber. No cry of wandering spotted stag or whistle of herding hind disturbed the deep brooding silence. The quiet of night was unbroken by the harsh cry of questing beast of prey—because there *was* no prey! Was all the jungle dead, then? Was it that the presence of a few wandering buffaloes had thus crushed all other wild life?

Such thoughts would come ; but, spite them all, what a charm in those wilds and that lovely river!

In one locality we brought a solitary mournful tiger to bag, and each of us got his first buffalo ; whiling away the time between by good sport with the *mahasir* at our very tent doors. By lashing together a couple of *dóngas*, or 'dug-outs,' we were able to construct a stable boat, capable of accommodating ourselves, retainers, gun and rifle, tiffin, rods, tackle, and boat-men. Embarking thus on one of those long still reaches, away we paddled ; shot rapids ; tarried awhile by some alluringly fishy pool or run, consoled by the music of the winch, and passing the while a woody hilly panorama full of striking beauty.

At night alone the buffalo approaches the river bank. Moonlight on a silent and deserted shore discloses some great black rocks, so it would seem, that stand in the shallows with the ripples glistening away from their feet. Hush ! Was not that a slow plashing in the warm water ? Look at that promontory of yellow sand jutting into the dark waters from darker woods ! An enormous shadow, clear-cut in the brilliance of a tropic moon, is creeping across it. There is the sound of profound breathings. Now, gently push the dug-out along the black shadow of this high bank, and wait. Slowly, ponderously, one—two—five—seven enormous creatures emerge from the gloom of the *sál* trees into the sandy shallows and, one by one, splash their leisurely way across them to a reedy islet. The shining ripples widen and slap tiny wavelets against our side. There is a distant crunching of gravel, and some low trees amid long grass on the island are being crushed through by heavy bodies. The buffaloes are moving slowly up-stream, feeding as they go among the rank herbage of the river-side.

Splash their leisurely way across.

At length the rustlings die away, and not a sound can be heard but the feeble chirping of crickets, an occasional low moan from an owl in the trees across the water, and the remotely-faint rushing of some distant rapid.

If we have the patience to haunt the sleeping river until the moon shall have crossed the sky to decline towards those wooded hills, those slow-moving monsters will at length return and seek the shore, and the woods that disgorged them earlier in the night will again close mysteriously over their huge forms.

Perhaps the skirt of that distant thunderstorm may extend and give the slumbering forest a slight shower. That would be well indeed, for by early dawn we should rejoice to find the fresh tracks so patent to our eager gaze. Here is the spot where the herd finally left the river-side; and, farther on, the immense indentations left by the feet of the master bull. The tracks of the herd lead a broad path away from the river towards the distant open grassy and sapling-studded country, where these pachyderms love to lie during the hot hours of the day; but the big fellow has made off elsewhere. Twice has he skirted the sandy shore and once entered a secluded back-water, where he rolled in the muddy sand. Here it was that the rain fell during the small hours of the morning, when he climbed the steep bank, and passed round that huge fallen tree, making inland.

The woods are waking now. A sudden commotion high above our heads, and a little shower of rain-drops; red Malabar squirrels on the limb of a forest giant, rousing to their daily play up mighty trunks. Those four melodious cuckoo notes—whistled now, long after, and in a far distant land they instantly bring us back to that enchanted forest—echo through the vistas of tall straight stems before us. Gradually we pass on. Glade land opens out, long grass receives us, still slowly pacing forward, eyes on ground, and a glance for on ahead. Again the tall-stemmed forest covers us. That bull is making for some distant ground! The *sál* forest thins again, and the ground becomes stony. Our little Máriah trackers evince greater caution, taking up the trail from the *sahib*, whose half-educated eye has lost the—to them—simple guiding marks. It is a little rising ground before us. Gently up to the top now, and put your head quietly round the trunk of that tree, rifle in hand. What! Not there? This little shallow depression among the knolls is well known to the Máriahs as a favourite lair of this very bull. But to-day we must pass on; he has only tarried here in seeming hesitation.

In such manner the *shikári* may encompass many a weary mile, during almost every pace of which all his senses have to be on the stretch. *Bubalus* is capricious. To-day he may be making for a distant spot, or, suddenly tempted by some, to us, unknown advantage, he may be loitering in the shade of those trees. Nay, at this moment he may be silently contemplating us, nose in air, horns sweeping his flanks, and ears and tail suddenly held still from their ordinary fly-flapping movements, ready to thunder suddenly away, and from a heavy gallop settle into that aggravatingly ceaseless pace that may carry him ten miles before we have a chance of finding his suspicions lulled.

But to-day we are in luck at last. Patience has its reward! Past days of toil are going to be repaid!

It is very hot in these stilly forests. The big rifle appears to weigh a hundredfold what it did when we left the sandy shore this morning; and, in spite of a pull at the water-bottle, our feet, lightly shod in an ancient pair of brown tennis shoes though they be, go not any too sprightly. See! A slight detour the bull made here to avoid a big fluted termites' heap, when suddenly—there is old Dabbi the Máriah crouched close to the ground; and the others, well to the rear luckily, all behind *sál* stems! As for me a tree trunk is what I most desire to simulate at the moment. Am I 'spotted'? Or do the khaki breeches and brownish coat in any wise resemble the corrugated stems of *Shorea robusta*! Dabbi however begins to crawl, crab-like, in my direction; so, very gently, down I go too. *Gondi* is the only language in which Dabbi and I have common knowledge, my share comprising a few names of animals and a common word or two; but hunters' language of eye and hand is a regular "Volapuk," carrying one all the world over, and there is no difficulty in learning that 'he' is lying in a slight hollow in that bit of a clearing ahead of us.

Delicious moment! Does the hunter not know it well, when the knowledge of having found his game, his presence all unsuspected, mingles with the suppressing of the eager desire to attack! Yes. The great beast is there; for the tips of a truculent pair of wide-curving black horns betray his position, and here are we planning how to get the better of his natural wile.

And a cunningly-chosen position the old bull has taken up! What wind there is it guards the weak spots of his defences. Clear ground to the other spots of the compass gives him a commanding view down-wind, while his post in the slight hollow affords that advantage of forcing an approaching enemy to show himself over the sky-line. If startled now, a few paces would take him among the timber up-wind, and we should not get in that well-placed shot which alone will prevent a pursuit infinitely more arduous than the whole of this long morning's work, or, perhaps indeed, his eventual escape.

Here, then, is the advantage of a strong binocular glass wherewith to scrutinize our ground and endeavour to eliminate the element of chance. Old *speiroceros* lies almost facing us, but his eyes are below the level of our present horizon. No. To creep stealthily in, *this* time, would not serve our purpose. Time is passing however, and something must be done. What if the bull should make off, warned by that subtle sense the operation of which we must have noted at times, and which is apparently set in motion by the concentration of mind bent on the hunted by the hunter ! What else but this indefinable transference of brain energy can it have been that on certain occasions has caused the originally unconscious then uneasy game to rise to its feet with vague forebodings, and display a mysterious disquiet unaccountable to the external senses of sight, hearing, or smell !

Well, here goes ! "Dabbi, my little friend, do thou stop here ! I, the slayer, will make a détour across the wind, and come in there, nearly behind of the *Barreh*, and among the *sál* trees into which he will make his way when roused. And then, good Dabbi, creep nearer, and show but that tiny black cranium of thine to him who, pondering, masticates in the hollow yonder ! "

The little Máriah's crowlike eyes blink. He nods reflectively.

* * * * *

It is with feelings of gratitude that the hunter at length creeps behind the afar-noted trees. The wide horn-tips are still down there, but are seen this time from *behind*. Fearfully is the breech of the cordite rifle gently set agape. Yes. Two shining cartridges are *still* there ! A perspiring palm is wiped dry on the clothing. The little Máriah should be at work now. A hot, oppressive silence broods in the glade, and the somewhat quick breathing of the sportsman must be checked.

Slowly, certainly, but with a suspicious tilt, the great sweeping horns turn towards the thin grass that must now cover my co-operator, and so remain motionless. Anon they are gently tossed from side to side in their resumed *rôle* of fly-whisks. What can Dabbi be at! Some minutes elapse. The great ears are slowly turned forward, then back; then suddenly forward again, with a twitch, and there fix stiffly.

A tiny dark object, away beyond the couched *Bubalus*, raises itself a moment in the yellow grass, then drops swiftly. The bull is on his legs instantaneously. What a monster he looks, even at a distance of two hundred yards: those betraying horns now laid back along the huge shoulders, and his stern looming gigantic through the *sál* saplings—a great black rock, immovable as the granite boulders of his native soil!

In a threatening attitude he takes a pace or two forward, away from me, and halts again, nose in air. I feel distinctly sorry for Dabbi, until reminded of his sprightly activity and ape-like powers of climbing.

After standing awhile in this attitude, the bull turned and moved suspiciously off, first at a walk, then at a gentle trot, slowing down to a walk again as he entered the fringe of jungle amid which his enemy eagerly awaited his coming. There was a spot where an ant-hill and the butt-end of an enormous fallen tree gave excellent cover, and behind this I had crouched, convinced that the bull would pass within a few yards and afford an easy and deadly shot; but, when that enormous bulk came into view, to my dismay he had turned, and was making off across rather open ground some hundred and fifty yards distant.

Anxiously waiting until he had passed behind a heavy clump of bamboos, I made a sudden bolt, and darted for a spot about seventy yards farther on, almost cutting his path. There was a very slight depression here, of which, by bending down, it seemed possible to take advantage. On the far side of this grew a few low *sál* bushes of the kind that often form a very thick undergrowth beneath the parent forest. Creeping forward, rifle held ready, I peered round them.

Not fifty yards away my huge quarry had just come to a standstill. His great head was turned sideways, nose downward, in comical bubaline fashion. He appeared to regard something in my direction in a quizzical manner out of the corner of his eye. I remember noting his extremely venerable appearance and the enormously powerful short thick legs, dirty white below the knee, while overcome with a sudden realization of my own puny proportions.

The safety-bolt had been pressed forward, and the massive breeched, taper-barrelled ·400 bore cordite rifle was half way to my shoulder, but—a huge curving horn covered most of the vital spot, at any rate would probably interrupt the bullet.

Slowly, very slowly, that venerable muzzle was raised; slowly the great ears hinged forward; the massive neck bent; and the obstructing horn gradually shifted round.

He is now gazing straight at me. The psychological moment has arrived. Nervously the sight comes to rest about the point of his mighty shoulder, quivers a little, and is forcibly, with bumping heart, held steady——

Bang!

These deadly new rifles! There is no smoke. Simultaneously, with the sudden sharp recoil, the bull gives a quick flinch and twist of his body, and, turning before the left barrel can be got in, blunders suddenly and heavily away.

Reloading as we go, we are after him, warily enough however, on the toes of the tennis shoes, eager for a chance turn to expose some vital place in that crashing lumbering grey-blue mass.

But is he not cantering strangely, bearing off ever to the left, and heeling over more and more like some squall-struck vessel! A stumble! The colossus slows into a trot, a walk, and, standing an instant, sways—poor old fellow!

Then he rolls ponderously on his side, and over on to his back—a sight as incongruously extraordinary as an overturned locomotive.

Need one expatiate further on the gazing, admiring, examining, measuring, and further viewing of the grand old fallen monster—on the clicking of the camera, the well-earned snack of tiffin, the cleaning and fondling of the cherished rifle, and the homeward path with lightsome tread?

All that the hunter has toiled for—almost all—is o'er; and a certain re-action is felt, mingled with that regret which will perforce push in after the downfall of very big game.

But that mighty head shall be accorded the post of honour on already well-trophied walls, and thereon live once more to recall those halcyon days in beloved jungles!

All too rapidly will those days pass, and, with them, perchance our youth; opportunity perhaps gone, 'wind' impaired, an Indian sun grown strangely fiercer than of yore, the hill-side somehow steeper. Until at last, the time of our exile o'er, we set our faces homeward—to the West.

Land of the East, farewell! thy hills grow dark,
On purple peaks a deeper shade descending;
In twilight copse the firefly lights her spark,
The deer, half seen, are from the covert wending.
A distant echo from thy stretching plains—
Some wandering witch-note of those far-off hills—
And then—'tis silent all! Dear jungles, fare ye well!

THE END.

The End

APPENDIX.

The Letters of Jhoot Singh.

APPENDIX.

Being the letters of one Jhoot Singh, process-server, táhsil chaprasi, and some time *shikári* in the táhsil of W—— to that most exalted, kind, brave one, Luchcha Ali Khan Saheb, Tahsildar of W——.

(All written in the Hindi language and character.)

The exalted one of high dignity, protector of the poor, appreciator of worth, the kind Khan Saheb Tahsildar, the brave, to him-wards.

Let it be known unto your honour that the petition of your dependant is this that yesterday evening that English *saheb* to whom your honour made reference he is arrived in camp here at P——. Further—— as it is known to your honour already those his servants who are his sepoy orderlies of whom there be four one a Kshatriya like your slave two Játs and one old Mussalman who have for some time-space been making endeavours to spy out the land these very people have previously to your slave's arrival found that there is a tiger in this jungle of P—— and had tied *hélas* and that tiger had previously to the arrival of that *saheb* eaten one *héla.* Further—— again last night was there tying of *hélas* and I had made representations before the *saheb* that on account of my knowing all this jungle and the state thereof he should permit me to examine the *héla* near Gat jungle which of all places the most favourite and the *saheb* said go Jhoot Singh and I will send one sepoy with in order to aid. Further—— accordingly I went to-day very early morning and when in the neighbourhood of Gat I said to the sepoy see brother it is good only for one man to examine with great carefulness for this cause remain resting here awhile and I will go to see that *héla* if it be *gára* or if it be alive and so he sat and I went and the tiger having made *gára* was sitting near (the kill) and by beating on a tree with my stick he ran away and by beating tree farther on he ran away more and went quickly and without doubt is gone from this jungle of Gat so I called that sepoy and said there is *gára* taken place and surely to-day there will be good hunting. Further—— and because there could not be found sufficient villagers for beating that jungle of which your honour will doubtless understand a reason so the English *saheb* sat vainly by night near the *gára* and in the morning I said we will remain here more days and tie more *hélas* for I know this tiger he is a very big old one and a great thief. Further—— it is the Patél of P—— that has much helped the *saheb* in this place and so I have threatened and struck with shoe according to your honour's order the rest is all well to-day the date the five May the signature of Jhoot Singh chaprasi.

The exalted, etc., etc.

Protector of the poor be it known to your honour that again that tiger that remained yet in jungle of Gat had eaten a *hèla* and that because of this occurring in a distant part when I was gone elsewhere it was that Mussalman sepoy that this time brought news and so the *saheb* walking in the jungle met me and ordered that you go collect villagers for the purpose of beating jungle and then by reason of my astuteness had I gone aside to see that place of *gára* and perform plans but as I approached near to it that old Mussalman who is a very cunning man he had seen me so I had gone forward to the villages and collected some beaters and when at the time of noon the *saheb* began to arrange for beating jungles he called me and said that Jhoot Singh dost thou know this jungle and in which direction the tigers are accustomed to run and proceed away in this place? So I agreed and went to make arrangements and with us came the sepoys except that cunning Mussalman he remained near to the *saheb* and when I had escaped out of the sight of those sepoys I went alone and taking with (me) some loin-cloth and white cloth of turban by arranging that cloth on bushes so that animal (tiger) did not run straight forward at the time of making the beat but ascended a little hill and went away to one side and the *saheb* called me and asked me this reason with great force and said 'Dyám!' afterwards were there more two beats but there was no further trace of that animal. Further—— the Kshatriya and one Jât had afterwards found the tracks that were going towards a far jungle and so there was an order to take camp near there and the *saheb* shot some deer and was coming there also. Further—— in this other jungle there remains never any tiger but it became known to me that the very animal has gone in the direction of the jungle of B—— and that the Mussalman also had gone away not saying any word and so I said to the *saheb* I will go to another good jungle also for the procuring of news and then I walked by night but first did I remain at the village S—— to execute some private works so when in the morning time I had arrived at B—— there was present that Mussalman sepoy and he spoke friendly words and was saying gladly see Jhoot Singh my brother how I am clever in obtaining of news for there is fresh news of two tigers in the *bandi* of T—— and wilt thou come this day after eating food and give help and I said first I will sleep and then will I eat and after that will I come—— but soon escaping from his view by cleverness at once I went to that *bandi* of T—— which is distant three *kós* and in that village I greatly beat Raoji patél and one Phagoo *shikári* although they cried with oaths that there is no tiger here nor gave we any kind of news and then I remained resting in their house and so after giving warnings I relented. Further—— when I was returned with lateness next morning to B—— I heard afar off a sound of gun twice in jungle nor were there any men left in that village of B—— on this my heart became fluid for I knew from this reason that there was beating and hunting of tigers. Further—— the *sáheb* had killed one tiger owing to the astuteness of that Mussalman and the Mussalman spoke sweet words with me saying see Jhoot Singh I have told my master that thou art a very good man and very clever on account of giving good news so he will surely give great reward but the younger Ját sepoy was then laughing very much not all at once restraining his behaviour but saying afterwards by a pretence and quickly how it was a big *tamásha* this tiger hunting and all the villagers climbing on trees but I knew that real reason of his laughter but by concealing my anger and making much sweet words and flatteries did I make all matters smooth and so even that Mussalman was becoming a little unsuspicious. Further—— and it is the petition of this slave that this foolishness be this time forgiven so will it in future not be thus to-day nine May the signature of Jhoot Singh chaprasi.

The appreciator of worth, the kind, etc., etc.

Be it known to the kind Khan Saheb brave one that this slave had received tidings that there has been a robbery in that his other house of which your honour perhaps knows that it lives in the village of K—— and there is much jewellery remaining gone so I had gone there to make enquiry into that matter and had left Govinda forest guard to do my work in my place during my absence but Govinda is an exceeding great fool and by reason of that word the *saheb* killed another tiger but I immediately caused to be written letters to all police stations and forest posts that our *Dipti Saheb* he is coming this side to hunt tigers and that on account of giving any help to this other *saheb* all people will receive much loss and beatings and trouble to their houses. Further—— it is the petition of this poor one that he may be forgiven also that for his stomach there is not enough pay therefore day and night is he praying before your honour that pay may be increased the rest is all well the to-day date thirteen May the signature of Jhoot Singh chaprasi.

Further—— I have sent word to the villages on that road which it is told that this *saheb* is about to proceed and have again warned all police and head-men that whenever there is become any news or hope of tiger hunting they must make great difficulties concerning all matters of supplies and the obtaining of coolies for camp work and especially for making beats in the jungle but such people are always fools and there is fear of the Mussalman who is showing cleverness like unto that of an old dog-fox also of the other sepoy people who on account of being foolish do not understand that it is better that our *Dipti Saheb* should obtain good hunting also are they in no way connected with me or with this *zillah* or there should easily be some sort of arrangements. Further—— your honour is both mother and father and nobody but you is protecting me and it is known to me that Prem Sukh chaprasi has told lies to your honour concerning the matter of three hundred rupees and the house of a certain man who had come from Hindustan and in this word there is no truthfulness and this will I show when I am returned.

The kind appreciator of worth, etc., etc.

May it be known to your honour that since several days because the English *saheb* who has come for hunting could find no trace of tigers then one of the sepoys came to village K—— where I was occupied in my private works and called me saying that come quickly and give help and so for the sake of my name which is very great in matters of *shikár* I went that very day and at the time of my arrival immediately that *saheb* called me and said that Jhoot Singh we people are unable to do any works without you for there is no help or news in anything and these rascal village people are giving trouble and certainly making villany then was I secretly glad for it is so known that they the village people have indeed well obeyed that order but looking sad I explained much loss was mine and bereave-ments so looking in my direction some time then the *saheb* struck kindly the hand on my back and said that Jhoot Singh I have seen no more tigers although there has been hunting of leopards and bears and some deer therefore am I about to march now many *kós* to the westward near the village of K—— M—— where I know are some tigers and so I ate apprehension and became glad that I had been called in that time for in truth are there many tigers in that place and moreover it is the best jungles in all the taluk and there was intention of reserving it for the hunting of the *Dipti Saheb.* Further—— again the *saheb* sent me forward to obtain news and this time by reason of the Mussalman being sick with ague I came to that place with another sepoy and immediately it became known to me that in the *nála* of P—— there are three tigers in the near neighbourhood. Further—— because the sepoy was looking always at my goings and comings for he had without doubt been told to do this by the Mussalman I could not go of myself and so the forest guard went by my order to that *nála* and took with his gun and in cool time of evening made two four sounds of gun also because there was confusion of hurry I had given him some newspaper of the *saheb* people to place on little trees near water for all that jungle was much beloved of tigers and there was fear that they might return or not all run away. Further—— during the moonlight night-time the *saheb* came without warning riding on his horse and slept lying on the ground and in early morning he rose and said come Jhoot Singh show me then this jungle of great fame that I have heard and so taking me with the sepoy went to that *nala* now because of that fool forest guard's mad work there were clear marks of boot left in that place and underneath them new footsteps of tigers and immediately the *saheb* saw and so was astonished and spoke no word. Soon we went a long way and then saw again that by madness that profligate man whom I had sent had not taken all away so there was remaining near some water in *nála* a piece of newspaper hanging on a bush. The newspaper was not like that one which is all big and is then folded into smaller size but was of separate large pieces that each were inside one in one and of excellent good size for putting each piece on a bush. Further—— the *saheb* spoke no word but began to look for marks of feet in the sand with signs of great anger and then saying O Dyám ! then after a space of time he pulled and took that newspaper and when he had read in it for a while he made sudden loud laughter and afterwards spoke in this manner that what is this word then Jhoot Singh that some enemy has placed not only white papers for the disturbing of tigers but also making such cunning choosing that he has placed this very one then making more laughters he said also that enemy is too clever for he has chosen such a newspaper that the tigers and other wild animals of forest will have great and true frightenings beside doubtless being stricken with painful sickness of the belly by the only looking at it. Further——meantime your slave not understanding and becoming doubtful remained silent by reason of uncertainty because the *sahebs* have strange ways like magic and often smile when they are about to strike or greatly anger themselves. Further—— the *saheb* again looking carefully at marks of boots and making a little map thereof with pencil he spoke no more anger words but again often making silent laughters so he returned to the encampment. Further—— when I was eating food the Mussalman sat and talked much secret words near the *saheb* and so when I had finished and had drunk water and was lying resting at that time that old man came to my direction and having spat on the ground said that Jhoot Singh it is an order that you now go to the jungle of B—— P—— for bringing *shikár* news but I pretended anger and gave abuse and so went at once before the *saheb* and made many words of people casting doubts on my works because some one my enemy in this village had done treachery in order to break my honour through jealousy and so after awhile again the *saheb* became unsuspecting. Further—— remained in this camp four-five days and himself the *saheb* went and arranged the tying of *hèlas* and every day in the morning time he went to see if *gára* had resulted and was loosening the *hèlas*. Further —— from another direction during night-time there came a strange tigress to this *bandi* and there was *gára* and beating of jungle but with fortune that ball missed and that day because of a great bravery which was performed by your slave in going near the tigress the *saheb* has become very pleased and made much praise of that work and the Mussalman and other sepoys are looking in my direction with great affliction. This is written by the hand of Lala a Kayasth in the village of B—— to the brave Khan Saheb the *salaams* of Jhoot Singh to-day date the 27th May.

To the exalted, etc. etc.

Be it known to your honour that the letter of your honour is arrived at me and before your honour's presence the kind appreciator of worth brave exalted one, the petition of this dependant is that the word of which your honour writes is only falsehood and lying word without doubt it has been made by some my enemy and how shall I tell lies to your honour and I have always placed your honour's orders in my heart thereby how shall I render helping to this *saheb* but day and night am I engaged with great cleverness and astuteness and make much endeavours according to your honour's orders but these sepoy people are in these days become very cunning and so my work is being spoiled and they are continually looking to my direction and giving deceits to me in such a manner that neither by disturbings of *nálas* nor by taking away of *hèlas* by night which is a dangerous work nor by placing of cloths nor by filling sand in waterpools nor by beatings of patéls and *shikáris* nor even by setting fire to open jungles nor by any kinds of deceivings is that remaining any more success but this is a true word that only two three other tigers have been killed. Further—— the reason of the killing of the big tiger of Karoa was thus-wise that by chance one Ját sepoy had tied a *hela* in some distant jungle and the tiger had eaten it and lay in rocks and so one Jaglia who is giving me help he was going there quickly and driving away the animal, but coming back he met that sepoy and that other the Mussalman, so they caught him and beat him with much strength so that he is lying helpless in his house. Further—— because of my well knowing all that jungle I knew where that animal's home remained and where he was doubtless gone to lie, so I told the *saheb* and persuaded him by many words and eating of oaths that all the roads of that tiger were known to me and so took him to beat another jungle where by reason of the smallness of the bushes a tiger remains not ever, in addition that tiger had left no footsteps so the *saheb* agreed. Further—— by reason of ill fortune that accursed animal had not gone to that other usual place but was even lying asleep in this very small jungle so by chance so it happened that there was successful hunting and because of this the *saheb* became very happy. Moreover that Mussalman could not speak by reason of that astonishing thing the mouth of your honour's slave also became stopped through wonder, but I gave flattering words to the sepoys and by reason of the days of his leave being finished that *saheb* is making much gladness on account of killing the big tiger during the last day. Further—— the *saheb* taking aside said to me that Jhoot Singh thou art a very good man and a clever *shikári*, tell me then of an altogether truth and as if holding the cow's tail that has there from thy side been at any time any treachery in the matter of hunting and was it truly thy some enemy who drove away the three tigers from that *nála* of P—— for I have heard about sounds of gun also in the evening before I came to that place. Further—— but I made answer with great sadness of countenance that it is your honour's pleasure that having killed tigers and made such good hunting that your honour is now making suspicions on me surely and without doubt some person my enemy has given false information but it is as your honour pleases and it is a word of great sorrow and to me there is great shame because of this word. Further—— then the *saheb* looked at me with sharp looking for some time and made mention of many kinds of deceivings and the tracks of the treachery which had come to his knowing and I became afraid for I knew now that the *saheb* although making dissemblings was knowing little and much. At last the *saheb* became unsuspicious and at the time of his departure he presented me with some rewards and gave promises of returning again for hunting and said that see Jhoot Singh in this zillah of W—— there are many villainous blackguards of which some are of greater rank than tahsildars but knowing of their astuteness I became watchful so it is come about that in spite of hindering and treacheries I have killed some tigers take therefore this reward because by reason of thy bravery and the good hunting of the big tiger yesterday I believe that thou hast eaten my salt without treachery. Further—— and then making many words of coming again in a future year and arrangements thereof the *saheb* became mounted on his horse and departed. Further—— those my enemies will be saying that this hunting of tigers is due to your slave that he is deceiving the Tahsildar *Saheb* but your honour knows that by my astuteness and great works of trouble that *saheb* was much prevented because otherwise many more tigers would have been killed and the hunting of the *Dipti Saheb* greatly spoiled. Further—— according to the orders will I proceed quickly this evening in order to make obeisance to the *Dipti Saheb* at the encampment of J—— and in the presence of your honour I am making petition that there may be increased pay and reward for the much work of this poor one and your honour is mother and father and to the kind appreciator of worth the exalted Luchcha Ali Khan Saheb Tahsildar the brave one the *salaams* of Jhoot Singh to-day date the second June the signature of Jhoot Singh chaprasi.

GLOSSARY

of such Hindustani words as do not bear their own explanation in the text.

Achcha. Good. Colloquially—"All right." "Very well."

Akhára. Arena.

Al-hamdu-l-illah! Praise to the Almighty!

Anjan (*Hardwickia binata*). A jungle tree of large size and handsome appearance: grows near water in hollows.

Aola (*Emblica officinalis*). A small, feathery-leaved tree bearing a light-green, polished, round, acid berry.

Ap ki kúshi. Your honour's pleasure—As it pleaseth your honour.

Babúl (*Acacia Arabica*). The thorny gum-Arabic tree. Very common on the plains.

Bachcha. Child.

Badmásh. Ruffian.

Baitak. Seat. Sitting place. 'Form' of hare or deer.

Bandi. Closed jungle. Government reserved forest.

Bandúk. Gun.

Ban Héla (lit. Jungle male buffalo). Wild buffalo. Also used to denote the bison in some parts.

Barra (or *Burra*). Big—large—important—of high rank.

Basti. Village—usually meaning a large village.

Bér (*Zizyphus jujuba*). A small and very prickly tree-bush, bearing quantities of a sickly, acid, little red-yellow fruit like a small crab-apple.

Bhagwan. The Omnipotent Spirit of the Universe. The 'Great Spirit' of the Hindus, to whom all other gods of the Hindu Pantheon are subject.

Bhálú. A familiar name for the bear.

Bhisti. Professional water drawer and carrier.

"*Bismillah-illahu-Akbar.*" "In the name of God the Almighty."

Chágal. A leathern kettle-shaped water-bag to hold drinking-water.

Champa. A curious small tree of pulpy fleshy wood, growing, when leafless, a camelia-like flower of very sweet perfume and waxen yellow-white petals.

Charpai (lit. four feet). A native wooden bedstead strung with cord.

Chinkára (lit. 'The Sneezer'). The Indian gazelle. Its warning call is a sharp sneeze or hiss.

Chirónji. A small soft-looking jungle tree, bearing a sloe-like berry of considerable sweet-acidity.

Chital (*Cervus Axis*). The Indian spotted deer.

Chhota (or '*chota*'). Small—of small importance—younger.

Dak. Post.

Dewar. Junction of *nalas.*

Dhamin (*Grewia elastica*). The Indian lancewood tree. Usually of small size; grows in coppices.

'*Dipty*' / '*Dipti*' } Sahib. Deputy Commissioner. (Indian 'pidgin'-English.)

Fakir (lit. a holy beggar). A dervish.

Gaoli. Cowherd.

Gára. The 'kill,' the prey killed by a feline.

Gári-wála. Cart-driver.

Gharri. Small mud fort.

Ghát. Mountain pass or path. Also, bathing or embarking place at a river side, etc.

Gônd. A jungle tribe of Kolarian (aboriginal) stock.

Hallál (lit. 'lawful).' Usually used to express animal food rendered lawful for Mahomedans by the orthodox throat-cutting ceremony.

Hazúr. 'Your Excellency.'

Héla. Male buffalo. Here used to denote a young male buffalo calf.

Hóli. A Hindu festival of a Bacchanalian, Eleusinian kind.

Jamadár. A kind of semi-military rank. A 'commander of a guard.' Here meaning the native assistant who controls a Government forest post.

Ját. A tribe of Hindus inhabiting the Delhi and neighbouring districts.

Jawári (*Sorghum vulgare*). Indian giant millet.

Jungle. The opposite of inhabited land; it may be either a pathless forest or a mere stretch of uncultivated grass and scrub.

Kadbi (or *Karbi*). Dried stalks of *jawári.*

Kamarband. 'Waist-binding'—Waist-cloth.

Karunda. Thorny evergreen bush, bearing a pleasant, slightly acid pulpy berry.

Káwit. A medium-sized tree with small leaves, bearing a hard round fruit the size of a cricket ball. The inside is soft, and when dried and filled with gunpowder is used as a bomb to scare animals from thick covert, caves, etc., in which they may have taken refuge.

Khákar (*Cervulus aureus*). The barking deer, rib-faced deer, or muntjak.

Khôra. A glen—small or big, or a deep ravine in a hillside.

Khubbar (or *Khabr*). News—news of the whereabouts of wild animals.

Kismat. Fate. Luck.

Koël. The Indian hawk-cuckoo. The 'Brain-fever' bird of Anglo-Indians; possessing a beautiful mellow note that, during the height of the hot weather, becomes broken and discordant, and then particularly irritating to those who suffer from the excessive heat.

Kós. Indian measure of distance, equivalent to two English miles.

Kowa (*Terminalia arjuna*). A fine forest tree, nearly always found on river banks; furnishing a dark-brown extremely hard wood. Has a very smooth trunk and whitish bark, with numerous smoothed knobs and gnarls : see the tree under which tiger is lying in the illustration 'At Home'.

Kúlhári. Small axe.

Kutki (*Panicum*). A small semi-cultivated grain grown in clearings on jungly hills by the Korkus. Has a small sweet grain not unlike sago. Grows about one foot high.

Lantuna. A thick, strong-growing, weed-like bush with harsh leafage and masses of strong smelling, reddish-yellow flowers. Forms a very thick under-wood.

Láthi. Large long cudgel, similar to a quarter staff.

Lótán. Mud-wallow or 'soiling'-pit (moss-hag) in which stags and hogs delight to roll at night when visiting water.

Machán. Raised platform. Watching-perch in tree or in fields. Any raised platform in tree or otherwise, from which the sportsman may obtain command of view and fire during a 'drive' or 'beat' for big game.

Máharaj. Great King. Salutation or mode of addressing a superior or somebody whom it is desired to conciliate.

Mahasir. (*Barbus Tor*). The 'Indian Salmon.' A large species of carp which takes the artificial fly or spoon or other spun dead or live bait, giving magnificent sport to the angler. Weight not uncommonly runs up to 50 and 60 lbs., but much heavier fish are occasionally taken.

Máro. (Imperative) Strike! Beat! Fire! (a gun).

Massak. *Bhisti's* water bag, carried over the back.

Mhowa (*Bassia latifolia*). A handsome oak-like tree, bearing a very-strong-smelling, sickly-sweet, deciduous flower with a fleshy edible *corolla*. When this flower is falling wild animals and jungle men are greatly attracted. *Darú*, a very strong native spirit, is distilled from it. After the flower falls, it forms an oval oily nut.

Mongoose (*Mangús*). The ichneumon of India.

Mót. An arrangement of leathern bag, ropes and pulleys, by which a yoke of bullocks draw water from a well for irrigation purposes.

Múrghi. Barndoor fowl.

Nála (also spelled *Nullah*). A water-course—usually meaning a dry water-course.

Nay (*Nahin*) *Sahib! Hom kaisa?*—No, Sir! How can I?

Nilgae (lit. 'Blue Cow.') (*Portax pictus* or *Boselaphus tragocamelus*). The blue-bull. The largest of the Indian antelopes, of a distinctly bovine type. Stands 14 hands at the wither.

Pagri (*Puggari*). Turban. Head cloth.

Palás (*Butea frondosa*). The kino tree. A bush rather than a tree. Bears bunches of magnificent flame-coloured flowers growing from *corollas* as of sage-green velvet, and has strong hard leaves.

Paláti. The stalks or plants of cotton.

Pancháyat. Committee or village conclave of five respectable members.

Pardah. *Purdah*. Curtain. State of seclusion or segregation.

Patél. Hereditary head-man of an Indian village.

Pawnee (correctly *Páni*). Water.

Pipal. (*Ficus religiosa*). The Indian pipal fig. A large tree with light roundish leaves turning to a sudden point. Light-coloured trunk. Rarely found far from human habitations. Its piercing roots will in time destroy the best-built lime-set wall.

Pipalda. 'The water by the pipal tree.'

Pug (*pag*). Footmark. Footprint.

"*Qui-hi*!" (correctly—"*Koi hai?*" or "Is there anybody there?"). A summons to an Indian servant by his master, and of the nature of "What ho without!"

Rabi. The cold-weather or later crop; usually consisting of low crops, as wheat, linseed, gram (pea), vetches, etc.

Ramnah or *Rumnah*. Stretch of grass-land set apart for the cutting of dry grass.

Rausa (*Andropogon Martini*). An Indian grass (lemon grass) from which a strong fragrant oil is distilled, of great commercial value, as it forms the basis of Egyptian and Turkish scents, and is largely exported for that purpose.

Ringhi. A light cart drawn by trotting bullocks.

Rumál. Kerchief.

Sahib. (*Saheb*). Lord. Master. A term generally used by natives of India to denote a European, and sometimes considerably misused.

Salai (*Boswellia thurifera*). An extremely common gregarious tree. Leafless from December to June. Tortuous, twisted, whitish-yellow, scaly, soft branches. Exudes a strong frankincense-like gum. As yet of no apparent use as timber or anything else.

Samálu. A weedy willow-like bush, growing in beds of streams.

Sámbar (*Cervus unicolor*). The largest of the *Rusine* type of Indian deer, and in point of size inferior only to the Wapiti of N. America. Exceeds 14 hands at the shoulder. Horns possess only six points. Maximum length 48¼ inches and very massive.

Sári. The single garment worn by Indian women.

Sendhi. The Indian date-palm. Sometimes, also, the juice of this palm.

Shabash! "Well done!"

Sháitán. Devil. Demon.

Shikár. A Persian word denoting 'Hunting', and used in India to express all kinds of the pursuit of game and fish, hawking, hog-hunting, etc.

Shikári. A hunter.

Sooar. *Súar*. The hog—wild or tame.

Taklai. A tree somewhat akin to the salai, but 'more so'. Grows larger than the salai, is less common, more leafless (being in leaf during June, July, August, and September only), and possesses an extraordinarily smooth, soft, skin-like bark which 'peels' in flakes.

Tom-Tom. Indian drum.

Tópi. Hat.

Tur. A species of pea growing on a strong straggling plant sometimes over four feet in height.

Ujár. Deserted. Overgrown by encroaching jungle.

Worli. A raised oblong mound of earth or stones serving as a landmark or the boundary of a field.

Zillah. District.